OMNI'S HIGH-TECH SOCIETY 2000

The year 2000. It used to conjure up images of futuristic lifestyles and new technology, but in fact, the year 2000 is less than a generation away. What kinds of new scientific, medical and societal changes are in store for us? What can we expect from current explorations in space and here on earth?

Let OMNI'S HIGH-TECH SOCIETY 2000 be your guide to a peek into the world of tomorrow. And have fun taking a quiz on your own ideas of what will be in store for all of us in the next century offered by Arthur C. Clarke, author of *2010*.

Welcome to the future!

THE OMNI
BOOK OF
HIGH-TECH
SOCIETY 2000

Edited by Peter Tyson

ZEBRA BOOKS
KENSINGTON PUBLISHING CORP.

CONTENTS

FOREWORD

The Edwin Hubble Space Telescope is scheduled to be launched from the cargo bay of the space shuttle in the summer of 1986. Costing as much as a new shuttle ($1.1 billion), the $12^1/_2$-ton telescope circling 368 miles above the Earth will be able to peer 10 times further into space—and as much as 15 million years in the past—than any terrestrial telescope.

The Space Telescope represents not only a triumph for astronomy but a symbol of our high-tech society and its potential. The technological leaders of the world must join together in directing this capability to solve the world's critical problems, like feeding the billions of undernourished people in Africa and other parts of the Third World. Cyril Ponnamperuma, director of the Laboratory of Chemical Evolution at the University of Maryland, addresses this grave issue in an essay in Part One of this volume.

Another crucial world problem that affects both rich and poor is the threat of nuclear annihilation.

11

Freeman Dyson of the Institute for Advanced Study in Princeton, New Jersey, thinks that we can avoid nuclear war by becoming less technological. In "World Unity in Space," Senator Spark Matsunaga of Hawaii, fast becoming the leading advocate for Mars exploration in Congress, explains why Russia and the United States should put their money into an international space effort rather than into star-wars defense.

In bringing about such goals, *Omni* has tried to help. For seven years, the magazine has published the most advanced scientific information and developments—leading-edge reports by preeminent scientists and expert science writers. With a unique blend of science and art, *Omni* has opened imaginative new vistas of what the world will be like in fifty, one hundred, and even, one thousand years. In doing so, it has shown how readers can take an active role in shaping that future.

OMNI'S HIGH-TECH SOCIETY 2000 anthologizes the best articles *Omni* Magazine has published on computer technology, robotics, lasers, biomedicine, energy sources (established and alternative), and all aspects of living, working and traveling in space. These articles discuss developments that could directly affect your future. For instance, would you have a robot in the home? If so, what chores would you want it to perform? Would you live on a space station or on the moon? With world population doubling in forty years and tripling 30 years after that, you may want to consider it. This book will force you to think provocatively about the future.

What do we mean by a "high-tech society?" A society that is high-tech is one that develops and incorporates into its culture the latest advances in biomedicine, science and technology, thereby improving itself. In this book, you'll learn about computers controlled by brainwaves, voice patterns, fingerprints, even the retina of your eye. You'll see how it will soon be possible to alter the genes of your children, not only to avoid serious genetic handicaps, but also to improve intelligence, coordination, or simply looks.

Or if you'd prefer to defer on your child's birth until a more auspicious time, you can already place a fertilized embryo in a cryogenic (frozen) bank for implementation in the mother's womb at a more convenient time. Besides corrective surgery for deformed fetuses, hope abounds for paralyzed or physically incapacitated people. Some may be able to move again, thanks to "born-again nerves" rejuvenated by electric pulses and various bionic implants.

Concerned about the ongoing energy crisis? Here, you can read about the alternative energy sources you won't find discussed in conventional magazines. One such energy form is magnetohydrodynamics. It's a formidable word, but also a cheap form of electrical energy that could make nuclear power and its attendant waste obsolete. Also included are articles about solar energy that could be fueling American homes from a string of solar-powered satellites orbiting 22,300 miles above the Earth.

While many of these outlandish ideas may be centuries ahead of their time, other technological breakthroughs of a similar magnitude may not be. IBM has already developed the first million-bit chip containing circuit elements only a fiftieth the width of a human hair. Ten years ago this would have been unthinkable. In "A Window on the Living Brain," Douglas Starr reports on how computer science, nuclear physics and medicine have been combined to create the PET scan, a revolutionary biomedical device that may provide new answers to the causes of senility, strokes, and even insanity. In the realm of space, Princeton physicist Gerard K. O'Neill believes that if current research continues, we could have a thriving space industry 200,000 miles above Earth by the end of this century. Within decades this "industry on high" could realize a profit of $100 billion annually.

Omni's Prophecy Quiz opens this volume. Predict when many of these breakthroughs will occur. Compare your answers with those of Arthur C. Clarke, the visionary and science fiction master who foresaw back in 1947 that orbiting satellites would be used widely in telecommunication. Even though the future is both boundless and, in the end, unpredictable, the Clarke quiz and this high-tech volume tell you what's yet to come.

—Peter Tyson

OMNI'S PROPHECY QUIZ

Take *Omni*'s PROPHECY QUIZ and match your wits against Arthur C. Clarke, author of the science fiction bestseller *2010*. Two *Omni* editors—well in touch with the future took the quiz and were only able to agree with Clarke, the great prophet of our space age, on 40 percent of the questions. Can you do better?

The PROPHECY QUIZ poses questions on breakthroughs in biomedicine, science and technology. It questions whether cataclysmic events, like nuclear war, will occur. Which planets in our solar system will man (not robots) have visited by the year 2050? Will the existence of an Unidentified Flying Object be verified in the next century? Can we ever expect a cure for cancer?

These are questions no one can answer for sure, but Arthur C. Clarke provides a strong intimation of what's to come. See if you agree with him (his answers appear in the back of the book.)

The twenty-first century is only 15 years away, and we must be prepared for it. Answer the following 50 questions and get a preview of the third millenium. Good luck! Then read the 63 articles presented here and discover what is happening now to make the future easier for all of us.

OMNI'S PROPHECY QUIZ

What will life be like in the year 2000 and beyond?

By Robert Weil and Peter Tyson

1) When will an ordinary person be able to buy a ride on the space shuttle?

    a. by 1995
    b. by 2000
    c. by 2010
    d. by 2020
    e. after 2020

2) Place the following medical breakthroughs in the chronological order in which they are likely to occur.

a. a human fetus comes to term in an artificial womb

b. most human genes (roughly 100,000) are located and mapped

c. a so-called human death hormone is isolated

d. artificial or bionic eyes are successfully implanted in a person

3) Will we establish extraterrestrial contact in the twenty-first century?

a. yes
b. no

4) Which of the following events will occur first in space?

a. a birth
b. a marriage
c. a murder
d. a suicide

5) Which of the following high-tech birthing techniques will be most prevalent in the year 2000?

a. in vitro ("test tube") fertilization
b. surrogate mothering
c. cryogenics (embryo freezing)
d. choosing the sex of your baby

6) If sex selection becomes reliable, will 21st century parents choose a majority of

a. boys
b. girls
c. 50/50 ratio

7) In the coming years, which *one* chore will people come to rely on their home robot to accomplish the most?

    a. housecleaning
    b. cooking
    c. laundering
    d. serving as a burglar alarm
    e. teaching the children
    f. acting as a pet or companion

8) What percentage of the American labor force will work at home via computer modem in 2000?

    a. 1%
    b. 5%
    c. 10%
    d. 25%
    e. 50%

9) Will there be a World War III?

    a. yes
    b. no

10) If World War III comes to pass, will we survive it?

a. yes

b. no

c. no, but we will seed other planets with our species

11) What do you think the typical 21st-century American family will be like?

a. a single woman with children

b. a mother and father with children (traditional family)

c. communal groups of couples who share childrearing and other tasks

d. a childless couple

e. single adults without children

12) What do you think the typical 21st-century Third World (or developing country) family will be like?

a. a single woman with children

b. a mother and father with children (traditional family)

c. communal groups of couples who share childrearing and other tasks

d. a childless couple

e. single adults without children

13) In the year 2000, what percentage of American fathers will act in the traditional role that mothers once assumed—i.e., staying at home, raising the children, etc.?

a. under 1%

b. 1% to 5%
c. 5% to 10%
e. 10% to 20%
e. over 20%

14) By the year 2010, how many years will you be able to add to your life with life-extension drugs and techniques?

a. 1–3
b. 5
c. 10
d. 20
e. over 25
f. none

15) When do you believe the Grand Unification Theory—which unites the electromagnetic, gravitational, and strong and weak nuclear forces of energy under one principle—will be proven?

a. before 1990
b. 1990–2000
c. 2001–2010
d. 2011–2020
e. beyond 2020
f. never

16) Name the most common global energy source in the next century.

a. oil
b. coal

c. fusion
d. fission (nuclear power)
e. solar
f. geothermal power

17) Which minority will be inaugurated as President of the United States first?

a. a woman
b. a black
c. a Jew
d. an Hispanic

18) Which one of the following scenarios will best characterize the state of Soviet-American relations in 2000?

a. widespread cooperation, including joint ventures in space and scientific collaborations on Earth

b. a wary detente in effect with arms limitations treaties working somewhat successfully

c. a continued arms build-up of weapons, both on Earth and in space, but no aggression (in essence, a status quo situation)

d. continued arms build-up, with limited military operations in progress on Earth

e. widescale nuclear war pursued only in space

f. nuclear war pursued both on Earth and in space

19) When do you think cryogenic freezing of an embryo (which would allow a mother to postpone childbirth for an indefinite length of time) will be-

come a safe and socially acceptable technique?

a. in your lifetime
b. in your children's lifetime
c. in your grandchildren's lifetime
d. never

20) What do you think the American minimum wage will be in the year 2000?

a. under $5.00
b. $5.00 to $6.00
c. $6.00 to $8.00
d. $8.00 to $10.00
e. over $10.00

21) Which one of the following alternative living environments will be used by the greatest number of people in the year 2050?

a. underground communities
b. underwater communities
c. space colonies
d. orbiting spacecraft

22) By the year 2000, which one of the following will the space shuttle be most used for?

a. as today, for scientific experiments and satellite repair
b. for routine passenger transportation to a space station or for pleasure (honeymoons, excursion trips, etc.)

c. for industrial cargo transportation, to a space station or moon colony

d. all of the above

e. the shuttle will no longer be used

23) Which of the following events will have occurred by 2010? (more than one answer is acceptable)

a. a computer will defeat a grandmaster at chess

b. a major earthquake will ravage the California coastline

c. terraforming will have begun on Mars

d. genetically engineered foodstuffs will virtually alleviate hunger in Africa and the Third World

24) Which of the following macro-engineering projects will be completed before the middle of the next century?

a. Planetran, a levitated tunnel subway carrying passengers from New York to L.A. in 20–60 minutes

b. an English Channel tunnel

c. a pipeline exporting Rhone river water under the Mediterranean to arid Libya or Algeria

d. a "Friendship Bridge" across the Bering Strait connecting Siberia with Alaska

e. all of the above

f. none of the above

25) August 6, 2045 marks the hundredth anniversary of the nuclear devastation of Hiroshima. Will we have done away with nuclear arms by that time?

a. yes
b. no

26) Can we expect a vaccine for the common cold (interferon, perhaps) within one generation (30 years)?

a. yes
b. no

27) Which will come first?

a. a cloned man
b. a bionic man
c. a 150-year-old man (with help from life-extension drugs)
d. a self-replicating robot

28) What will be the most polluted city on Earth in the year 2000?

a. New York City
b. Los Angeles
c. Tokyo
d. Bangkok
e. Mexico City
f. Cairo
g. Sao Paulo

29) Which city will boast the largest population at the turn of the century?

a. New York City

b. Los Angeles
c. Tokyo
d. Rio de Janeiro
e. Mexico City
f. Shanghai
g. Sao Paolo
h. Calcutta

30) Which of the following types of fuel will most likely power our spaceships in the next century?

a. fusion
b. fission
c. solar power
d. antimatter, such as boron fuel
e. conventional rocket fuel
f. other

31) What will be the primary use of orbiting satellites in the coming century?

a. telecommunications
b. solar energy receivers/transmitters
c. weapons, as the ASATs
d. cargo holds and fueling stations for shuttles

32) Keeping in mind the ravages of inflation and the rising costs of paper, what will you pay in the year 2000 for a magazine that costs $2.50 today?

a. $3.00
b. $5.00
c. $7.50

d. $10.00
e. $15.00
f. over $15.00

33) Are any of these drugs likely to be commonly used in 2000? (more than one answer is acceptable)

a. energy-boosting medicine
b. memory-enhancing medicine
c. proven aphrodisiacs
d. intelligence-boosting medicine
e. life-extension drugs

34) The first permanently manned space colony will be established by which one of the following groups or nations?

a. United States
b. Soviet Union
c. European consortium
d. China
e. there will never be a viable manned space colony

35) Who do you think will be the world's technological leader at the turn of the century?

a. the Americans
b. the Russians
c. the Japanese
d. the Germans
e. the Chinese

36) Robots and computers will make which of the following jobs obsolete in the year 2010? (check more than one, if desired)

a. bank clerks
b. newspaper deliverers
c. toll and ticket booth operators
d. telephone operators
e. short-order cook

37) What will be the average life expectancy of an American in the year 2000?

a. 66–69
b. 70–73
c. 74–77
d. 78–81
e. 82 or over

38) Electronic mail will render the American post office (in its current manual delivery state) obsolete in 30 years.

a. true
b. false

39) It's New Years Eve, December 31, 1999. How many people will be popping champagne corks in space?

a. none
b. 10–20
c. 21–50

d. 51–100
e. 101–1000
f. over 1000

40) A so-called "greenhouse effect" long predicted by scientists will cause extensive damage to coastal areas within the next 40 years?

a. true
b. false

41) By A.D. 2000, how many nations will possess workable nuclear weapons?

a. 8–10
b. 11–13
c. 14–18
d. 19–24
e. over 25

42) How will most cars be powered in the year 2010?

a. gasoline
b. gasohol
c. electricity
d. steam

43) There are approximately four and one-half billion people alive today. How many will there be in the year 2000?

a. 5–6 billion
b. 6–7 billion

c. 7–8 billion
d. 8–9 billion
e. 9–10 billion
f. over 10 billion

44) What will be the typical classroom of the 21st century?

a. group of students listening in school to human teacher (traditional)
b. group of students listening in school to robot or computer teacher
c. each student at home with computer terminal

45) Will Venice be under water (uninhabitable to the city's population) by the end of the next century?

a. yes
b. no

46) "That's one small step for a man, one giant leap for mankind," remarked Neil Armstrong on July 20, 1969. Will man be living on the moon 50 years later (2019)?

a. yes
b. no

47) What would a 21st-century man say is the single greatest invention or discovery of the 20th century?

a. computer
b. theory of relativity

c. polio vaccine
d. splitting the atom
e. television
f. satellite
g. automobile (late 1800s)

48) In the year 2050, will the world's wealth be

a. more evenly distributed
b. less evenly distributed
c. about the same as it is today

49) Given that painting is the most ubiquitous manifestation of fine art today, what will most artists be working in during the 21st century?

a. painting
b. sculpture
c. photography
d. computer and holographic art
e. a new art form as yet unexploited or uninvented

50) What is the most *difficult*, perhaps impossible, challenge facing man in the 21st century?

a. alleviating world hunger
b. reducing or eliminating nuclear weapons
c. finding alternative energy sources to replenish depleted reserves
d. stabilizing world population
e. colonizing outer space

PART ONE:
PREPARING
FOR 2000

*"Real generosity toward the future
lies in giving all to the present."*

—*Albert Camus*

IMPROVE FOOD PRODUCTION

By Cyril Ponnamperuma

Food is the single most important requirement for life. The need for food is universal in the entire biosphere, and the success with which each individual obtains the elements and compounds essential for an adequate diet determines ultimate survival. With the explosive growth of world population, food has become global priority number one.

Although American dietary patterns might suggest otherwise, the moment of decision is upon us. A sense of urgency pervades scientific talk. In a 1983 address to the American Chemical Society, Nobel laureate Norman Borlaug, father of the Green Revolution, commented that "expanding food production fast enough to meet the increasing needs of a large and growing population over the next four decades will be vital to the survival of civilization."

In the sphere of foreign policy, the need to confront world-hunger problems has also come to the fore. The Presidential Commission on World Hunger, which concluded its studies under the Carter Administration, recommended that beginning in the Eighties, the United States should make the elimination of hunger the primary focus of its relationship with the developing countries. The prospect of disaster is at hand. It is closer than most people realize or are prepared to admit.

By 2015 our planet will be the home of almost 8 billion people, double today's population. It will not suffice, however, to double our food production; we must at least *triple* it. Two thirds of humanity are already suffering from inadequate nutritional balance, as the experts would say. In street parlance, they are starving. The gap between the billions of hungry people and the amount of food needed to feed them is constantly widening.

Population reduction is the obvious answer. But the numerical stabilization of the human race will not be achieved in a decade, nor in two, but perhaps in half a century it will. For at least another generation we must turn to science and technology to provide food for humanity. This is a formidable project. In the next 40 years alone, world food production must be upped by at least as much as it was increased during the entire 12,000-year period from the beginning of agriculture to the present day.

The choices are bewildering. On one hand, there is dire pessimism; on the other, a certain scientific optimism. After the World Food Conference, sponsored by the United Nations, there were even some scientists who advocated the totally unthinkable and absolutely abhorrent solution of triage: Let the hungry die of starvation, they said, while the strong conserve available supplies of food for themselves and their families.

Then there are those who profess a certain exuberant hope that science can solve all problems. Francis Bacon gave us his idea of utopia. The modern proponents of this utopian ideology quote the significant developments in science—from the conquest of space, to the harnessing of the atom, to the decoding of DNA. The Apollo program was without question a supreme triumph of science and technology. The casting off of the shackles that bound us to Earth and gave us the exhilarating freedom to explore the universe will be recorded as one of man's greatest achievements. But perhaps there is a fallacy in the line of sanguine reasoning that suggests science can be a global elixir. The truth may lie somewhere between the poles of dismal pessimism and undue optimism.

How can the world food supply be increased? Is it possible for man to produce some food independent of climate? The chemical synthesis of food is a tantalizing area of exploration. If we can make material for our shirts, can we not make the substance of our lunches? Carbohydrates arise from the fixing of carbon, hydrogen, and oxygen. Proteins result from the same three elements, with nitrogen thrown into the bargain. The laboratory of nature achieves this result through the complex process of plant photosynthesis and animal metabolism. In the laboratory of modern chemistry, the shortcut from molecules to meals is within scientific reach. There is an intriguing science-fiction story about a gourmet restaurant, where the only raw material that enters the building is coal. Such a concept may not be a mere technological fantasy.

It is commonly believed that nature knows best. Molecular biology has given us ample evidence that in many instances the ways of nature may be wanton and wasteful. In the breeding of plants, the reduction of respiration and the improved efficiency of photosynthesis might double the yield of our crops. Enhanced biological nitrogen fixation, accomplished by exploiting the symbiotic relationship of certain algae with the roots of cereals—the Azolla with rice, for example, a circumstance understood by the ancient Thai and Vietnamese and rediscovered today—is a potential area for active research. Epoch-making discoveries of recombinant DNA have opened horizons of wondrous proportions. We are on the threshold of major new advances. The Green Revolution will yield to the Gene Revolution.

Since 1971 Cyril Ponnamperuma has been professor of chemistry and director of the Laboratory of Chemical Evolution at the University of Maryland.

AVOID NUCLEAR WAR

By Freeman J. Dyson

Nuclear weapons are deeply entrenched not only in the concrete silos of Montana and Siberia but also in the structure of international relations and in our ways of thinking. It is difficult to imagine the process of transition that could take us from the world of today to a time when nuclear weapons would no longer be important. But the fact that a historic transition is unimaginable before it happens does not imply that it will never happen. History is full of examples of transitions that upset deeply entrenched institutions and deeply held beliefs.

It has happened not infrequently that a dominant technology, accepted by contemporary observers as permanent, disappeared from the scene with astonishing swiftness. Sometimes a technology disappears because it is replaced by something more powerful: Sailing ships succumb to steam, and canals succumb to railroads. Sometimes a technology disappears because it is replaced by something less powerful; there may be social or political forces that cause a less powerful technology to prevail. I call a transition from less to more powerful technology a transition of the first kind, and a transition from more to less powerful technology a transition of the second kind. Transitions of the first kind are familiar to us. Transitions of the second kind are rarer and less well-known. Since the transition to a world without nuclear weapons must be a transition of the second kind, it is important for us to study transitions of the second kind with special care to understand how and why they have happened.

In his book *The Camel and the Wheel*, Richard Bulliet, a historian of early Arab civilization, describes a striking example of a transition of the second kind. He demonstrates with ample documentation that in Roman times the entire Arab world, extending roughly from Tunis to Afghanistan, based its economic life on the same infrastructure as the Roman Empire, namely, on the technology of wheeled vehicles and paved roads. South, east, and north of the Mediterranean, the basic unit of freight transportation was the oxcart. About A.D. 500, a few hundred years before the rise of Islam, a drastic change occurred. Throughout the Arab territories, caravans of camels took over the freight business, roads fell into disrepair, and wheeled vehicles disappeared. For more than 1,000 years, until Europeans moved in with steel rails and locomotives during the Industrial Revolution, the camel reigned supreme.

Another transition of the second kind, described by Noel Perrin in his book *Giving Up the Gun*, occurred in Japan in the seventeenth century. In the sixteenth

37

century, after the first European ships visited Japan, Japanese swordsmiths quickly learned to make guns. They manufactured guns of superior quality. Large numbers of Japanese guns were exported, and still larger numbers were used by Japanese armies abroad and at home. Perrin illustrates his book with old Japanese drawings of seventeenth-century warriors carrying and firing guns. For half a century the corps of samurai was heavily addicted to guns. The warriors fought gun battles with great losses of life. The losses were so heavy that the leading samurai became convinced that guns were ruining their honorable profession. They decided to go back to fighting with swords. For two and a half centuries the sword was reinstated as the basis of military power, while guns were used only in small numbers for ceremonial purposes. The supremacy of the sword was maintained until 1879, when the samurai were defeated by a new-style army intent upon modernization and armed with European weapons.

These two transitions of the second kind have much to teach us. In both cases, the driving force of the transition was the political power of a skilled, professional elite—the camel drivers in Africa and the samurai in Japan. In both cases the ideology of the transition was conservative, aiming to perpetuate an old social order and a traditional way of life. In neither case was the transition permanent, but it lasted more than 1,000 years in Africa, more than 200 in Japan. If we could successfully abolish nuclear weapons and make the abolition stick for 200 years, that would give our species time to adapt itself to new technologies and to tackle some of the other urgent problems of survival.

A practical program leading toward the abolition of nuclear weapons must be based upon three principles. First, it is not possible to replace something with nothing. To replace a wheel we need a camel. Our camel must be a robust and versatile technology of nonnuclear weapons capable of defending our interests and our allies without destroying us. Second, the only political force strong enough to abolish nuclear weapons is the military itself. The move away from weapons of mass murder must be presented to the public not as a response to fear but as a response to the demands of military honor and self-respect. Third, the military establishment of the Soviet Union must be allowed to share equally in shaping the program. The stabilization of a nonnuclear world is a conservative objective, and the hope of achieving it rests mainly on the profoundly conservative traditions of the military professionals in all countries. To succeed, we need to have on our side not only the camel drivers but also the samurai.

Freeman J. Dyson is professor of physics at the Institute for Advanced Study, in Princeton. His most recent book, Weapons and Hope *(Harper & Row), discusses the struggles man must yet face in abolishing nuclear weapons.*

PART TWO:
COMPUTER
REVOLUTIONS

*"The real danger is not that computers
will begin to think like man
but that man will begin
to think like computers"*
—Sydney J. Harris

MEGACHIP

By Richard Wolkomir

"What's that modem's baud?"

"Ready to boot?"

"What K you got in EPROM?"

"Hey, man, dump the screen!"

"You running a Winchester?"

Peek into the computer room at Anywhere High School, USA, and you'll find the local technojocks idling at the keyboards, slinging lingo back and forth. It's like NASA's Mission Control, this brotherhood (and sisterhood) of the micro. Out of the way, old-timers, here we come: the merry chipsters, ready for the microcomputer's tomorrow and the supermachines.

In California's Silicon Valley and other high-tech bastions, such as the arc of electronics companies around Boston, these New Age computers are now taking shape. Ultrapowerful, they promise to jerk the entire society around. As Chris Morgan, a vice president at Lotus, a leading software company, puts it,

"This is going to be the next industrial revolution."

Any forty-year-old Methuselah looking into the computer room will remember when the machine was a primitive beast called UNIVAC, big as a boardroom but dumb as any of today's $12.95 loss-leader calculators at Radio Shack. He isn't completely computer-illiterate, this product of the prechip Tube Age; on his office desk sits the ubiquitous IBM PC. But like great-grandpa driving his first Model T, he has an urge to say giddyap when he turns on the machine. The brotherhood, on the other hand, seems to have begun every morning since they were weaned, with a bowlful of transistors, milk, and sliced bananas. Bring on the supercomputer—they're ready. Just as Dad was into '56 Fords and overdrive, the kids are into Macintoshes and 32-bit processors.

Look up all your data banks! The high-school technojocks don't need Goodyears to get around. They can punch a key and go anywhere. Like the car in its day, the computer is reshaping society to suit itself. Of course, it's still warming up, but this analogy has not been lost on the microcomputer industry.

"Right now, compared with the automobile, computers are at about the year 1915," says David Kay, vice president of the Kaypro Corporation.

"We need to have an infrastructure like the one developed for the car," Alladi Venkatesh, a University of California management expert told a group of computer professionals in Boston in early 1984. "For cars, we have highways, streets, parking lots, gas stations, and repair shops. If computers are to reach the popularity of cars, they need something similar. That means computers that can do our shopping for

43

us, and provide electronic mail services, library and data retrieval, education access, as well as access to a wide variety of entertainment."

It also means computers that can think back at you—that is, machines that can actually sense when you need help and what specific help you need. But that takes more power than today's microcomputers command. Thus, at the moment, the computer industry is engaged in what any graduate of the hot-rod Fifties can easily understand: a horsepower race.

In the sleek-and-low palaces of the high-tech companies, laid back among Silicon Valley's palms and pines, the hardware nabobs are sloshing in their hot tubs, pondering ways to torque up their machines. But—wry twist!—they are not thinking of those kids in the high-school computer room, the electronic hot-rodders. Komputer Kids, face it: You are a wee market. The nabobs have declared you obsolete. The future—twist again!—is all those Methuselahs out there who don't know bauds from bytes and speak no Pascal.

The nabobs want a computer in every florist's shop and dentist's office and two in every suburban split-level and ranch. That means programs so easy and slick that old Methuselah won't even notice he's using a computer. It also means programs of dazzling complexity, requiring super-powerful machines.

"In just a few years, we'll have machines with twenty-five times the power of today's IBM PC," says Kay. "Programs will have advanced to the point of being able to sense what you don't understand and help you along. When that happens, a huge market will open up because nobody will have any excuse *not*

44

to use a computer."

Leading to this Oz of bullet-fast micros with memories like the national archives are many yellow-brick roads. And the engineers are following all of them.

For instance, IBM has just developed a new chip that stores 1 million bits of information, nearly four times the capacity of today's best chips. Capable of holding approximately 100 pages of double-spaced typewritten text, the chip is the culmination of improvements in both photolithography and processing technology. These advances made it possible to fabricate circuit elements on the chip as narrow as one micrometer—about a fiftieth the width of one human hair. Consequently, the IBM designers can pack in more circuits, making the chip extra dense.

Other engineers are working on bubble technology, an alternative to silicon chips for computer memory and logic devices. These units contain tiny blobs of magnetism—called magnetic bubbles—that can move about under the influence of magnetic fields and electric fields. By changing position, these magnetic bubbles can record information in binary form. Bubbles have several advantages over ordinary chips: They are more rugged; they retain their memory even after the power is turned off; and they can store more data. Consider the Intel company's latest bubble system. It can store 4 million bits of information—roughly 400 double-spaced typewritten pages—on a device the size of a tack's head. Researchers say the technology could theoretically lead to a *billion*-bit computer no bigger than a portable radio and powered by flashlight batteries.

In the meantime, bubble technology has two drawbacks: Bubble memories are more expensive than standard chips, and they work more slowly. But rising production will cut costs. And according to Mark Kryder, director of the Magnetics Technology Center at Carnegie-Mellon University, engineers are now striving to speed up bubble devices. "Silicon is clearly much further along the learning curve and slowing down," he points out, "while bubble research is still early on the curve, with a considerable distance to go."

Bubbles already have many applications in robots and other systems where grime and vibration can maim standard chips. For example, they are now incorporated in tiny computers that fit in briefcases and, in the future, may supplant magnetic tapes for use in space shots. Kryder reports that the Japanese also have a major push under way to incorporate bubble technology in personal computers. "They let you make a smaller machine," says Kryder, "and the bubble's ruggedness can be a big asset because the average consumer is not notoriously careful with disk drives."

Other researchers believe the next century's computer chips will be made not of silicon crystals, but of large organic molecules. Such biocomputers might simulate the human brain, processing myriad amounts of information at once, making decisions, drawing conclusions, weighing evidence, perhaps even exhibiting creativity. Biological computers, however, are still theoretical. At best, they are many decades away.

Closer to reality is a souped-up silicon technology called parallel processing, which industry experts say is almost ready.

In parallel processing, the computer contains several chips, each specializing in a specific job. One, for instance, may handle calculations; another, memory processing, and so on.

"You can put many interconnected computers on one chip, and they can work on different parts of a problem simultaneously, like the neurons in your brain," says Ronald Krutz, director of the computer-engineering center at Pittsburgh's Mellon Institute, a branch of Carnegie-Mellon University that does consulting work for industry. He says the advantages are high speed and the ability to handle programs far more complex than today's software. Parallel-processing computers, for instance, might well carry on conversations in ordinary English. Engineers at Carnegie-Mellon and throughout the computer industry are currently wrestling with such difficult problems as how to control parallel processing's multiple simultaneous operations without losing the speed advantage. The task is formidable, but most industry experts are highly optimistic.

"It will take a while, but the cheapness of processors will make it happen within five years or so," says Mike Jones, vice president for engineering at Peachtree, a leading software producer. "The result will be computers that are much faster, much easier to use, and that allow you to work on several tasks at the same time."

As just one example of what parallel processing can do, Kay suggests that your computer and telephone would be connected. "A call comes in while you're doing word processing, and a window opens on your screen to tell you who is calling," he says. "Or you might bring up information from a database and plug it directly into the report you're writing." The industry buzzword, he says, is *multitasking*, meaning computers that can do several jobs at once. For example, while you are writing a letter, the computer might be calculating sales figures you need, preparing a pie chart, and printing out 5,000 envelopes, drawing the addresses from a database. Reseachers are confident that such power will lead, in a decade or so, to computers that can see, listen, talk in ordinary language (such as English or Japanese), learn, and make judgments.

Even more immediate will be the impact of yet another technology: videodisk storage. Lasers write information on the disks in binary form, burning a microscopic hole in the disk to represent *one* and leaving a blank space to represent *zero*. The lasers also read the inscribed disks. Videodisks, of course, already allow owners of videodisk players to see movies or Michael Jackson's latest see-it-while-you-hear-it performance. The next step will be to mate the personal computer to videodisks, and it is coming soon. In fact, the computer industry has been humming with the news that IBM recently ordered 1.5 million compact laser-videodisk drives, possibly as an addition to the firm's PC line.

Videodisks offer immense storage capacity: One new disk can hold the equivalent of 2 *million* typed, double-spaced pages of data on a single 14-inch platter. They also offer visuals comparable to motion pictures, which are light-years ahead of the simple graphic displays now available on personal com-

48

puters. The possibilities are intriguing.

"You can perform very exciting graphic simulation with the technology. For instance, you could play a game of computer football in which the players on the screen are actual NFL athletes," says George Heilmeier, senior vice present and chief technical officer at Texas Instruments, in Dallas. "Simulation games like this could be highly educational," he adds. "Imagine exploring the moon by gliding over moonscape based on real NASA footage, or teaching yourself to fly and being able to safely see the consequences of your maneuvers. If you're too light on the throttle, well, then you plow into the power lines!"

He says that tomorrow's encyclopedia will probably be stored on such a computer-videodisk machine. "Suppose I wanted to look up something on supply-side economics," he said. "On the left side of my screen I might see [supply-side economist] Arthur Laffer delivering a lecture on his theory, and on the right side I'd see an outline of his ideas." The possibilities, of course, are enormous: Look up *tiger* in your computerized encyclopedia, and up comes a sinewy Bengal, bounding through the Indian jungle, while a leading zoologist, interrupted by an occasional roar, describes its physiology, behavior, and ecological niche.

Video-computer systems already are beginning to appear in video arcades. You can get airsick, for instance, dogfighting in an advanced jet plane from Clint Eastwood's movie *Firefox*. Computerized training courses are also available on videodisk. But Heilmeier notes that the disks are not yet interactive; so the computer user cannot write on them or change their contents and store his own information. According to Heilmeier, truly interactive computer-videodisk equipment is approximately three to five years away.

Norman Weizer, a senior analyst for the computer industry at Arthur D. Little, Inc., the international consulting company headquartered in Cambridge, Massachusetts, says that videodisks will eventually contain both a program—for instance, word processing—and the instruction manual needed to operate it. The user will then have the option of either studying the instructions on the screen or of having them printed out. Among other things, the manual will offer audiovisual how-to demonstrations. "You could get a couple of hours of video instruction on the disk in addition to the program," he says.

"We could put our entire software library on one videodisk," says Peachtree's Jones. "The disk drive, a peripheral attachment to your computer, will eventually cost about two hundred fifty dollars, and a disk will be about ten dollars."

"The density of storage in these laserdisks is spectacular. The entire Library of Congress card catalog can fit on just two of these disks," says Lotus's Chris Morgan. He adds that read-only disks will be available for computers in just a few years. Disks that a computer can both read and record new information upon (read-write disks) should be available in about seven years.

By then, he thinks, the video images will be as sharp as reality: "When holographic displays come along, you'll have live performances in your living room with three-dimensional projections."

Denser chips, magnetic bubbles, parallel processing, videodisk storage—as such technologies reach the marketplace over the next three to seven years, computers will acquire ever larger memories. And they will be able to process ever more complex programs in less and less time. As a result, software companies will be able to produce far more complex programs. Yet, because of that underlying complexity, the programs will be so simple and natural to use that any bright orangutan could operate a computer.

"I'm an ex-programmer for mainframes, and I know all the languages—I'm computer literate—but I don't see any reason at all why my twenty-year-old son needs to be," says Weizer. "In the future, *computer literate* will mean nothing more than knowing how to use software."

As an indicator of the direction in which computing is going, many industry experts point to Apple's new Macintosh computer. "It's a major breakthrough in many ways—it's hard to get people away from that machine," says Morgan. The Macintosh can process 32 bits—or pieces—of information at one time, which makes it roughly twice as powerful as the IBM PC. It also uses a new 3.5-inch plastic-encased floppy disk—something like a tape cassette—that many observers believe will become an industry standard because it's rugged and fits in your pocket, much like a cigarette pack. It is Macintosh's easy-to-use features, however, that suggest the most important trend in computing.

For instance, instead of typing out commands on the keyboard, the user can roll an ashtray-size electronic gadget, called a mouse, around on his desk to manipulate an onscreen pointer. By aiming his pointer at appropriate drawings on the screen, he gives the computer orders. For instance, if he wants to throw away something he's written, he points to a little picture of a garbage can. Other computer makers are moving in the same direction. Hewlett-Packard, for example, has developed a new computer that can be given a series of commands simply by touching various spots on the screen.

"Mice are good. I've run a mouse over pipe ashes, and it continued to work, but a messy desk can be a problem," says Weizer. "It's also annoying to have to remove your hand from the keyboard to work the mouse; so I think that we'll see increasing use of a one-finger joystick mounted on the keyboard to move the pointer around on the screen."

Despite such caveats, he says the Macintosh hints at how easy machine/human communication will become in the future. "Already, with just one hand on a mouse, by pointing to little icons on the screen, you're doing complex data processing that is hard even with a mainframe computer," he says, adding that piloting tomorrow's computers will be even easier. Today, for instance, an executive must use a keyboard to ask his computer: "How many salespeople do we have working the Midwest this week?" But in a decade or so, he might simply ask the question aloud.

"Voice recognition is difficult because of the problem of understanding different regional accents. Computers that can understand voice commands should be available in ten to fifteen years," said Jones. Ronald Krutz, of the Mellon Institute, notes that some speech-recognition devices are available already, but that they are primitive. "For true voice communication with microcomputers, we'll need lots of processing power and lots of memory," he says. The human side of the equation could also prove difficult to solve. Observes Weizer, "I don't know how long it will take for people to feel really comfortable talking to machines."

Meanwhile, as machines develop more power, software designers will develop entirely new kinds of programs. Just what form they will take is still unclear, but some of the latest programs are indicators.

To considerable fanfare in computer circles, Living Videotext, Inc., a small Palo Alto, California, company, recently introduced a new program called *ThinkTank*. Essentially, it is an idea processor, according to the company's president, Dave Winer. The program generates an onscreen outline that lets you organize and rearrange thoughts. Suppose you are planning a new store that will sell computer software. You type in a possible name, SOFTWORLD, which appears on the screen. Then you could create categories to think about: customer populations, suppliers, advertising themes, and so on. Then you could brainstorm, slapping down ideas under the different categories as you go, switching them around changing the categories, refining the ideas.

Eventually, your computer will have in its memory a definite plan for the new store, complete with details for financing, starting up, and eventual expansion. Such a program is a harbinger of software to come because it is useful to virtually anyone, whether he is plotting a corporate takeover or planning an awards banquet for the local bowling club. Programming must evolve in that direction—universal usefulness—

before the industry can achieve its cherished goal of a micro in every split-level.

"*ThinkTank* is a prototype for a new kind of programming. It's going to be a mass market, and we're going after that," says Winer. "You're also going to see computer networking so that we're no longer working as isolated little islands. Computers are going to link us together so that we can accomplish what individuals cannot."

A step toward that networked nation is now under way at Carnegie-Mellon University, where campus workers are currently stringing fiberoptic cables from building to building. By 1986, the university will be a microcosm of the city of tomorrow: Its microcomputers—approximately 7,000 of them—will outnumber people, linking freshmen, deans, janitors, and everyone else on campus to a central data bank and to one another. Students, for instance, will write term papers on computer terminals and send them electronically to their professors, who will grade them on the computer and electronically return the annotated versions. IBM and Carnegie-Mellon are cosponsoring this scale model of the computerized future.

"I used to work at Xerox's Palo Alto Research Center, where we had this kind of system, and the effect was a much higher quality of communication between people," says James Morris, director of Carnegie-Mellon's Information Technology Center. Morris is designing the programming for what university students already are calling Computer U. One reason, he says, is that written communication forces pupils to express thoughts more clearly than they would in everyday speech, while electronics speeds up the tempo of communication. "You can involve more people in a discussion because they don't have to be there physically," says Morris.

Eventually, he says, the university may extend the computer connection out into Pittsburgh, first for off-campus students and eventually for the entire city. But computerization already is having an effect on education at Carnegie-Mellon.

"A good example is history. Traditionally, undergraduates have been unequipped to do genuine research," says psychologist Jill Larkin, director of Carnegie-Mellon's Center for the Design of Educational Computing. "Now the history department has a database of grievances filed by people in different parts of France just before the French Revolution. Students are tapping into the database to do studies that actually increase our knowledge of the revolution's causes."

The unknown quantity in the computerization program, she says, is its psychological and sociological effects on students. "The best analogy is the advent of the mass-produced automobile—I don't think *anyone* at that time guessed that the car would completely rearrange society.

"You have to realize that tomorrow's microcomputers will be as powerful as today's mainframes. We're working with IBM right now to develop them," Larkin adds. "I think we're putting together a prototype of what will be common throughout society. Lord only knows what it'll be!"

As the computer revolution takes hold, the big winners may be schoolchildren. So says Judah L. Schwartz, professor of engineering science and education at the Massachusetts Institute of Technology and a leader in the new field of educational computing. "Technology is no problem—it's here now," he says. "But we have to learn to use the technology to support what education really is, which is the process of helping people to ask questions about the world around them." He believes that teaching children to program is unnecessary. "That's like giving them a machine shop and saying, 'Go build your own tools.' I say given them the tool kit—a screwdriver and a word processor are both tools."

At MIT, Schwartz and his associates are developing programs that will put computers to more effective use in classrooms. One of these programs lets students learn geometry by exploring for themselves the relationships between different figures. "For instance, you can put up on the screen any triangle you want and do anything to it that you want. Then you can formulate theories and keep trying them out on different triangles to see if they hold up," says Schwartz. "We've tried it with tenth graders, and they've discovered *new* theorems, and we've had slow learners duplicate every theorem in the book."

Tomorrow's microcomputers, souped up with artificial intelligence, glistening with user friendliness, are sure to affect everything from tenth-grade geometry classes to Fortune 500 decision making. No one is quite sure, however, where the computer revolution will take us.

"The car analogy finally breaks down because the car is a static tool—it just gets you from here to there. By contrast, the computer is open-ended, with no limits on its ultimate uses," says Lotus's Morgan.

"That's why the effect of the computer will be both more profound and less predictable. Except for the human mind, the computer is the first open-ended tool ever."

According to Texas Instruments's Heilmeier, tomorrow's computers will be ubiquitous but inconspicuous. Everything from your toaster, to your home's heating system, to your car will be controlled by tiny, internal computers. You will not even know they are there. And as computers become ever more potent, they will shrink. Eventually, says Heilmeier, you may carry your computer in your shirt pocket, plugging into a terminal—probably your telephone—to access databases. But even before the pygmy computer arrives, computers will be doing a bigger share of our thinking.

"Within the next five years, expert systems—artificial intelligence—will be in the personal-computer marketplace. That, in turn, will impel our entire culture to start thinking in a more productive way about the nature of knowledge. The impact will be analogous to the introduction of books," predicts Ira Goldstein, director of the Application Technology Laboratory at Hewlett-Packard's Palo Alto laboratories.

He says that programs will soon be available to serve as your tax adviser, attorney, or personal physician. Because the programs will be intelligent enough to make judgments, they will be able to serve as librarians. "You call up a database and say, 'I want to know about dangerous animals in North America,' " says Goldstein. "The program decides that you must mean dangerous to *people*. It decides you probably

57

mean large animals, not disease-bearing microbes, that you mean extant animals, and it asks you questions if necessary. In other words, it thinks."

In about ten years, he forecasts, we can anticipate the debut of machine learning, which will allow us to program our computers by talking to them, much as we might talk to a student. And in 15 years, he says, "machines will be learning from one another across a worldwide network and from their own observations. We'll no longer be able to say that in all situations, people are always smarter than computers.

"My grandchild's best friend will probably be a computer," Goldstein continues. "It might well be that every child will grow up with a computer nanny who, in time, will change with him, becoming his lifelong companion. It's difficult to imagine how such a society will work, but the potential is much greater than the risk."

LITERATE COMPUTERS

By Phoebe Hoban

Instead of using artificial languages to communicate with their computers, some programmers are now teaching their machines to understand an old and complex language: everyday English.

Researchers in artificial intelligence are developing systems that may eventually make man-machine communication as natural a process as human conversation. "If computers are ever really going to become household appliances like the TV or radio, there is no question they will have to use natural language," says Kenneth Lim, of Dataquest, a California market-research firm. "The average Joe Public is never going to want to learn BASIC. You have to program the computer to be people-literate."

BASIC is a programming language used in applications that range from calculating a return on an investment to playing games. Writing computer instructions in BASIC or other common artificial languages requires strict adherence to rules. Misplacing a quotation mark, for example, can cause a program to quit, blocking the flow of data. By contrast, people continue conversations in ordinary English even when a previous phrase is ungrammatical or ambiguous.

Cracking the human communication code and teaching it to computers, however, is a challenge. Which comes first—form or content? Is it possible to comprehend the meaning of a group of words without first defining that group's structure? These and other fundamental questions have kept researchers busy since the Sixties. Now their work is beginning to pay off. And by late 1985, several companies plan to introduce the first natural-language programs for personal computers.

Like people, these programs will differ in how they use language. For example, one program, marketed by Artificial Intelligence Corporation, approaches English armed with a rich knowledge of grammar. The *Intellect* program understands such normal English questions as, "What is the average salary of unmarried managers in the Rochester division?" and searches databases for answers. *Intellect* reacts to such questions by diagraming the user's command or query to outline its basic structure. Then it uses a built-in dictionary to interpret individual words, then phrases, until it has built up an understanding of the entire statement's meaning.

The $69,500 system deals equally well with incomplete or ungrammatical requests, and it adapts easily to different databases—features that have won acceptance for *Intellect* in some 150 locations, from Aetna Life Insurance to Du Pont. And its designers signed an agreement designating the system as the off-the-shelf natural-language program for IBM mainframes. Coming up: a personal-computer version of the program, which could be available by the end of 1985, for under $500.

Another set of programs, marketed by Cognitive Systems, Inc., favors semantics—meaning—over syntax or grammar. Cognitive's founder, Roger Schank, believes that the key to all language is knowledge itself. "You simply can't talk about what you don't know about," Schank says. Based on the artificial-intelligence research Schank pioneered at Yale, each knowledge-based program avoids syntactic analysis and goes straight for the underlying meaning that each word represents. This model breaks down language into fundamental concepts rather than parts of speech. Any action, for instance, is categorized as 1 of 11 basic concepts. One of these, for example, is the idea of possessing something. These concepts are understood within a specific context supplied by a "script" that's based on knowledge of such real-life scenarios as reading a newspaper, having an argument, or analyzing stock-market prices. Because the system is not bogged down by grammar, it operates with equal facility in any language.

Since the vocabulary used cannot be separated from the information it conveys, Schank's programs are not just transistors. They are virtual experts, or "advisers," in their specific field or domain. One Cognitive program, *Explorer*, was developed for an oil company. In response to natural-language questions, it consults a database, retrieves information, and converts it into maps of oil wells. Another program, *Marketeer*, was developed as a natural-language interface for *Access*, a marketing-analysis database from Dialogue, Inc. And *Broker* accesses information from Standard and Poor's stock-market database, *Compustat*. The company is now developing advisory systems, costing between $250,000 and $350,000, to provide linguistic fluency and decision-making support in personal investment and tax preparation. "Our advisory systems are basically computer models of human experts," Schank explains.

For the future the company is considering a way to offer such computer expertise to owners of personal computers. Using a modem—a device to connect home computers to distant mainframes via telephone—anyone could tap into the wisdom of Cognitive's advisory systems, paying only for the amount of time they were connected. Users could pick up advice on investments, for example, almost as easily as dialing a long-distance call.

Symantec, a spinoff of Machine Intelligence Corporation (which makes robot vision), has ambitious plans for its natural-language system. Based on work first done at Stanford Research Institute, the company is developing a $300 to $500 program that combines rules of syntax and semantics with a proprietary database management system (DBMS) designed for the IBM personal computer. A businessman could use the system to keep his own file of personnel and sales data that could be accessed easily using ordinary English. An earlier version of the technology, called *Straight Talk*, is currently available for $660 as a natural-language interface for the Dictaphone System 6000 word processor.

Meanwhile, one company already markets a widely

used English-language system for personal computers. Mention *Savvy* to anyone in the artificial-intelligence community, and you will immediately trigger a semantic debate. Developed by Excalibur Technologies Corporation, this $349 to $950 tool talks to computers but ignores such niceties as semantics and syntax completely. Instead, it concentrates on recognizing letters of the alphabet as they are punched into the keyboard. It uses a pattern-recognition system—matching up strings of characters—to identify key words and phrases typical of the user. The Savvy system may not be artificial intelligence, but it is already popular with Apple II users, and the company is introducing a model for the IBM personal computer.

What's next for *Savvy*? Natural-language interfaces for personal robots. *Savvy* has developed a general-purpose interface that will be marketed for the RBX5 robot manufactured by RB Robots, of Denver. And, says company spokesman Nelson Winkless, this interface could be adaptd to other robots, like Heath Company's Hero. In fact, predicts *Savvy* president Jim Dowe, the personal robot and the personal computer will eventually merge into one mobile, intelligent system capable of humanlike decision and behavior.

In research-and-development laboratories from Bell to Bolt Beranek and Newman, work is already under way on the next generation of natural-language technology—programs that can combine the in-depth knowledge of an advisory system like *Explorer* with the adaptability of a query system like *Intellect*. "What's hitting the market now is just the tip of the camel's nose under the flap of the tent," says William Woods, of Bolt Beranek.

Widespread use of natural-language systems for computers is still a decade away, believes Ken Lim, of Dataquest. "But each piece of technology further closes the gap between man and machine. Someday," Lim predicts, "the human brain may actually be able to think commands directly into computers." Until then, we will have to be happy with machines that understand slang.

LOCKING UP DATA

By Daniel Kagan

Hackers are able to crack password codes and wander the phone lines, trespassing through data banks. Industrial spies raid secret data files, snatching new product designs. Computer criminals enrich themselves, plundering electronic fund-transfer networks. The Defense Department is positive—almost—that its top-security computer systems are invulnerable to penetration by outsiders or, worse, insiders with evil intentions.

Suddenly data security is the most important issue in the world of computing. In a few years the key element in the most tamperproof computers may not be a password, a secret personal I.D. number, or a data-encryption system. Instead, it may be the authorized user's fingerprint, or the unique blood-vessel pattern in the retina of his eye, or the length of his fingers, or the lines that crisscross his palm. It could be the one-of-a-kind characteristics of his voice or the pattern of his brain waves. In fact, it might actually turn out to be something even harder to quantify—the very *style* with which he uses the computer. It may be the idiosyncrasies of the way he logs on, the order in which he habitually executes commands, the rhythm with which he taps the keys, the pattern of mistakes he consistently makes.

As the future user goes about his computing tasks, a software program would monitor a previously entered statistical "profile" of these behavioral elements and compare them with his actions. As long as his habits remain the same, the program—let's call it the behavior analyzer—will continue to grant him access to the data for which he is authorized. But should his pattern of use vary considerably, the behavior analyzer assumes a bogus operator is tampering with the system and terminates the man-machine communication.

The behavior analyzer would recognize the user's operating profile in the same way telegraphers in the last century could recognize one another's Morse code signals. Each telegrapher had a recognizable "fist," a way of tapping out his dots and dashes, pausing here, slurring there—a rhythmic tattoo as distinctive as a signature.

This concept is so new it doesn't have an official name yet. It's being researched by SRI International, in Menlo Park, California, under the guidance of Donn Parker, one of the acknowledged masters of computer-security theory. The work marks a move away from I.D. verification based on what the operator *has* (like a magnetic-stripe card) and what he *knows* (like a password)—since these can be lost or stolen—toward using what the operator *is*. Because behavioral and physical dimensions are measured, the new systems of safeguarding data could be classed as both psychometric and biometric. In several other security systems, some of which will be operational later this year, the approach is purely biometric: Authorized users are identified by unique body characteristics.

"You can't leave your body at home like a card or a key, and no one can steal it," quips Tom Catto, of Palmguard, Inc., in Beaverton, Oregon. His company's contribution to biometric data security is the PG-2000, and although it can't foretell the future, it can identify you by reading the lines on your palm.

The PG-2000 looks at a 2"x2" area of the palm. The hand is placed over an opening in its reader unit and aligned by means of pegs between the fingers. Below the opening is a glass plate, and behind that is a solid-state camera made up of an array of photodiodes. The camera works much like a vidicon tube, and when a light inside the reader flashes, its 100-by-100 cell array captures and digitizes an image of the target palm into 10,000 bytes of information. This palm pattern is then stored as a template in the host computer the Palmguard is protecting. The process takes about three seconds, and the palm image can't be faked, even if someone were to sever the hand of an authorized user and try to pass it through the procedure.

"There's a time factor here," Catto explains. "As soon as the blood stops flowing through the tissues, the lines on the hand change. It's almost immediate." That means it's too short a time for amputation to be useful. Constructing a latex facsimile won't work either.

According to Catto, the PG-2000 is extremely accurate. Its Type I error rate—that is, refusing access to an authorized user with a template in storage and making him repeat the process—is slightly less than 1 percent. Its Type II error rate—mistakenly allowing someone with no clearance to pass through—is 0.00025 percent.

These high levels of accuracy are comparable to other biometric devices. The EyeDentifyer spots authorized computer users by reading the one-of-a-kind patterns formed by the network of minute blood vessels across the retina at the back of the eye. This acts as an eyeprint, analogous to a fingerprint but, says EyeDentifyer's Dennis Porter, much more accurate. He puts the device's Type I error rate at 0.01 percent and its Type II error rate at 0.005 percent.

To operate the unit, you look through something that resembles a large pair of binoculars mounted on a swivel base. One eyepiece is active and does the work; the other is a dummy. Inside the unit, a tiny 10-watt bulb glows, its light filtered of all wavelengths but the harmless infrared. This beam is focused on the fovea at the center of the retina, illuminating it to produce the distinctive blood-vessel pattern and bouncing it back to be picked up by a photocell array in the device. This retinal pattern is converted to a digital signal. The bits of data are then stored in the host computer as the user's template. The I.D. process takes about five seconds.

The granddaddy of biometric-security systems is the Stellar Systems Identimat, which reads hand geometry—the finger length of four fingers, minus the thumb. Like retinal patterns and palm- and fingerprints, finger lengths are a "uniquely identifiable trademark of individuals," according to Stellar's Kent Serling. The Identimat has been around since 1968, long before computer technology required routine close data supervision. The device's operation is simple.

The hand is placed on the unit so that the fingers rest along four grooves that have strips of photocells along their bottoms. An 800-watt blast of light illuminates the hand from above, tripping the exposed cells, which record finger lengths. These data are made into a template, which is stored in the machine.

The Identimat is the first and longest-lived biometric security device: It has been used for years to guard not data but entryways at such high-security locations as nuclear-fuel-processing plants, military areas, and other sensitive high-technology-research zones.

Back in the mid-Seventies Texas Instruments (TI) invented another biometric security device, a voice-pattern identifier, as part of a security-research contract with the Air Force. In fact, TI installed a voice-pattern doorway-security device at its own facilities in 1974. It is still in use there, as is one sold to Allied General Nuclear Services, in North Carolina. At $100,000 per unit, these were extremely accurate but too expensive to market; so these two are the only ones in existence. With the release of its new TMS 320 signal-processing chip this year, TI expects some entrepreneurs to use the processor to program a less-expensive voice-recognition device for widespread use as a data protector.

At the moment, the only fully operational biometric I.D. system in widespread use is the Identimat. The newer, more sophisticated systems are "developmentally operational," according to Mike Eaton, director of the entry-control-systems division at Sandia Laboratories, in Albuquerque, New Mexico, which evaluates all new biometrics as they are introduced. But right now, they are all still too expensive for wholesale use in typical multiterminal computer systems in business, banking, and other fields. "The next breakthrough," says Eaton, "will be to get single-unit costs down from the five-thousand to ten-thousand-dollar range to the one-thousand-dollar range."

That would make the ultimate goal a reality: installing an EyeDentifier, Identimat, Palmguard, voice-recognition system, or other device at every terminal on every existing mainframe-computer system where security is important. The foolproof biometric-authentication step would be added to the familiar routine of logging on with an I.D. number and/or password. The system would keep fund transfers secure, keep the engineering boys out of the accounting data and the accounts people away from new-product designs. And it would completely outfox hackers, since they could not enter the system without the proper biometric I.D.

Perhaps the ultimate biometric identifier would be one that would read, average, digitize, and store for comparison every authorized user's brain-wave pattern. All that's necessary will be for someone to develop a safe, easy way to administer an electroencephalogram without using contact electrodes or a bulky helmet. Even then, the human brain will still be the key to unlocking crucial knowledge.

SMART TV

By Len Hilts

You are watching the summer Olympics of 1988. The TV cameras follow the breathtaking finish of the 1,500-meter run as three athletes sprint abreast down the stretch. Just as they reach the tape, you hit the FREEZE-FRAME button on your remote-control handset. Then you touch PRINT, and the printer beside your TV starts chattering.

Without waiting for an instant replay, you recall the frozen picture—now stored in the TV's memory—to the screen and see an unparalleled sports-action photo of a historic finish. A few minutes later the printer finishes its reproduction of the picture, and you have a permanent record of the great event.

This little scenario is possible because your 1988 TV set belongs to the new "third generation" of television. First there was black and white. Then there was color. And now television has gone digital. It has evolved from an analog device into a digital computer with a monitor. As a result, it can do dozens of things never before possible. And every year, the TV-computer acts smarter and is more responsive to viewers' interests.

Some of the new capabilities, in addition to freeze-framing and printing, include ghost-free images; a fantastically sharp picture, thanks to a screen with twice as many lines of resolution as today's TV's; self-diagnosis of malfunctions; constant automatic upgrading of color quality; handset-controlled zoom; and a second picture inset into one corner of the screen so you can watch one program while monitoring another. Overall, the technology means viewers can be more active participants in the shows they watch.

You won't have to wait until 1988 for digital TV to arrive. Major manufacturers such as Zenith, GE, and Sony are expected to market sets with digital circuitry by the end of 1984. No one knows which features will be on the first digital sets, but manufacturers won't need more than a few years to produce a whole new kind of TV.

In a way, digital TV began in the late Sixties, when our astronauts relayed photographs from the moon. Most people were impressed by the quality of these pictures but didn't question how they were sent. After all, we had had Wirephotos for a long time, and the electronic transmission of photographs didn't seem all that unusual. But in fact, the beaming of pictures from the moon was a sophisticated exercise in digital electronics. The pictures were broken down, dot by dot, into binary code and sent to Earth as a stream of 0's and 1's.

Here the code was translated, line by line, back into a picture. The digitizer doing the work took its reference points from the code, then thoughtfully interpolated more lines and dots to fill the gaps in the picture, giving it better detail than a standard TV would.

Designers of TVs began to adopt digital circuits shortly after that. The first use came in remote-control units, which replaced older mechanical systems and made computerized channel selection possible. Then Zenith eliminated the old horizontal- and vertical-hold controls, replacing them with a digital circuit to do the job automatically.

In 1985 we'll see a quantum leap in the analog-to-digital evolution, as digital control is extended to the processing of the TV picture itself. It will be possible, thanks to VLSI (very large scale integration) chips, developed by ITT Semiconductors in a research project that lasted more than five years.

These chips are a kind of signal-processing factory inside the TV set. The analog signal transmitted by a television station is received by the TV's antenna and relayed into the set, where it is broken up into a digital signal by the VLSI chips. Once the signal is in digital form, it can be processed in many ways. First, it can be cleaned up by removing the noise and clutter that could cause ghosts on the screen. Then it can be enhanced by scan conversion, the addition of more lines. The pictures generated by television receivers in North America comprise 525 horizontal lines. An additional line between each existing line can be interpolated by the computer, thereby doubling the resolution and providing an extremely sharp picture.

Carl Michelotti, vice president of color-TV engineering at Zenith, says of the digital operation: "One of its big advantages is its storage capability. In digital TV you can store picture information. You can examine it in storage and, if acceptable, pass it on to the screen. If it isn't good because of a ghost or because it doesn't do something desirable, you can perform electronic surgery on it. After the image has been corrected, the computer passes it on. In an analog system, you can't do that."

Once the digital circuitry has done its work, the signal is translated back into analog form and sent to the TV screen. The important difference between an analog TV and a digital TV is that the digital set functions like a computer. But instead of getting its information from a keyboard, as a computer does, it gets it from the signal provided by an antenna, cable, telephone line, or satellite dish. The signal is controlled by software—computer instructions—that is built into the set.

Many of the future enhancements in digital TV will be the result of revisions made in the set's software programming, rather than in the development of new hardware. TV designers look on this feature as one of the great advantages of digital TV.

If you know anything about computer graphics, you already have an understanding of how digital TV works. Once the set has the picture information in digital form, it can process it just as a computer processes graphics. The zoom effect, the freeze-frame, and the inset picture are different types of computer graphics.

The new ITT chips that make up the digital factory replace about 350 resistors and other parts and do the work of approximately 300,000 transistors. Engineers expect chips to increase the reliability and longevity of television sets, just as earlier TVs were improved when solid-state circuits replaced tubes.

TV engineers realize that television is no longer just an entertainment medium. Many of the practical chores planned for the computer—home banking, instant news coverage, and electronic shopping, for example—now can come into your home through the TV screen. A separate computer installation won't be necessary.

Zenith's Michelotti says, "The transmission of data is digital; so as digital TV develops, a whole new generation of services involving data will develop. The data can come from any source—including off-the-air transmission, cable, and telephone lines—and then be processed in the TV set. Right now we can't even guess at what those services might be. But as people see a need, digital-TV technology will make it possible for them."

MOLECULE MACHINES

By Anthony Liversidge

Arthur Olson may be treading the path to immortality. A molecular biologist at the Scripps Clinic, in La Jolla, California, Olson is sitting in front of a computer screen that is filled with colored balls and arrows, like firework bursts in a night sky.

The lights represent the structure of two molecules—the arrangement in space of their atoms, connecting bonds, and electronic force fields. Twisting a bank of knobs beside the keyboard, Olson steers one molecule forward so that a protruding part of it enters a cavity in the other structure. He is trying to find out how well a protein structure fits into the receptor site of another protein.

Olson is refining one of the most promising applications of computers: sophisticated graphics programs that provide chemists with beautiful, three-dimensional simulations of molecules—images they can instantly shrink, expand, swivel, or merge to form more complicated structures.

A quantum jump ahead of the Tinkertoy-like models that have long been used to visualize molecules, computer graphics are causing a revolution in organic chemistry, enhancing the creativity of chemists, much as word processors have boosted writers' output. And if, as some hope, artificial-intelligence techniques are successfully joined to the new technology, the ultimate benefits to human health may be astonishing.

This modeling technology is already proving indispensable in designing new drugs, according to organic chemists at pharmaceutical companies such as Hoffmann-La Roche and Merck. Using a computer and sophisticated software, they can narrow down choices and save the labor and time of synthesizing tens, perhaps hundreds, of alternative compounds.

Several drugs designed with the aid of computers have reached the stage of clinical trial, though none have yet been marketed. Many drug and chemical companies are making huge investments in the best equipment available—Du Pont is committing some $24 million to provide every lab in its research division with a state-of-the-art computer terminal.

Proteins, biochemicals of staggering complexity, are obvious candidates for computer graphic design. Although proteins are nothing more than long strips of amino acids, they rarely exist in nature in this simple, linear configuration. Instead, these ropelike molecules twist, turn, and fold in on themselves to form elaborate knotted structures, each protein assuming its own unique three-dimensional architecture. To act on a protein, then, a drug must precisely match that protein's contours and join to it in the same way that a child's Lego blocks fit comfortably together.

Consider a body protein known as renin, which has been linked to high blood pressure. A commercial race is now under way to develop a drug that will block renin's action. One front-running team, led by Daniel Veber, at Merck & Company, is using computer modeling to refine several "very good" renin inhibitors they have designed. The polishing is done by docking a suggested structure into a key receptor site on the renin molecule and then chemically redefining it for a closer fit.

Such docking is exactly like landing a Boeing 747, says David Pensak, who heads Du Pont's modeling effort. "Crashing through a hangar or overshooting the runway is analogous to a drug molecule coming out the back side of an enzyme." Pensak is considering buying a pilot-training simulator for the chemists in his program.

Researchers at Cambridge University, in England, gave a hint of what is to come when they used computer graphics and genetic engineering to invent a better enzyme. Enzymes are the large class of proteins that catalyze and control all chemical reactions in a living cell. The group changed the structure of one enzyme to make it bind better to another molecule, thereby improving the efficiency of a chemical reaction.

Greg Winter, coordinator of the project, sees this success as a step toward eventually making proteins as yet unknown on Earth—proteins that would incorporate amino acids other than the standard 20 found in living beings. The computer graphics he used were relatively elementary, he says, but the new Evans and Sutherland equipment they have just installed will be much more useful. "We're on our way to creating the first alien life form," Winter says.

At present, computers are totally dependent on input data, which are often sketchy; the computers don't do any creative thinking for the chemists. Pensak judges that it will be at least five to ten years before the computers can do the modeling themselves. None of today's programs could have replaced James Watson, for instance, who won the Nobel Prize in 1962 for his part in the discovery of the double-helical structure of DNA, the molecule that carries genetic information. "The computer is incapable of generating wholly new structures," says Pensak. "It took Watson's genius to recognize DNA could be a spiral chain."

But what of the future? Expert systems, programs that mimic expert decision making, are being developed; chemical engineers will soon put them to work. Intelligenetics, of Palo Alto, California, for example, markets both artificial-intelligence (AI) programs for the biotechnology field and database programs that draw on huge gene banks in Washington and Europe. Since genes serve as blueprints for proteins, these DNA data banks will help scientists explore how variations in protein structure are reflected in the underlying genetic code.

Robert Langridge, professor of pharmaceutical chemistry at the University of California at San Francisco and a leader in developing sophisticated modeling programs, hopes that computers will eventually be able to depict the exact shape of a protein merely by analyzing its genetic code. To do so, however, the AI program will have to recognize the DNA sequences that determine how proteins fold into zigzags and loops, which in turn determine their exposed surfaces and thus how they react with other molecules.

That capability would indeed be marvelous, agrees Columbia University's Barry Honig, professor of biochemistry and molecular biophysics. "Anyone who came up with that program tomorrow would be awarded the Nobel Prize in chemistry, physics, medicine, and peace combined." Is it pie in the sky? Langridge says, "There are so many problems to be solved, but we like to think it might happen in the order of a decade."

Such programs would usher in a strange new world of tiny biological workhorses—proteins custom-designed to carry out such dreams as mining gold from seawater, regenerating lost limbs or teeth, or even achieving immortality.

Immortality? "It's conceivable," says Honig. "Everything is chemistry. If we can figure out how it works and how to affect it, everything we experience can be modified. And most biological functions are controlled by proteins. Why shouldn't we live as long as whales?"

CHURCH ON A CHIP

By Phoebe Hoban

"There's an old story," recounts Rabbi Irving Rosenbaum, head of Chicago's Institute for Computers in Jewish Life, "about a scientist who builds a computer that he programs to be omniscient. Then he asks the computer, 'Is there a God?' And the computer replies, 'There is one now.' "

Although computer worship has not yet spread beyond a few fanatical IBM and Apple stockholders, an increasing number of religious groups are using computers to teach the Word. Religious software ranges from an electronic version of the Responsa—a library containing more than 2,000 years of Jewish law—to Bible-based video games with names like *The Philistine Ploy* and *Samson and Delilah* (billed as the adventure games that took three thousand years to create).

By far the closest thing to a bona fide computer church is the One Attunement Group, created by Peter and Trudy Johnson-Lenz, a husband and wife programming team. As part of a National Science Foundation study, the Johnson-Lenzes became early participants in the

81

New Jersey Institute of Technology's Electronic Information and Exchange System (EIES).

"Traditionally, people gather in the same place at the same time to meditate and worship," explains Peter Johnson-Lenz. "But one of the central aspects of a computer network is that it is asynchronous and needs no meetinghouse. Since God is supposed to transcend space and time, why couldn't we take advantage of the abstract nature of the computer medium and share in the spirit electronically—tuning in with different people around the globe and around the clock?"

The One Attunement Group went online in 1980, just hours before the tragic murder of John Lennon, and became a place where EIES members congregated to share their grief. Currently, this electronic chapel has about 100 international members.

The format of the One Attunement software was inspired in part by the Scottish utopian community Findhorn, whose members begin each day by clasping hands in a circle to attune with one another and themselves. Programmers also drew on the traditions of Hicksite Quaker meetings, in which members take turns sharing meditations or inspirations. WELCOME TO THE ONE ATTUNEMENT GROUP, the program begins. WOULD YOU LIKE TO ATTUNE NOW? (PRESS Y FOR YES, N FOR NO.) NOW CLOSE YOUR EYES, PAUSE QUIETLY FOR A FEW MOMENTS, AND BE HERE NOW. ATTUNE YOURSELF WITH YOURSELF AND THE UNIVERSE AND, SO, WITH ALL OF US. PRESS RETURN WHEN YOU FEEL ATTUNED. Random selections from 110 spiritual quotations, from sources as diverse as Zen Buddhism and Antoine de Saint-Exupéry (author of *The Little Prince*) flicker onto the screen. IF YOU ARE MOVED BY THE SPIRIT, the computer instructs, PLEASE SHARE YOUR INSPIRATION NOW. At this point, individual inspirations can be entered or inspirations from other members can be scrolled up. Finally, this message materializes: THANK YOU FOR SHARING THE SPIRIT WITH US. GO IN PEACE. The One Attunement Group is currently available only to members of the EIES computer network, but the Johnson-Lenzes will soon introduce software that will enable it to run on a personal-computer-based network.

"The temple of the Philistines—you're at the top—but you are a prisoner—at least Samson is—and you control his incredible power with nothin' but a joystick!" reads the flier for *Samson and Delilah*—one of 100 religious programs from Davka Corporation, a division of the Institute for Computers in Jewish Life. Other games, complete with vivid graphics and spooky music (there's even a synthesized shofar—the ram's horn sounded on high holidays), are *Bible Baseball*, a quiz game; *The Game of the Maccabees* ("The Maccabees need you—Antiochus the emperor demands to be worshipped as a god—are you going to stand for it?"); *Catch a Hamantash* (the object is to prevent flying Purim pastries called Hamantashen from squashing); and *Crumb Eater*, a Pac-Man-style Passover game. And if you want your computer to speak Hebrew, Davka has a computer chip called *Hebrew Hardware* that plugs into the Apple II and generates Hebrew letters. There's also a program that runs through the steps of the Passover Seder ritual, and even a kosher cookbook, *Jewish Compu-chef*.

This may sound like somewhat frivolous fare. But Rosenbaum relates it to an ancient Jewish custom: "When a youngster first went to school, his teacher would smear the pages of his books with honey to make it sweet. These days the sweetener is a computer."

The more mystical side of digital Judaica is the huge Responsa database developed in conjunction with Israel's Bar-Ilan University. This electronic library contains 38,000 documents of Jewish custom and law, dating back several thousand years. Talmudic scholars can consult the database to shed the light of the ages on modern dilemmas. Ponder this question: With all this high-tech religion, can a robot be a member of a minyan—the traditional ten-member Jewish prayer group?

After the two key words, *robot* and *minyan*, are punched into the system, it takes the database less than a minute to search 600 million bytes and spit out 59 related citations. One holds the answer, attributed to a sixteenth-century rabbi, Zevi Ashkenazi. An android—or golem—cannot be counted as part of a minyan because no matter how intelligent this being is, it is not human and therefore not responsible for its actions or obligated to fulfill the commandments.

Have you ever wondered how many bytes there are in the Bible? Bible Research Systems, of Austin, Texas, has squeezed the King James version of the Good Book onto a set of eight double-sided disks. This technological miracle was performed using a proprietary program developed by company founders Kent Ochel and Bert Brown. It condenses 36 million bits of data that could have filled 50 disks. This aptly named software, *The Word Processor*, accesses any verse in the Bible by searching for key words, phrases, sentences, or even character strings. And a new program, called the *Transliterator*, provides the Greek root of every word in the King James text. Both of the programs cost $200 and run on most personal computers, including the IBM PC, Kaypro, Compaq, Columbia, and a number of Apples. There is also a Macintosh version in the works. *The Word Processor* has been shipped all over the world, from Chicago to China, but perhaps one parish in Phoenix, Arizona, holds a vision of future religious services.

There, a televised pastor tends his flock, all of whom can use a reference code printed on the TV screen during the sermon to scroll up accompanying Bible text on their home computers.

A host of other religious software is also being developed. Sat Tara Khalsa, president of the Chicago-based Kriya Corporation, maker of the best-selling program *Typing Tutor*, is a member of the Indian Sikh religion. He is developing a database that will contain holy scriptures, dietary and nutritional information, as well as some of the 2,000 yoga exercises practiced by his sect. Computerized catechism may soon become standard in some Catholic schools, thanks to a program called *In Christ Jesus; Testing Program and Computerized Inventory*, developed by the Benziger Corporation, a Catholic publishing house in California.

And there's some spinoff software from the giant Mormon genealogical database, which has been computerized for the last decade. The $35, six-disk *Personal Ancestral File* should help members of the

Church of Jesus Christ of Latter-Day Saints, and others, trace their ancestry.

With computer screens scrolling out holy texts (some in their original language), are the faithful in any danger of deifying a mere machine? Rosenbaum doesn't believe so. "Computers will never be rabbis or serve Communion. If you use a tool such as computer technology for teaching ancient truths, then technology becomes the handmaiden of religion rather than its master. But," he warns, "any device can be used for good or evil. It depends on the user's intention whether it serves God or the devil."

"A computer is no more an idol than a church pew is," says Peter Johnson-Lenz. "God is in people, not in a machine." Moreover, he points out, computers can enhance the spirituality of religious ritual because in an electronic church, "you can't see if someone is fat, short, beautiful, or ugly. People are pared down to pure spirit."

But Orchel's judgment is the most down-to-earth: "Once you've used a computer for a few weeks and seen how many bugs you can run into, you realize it is not a god in any way, shape, or form."

MONEY MACHINES

By Anthony Liversidge

Recently a computer on Wall Street took a long, hard look at a hill of beans. And based on the computer's performance in predicting the future of the soybean market, designers of the system are now certain that artificial intelligence can make money grow like a beanstalk.

According to Manhattan's Raden Research Group, their computer spewed out its forecast for an 18-month period based on an analysis of five years' worth of data on soybeans. It was only a test. But Raden's thirty-nine-year-old president, Dave Aronson, says the computer would have generated up to three times the profit of technical models currently used by traders. Aronson is confident that the program will enable a computer to examine any financial market and to develop sound and profitable investment strategies. "The model seems to anticipate trends," Aronson says. "Technical analysts usually recognize a trend only after it appears."

For all their fast moves in money matters, the pin-striped professionals of Wall Street have so far been slow to embrace the computer as a partner in making investment decisions. Brokers have used hardware and software mainly for data transmission and calculations. But with the continued success of Raden's program and others like it, money managers and financial institutions may soon be buying and selling according to trading strategies produced by their computers, not merely their own intuition and experience.

"We can now give the computer general historical data of a market," Aronson says, "and let it tell us what to look for. It will build its own model."

Raden's methods of computerized pattern recognition resemble those that have already proved helpful in medical diagnosis, weather prediction, and oilfield exploration. Once loaded with the Raden program, called PRISM (Pattern Recognition Information Synthesis Modeling), the computer is fed many of the variables involved in determining the way, say, soybean prices move. Having analyzed how the market works, the computer makes its prediction and then suggests what action to take.

PRISM goes beyond current statistical methods used by Wall Street forecasters. As Aronson points out, conventional techniques depend on human understanding of market forces. Analysts using these techniques load the computer with a model of these human concepts, rather than allowing it to work out fresh principles. Traditional methods are like "baking a strawberry shortcake from a recipe," Aronson explains. "You are provided with the recipe, and you just follow the directions, using the ingredients you are told to use."

PRISM, however, is like "putting many possible ingredients on the table and combining them in a variety of ways until the result is close to the idea of strawberry cake that the cook has in mind"—or something better than the cook ever dreamed of. PRISM works by accepting up to 500 different variables that money managers, traders, and other experts suggest may have a bearing on trends in a particular market. By analyzing historical data, PRISM draws correlations too complex for a human to detect. Then it packages the data into a model of the way the market works. It keeps the design of the model as simple as possible, however, using only the variables it finds most important.

Raden now plans to apply the program on behalf of its first client, a meat corporation interested in the cattle market. Already signed up, the company will pay $30,000 and a monthly retainer, dependent upon the quality of the results, for the privilege of having the electronic seer's advice.

Computerized pattern recognition has proved successful in other areas. Another consulting company, Entropy Ltd., has established a good track record in forecasting weather, the breakdown rate of nuclear-reactor cores, and the life expectancies of individual heart and cancer patients. Entropy's president, Ron Christensen, reports that he tried the technique on gold-bullion prices and scored high. "We were sixty-eight to seventy percent correct in predicting market movement one day ahead," he says.

Other experts in the prediction business are cautious about whether Raden might have discovered the alchemic touchstone. "Most of what is important in finance is nonnumeric—political events, trade barriers, people's perceptions," says Gene Pettinelli, of American Research and Development, a Boston research firm with an interest in artificial intelligence. "You cannot capture all the important data relating to, say, soybean moves."

Raden, however, is forging ahead. There are plans to have PRISM produce a number of other models by the end of this year, one of them predicting the course of the Dow-Jones average. An investment fund is "down the line," says Aronson. How profitable might a good PRISM-produced model be, once up and running?

"You could be talking several hundred percent a year," Aronson believes. "If it works, we'll be very rich."

PART THREE:
IN SEARCH OF
ARTIFICIAL
INTELLIGENCE

*"The real problem is
not whether machines think
but whether men do."*
—B.F. Skinner

Viewpoint: On Artificial Intelligence

By Marvin Minsky

As the era of the robot approaches, we must continually ask ourselves the question of how intelligent machines might change our lives. We're rapidly adjusting to using automation in our science, art, and businesses. But so far machines have helped us mainly with the things we hate to do. What then will happen when we face new options in our work and home, where more intelligent machines can better do the things we like to do? What kinds of minds and personalities should we dispense to them? What kinds of rights and privileges should we withhold from them? Are we ready to face such questions?

Today our robots are like toys. They do only the simple things they're programmed to. But clearly they're about to cross the edgeless line past which they'll do the things *we* are programmed to. Already there's so much power in those arcade chips that one might think the toys are playing with our kids.

Most robots rolling around these days are mere

fakes, remote-controlled by people hiding out of view. A few, though, do some things that real robots ought to do, like sensing the sounds of certain words and acting on those words and phrases. And as they reap the fruits of research, these machines will show more visible signs of having minds.

For years there exited an odd paradox: We learned to make computers expert in many special skills but couldn't endow them with much ordinary, common sense. Why not? The reason was so simple it was hard to see: We're all so accustomed to using common sense that we take it for granted, but it's actually the most complicated thing we do! An "expert" can get by with a few kinds of highly specialized information, but a sensible person needs a large body of general knowledge. We'll have to wait awhile longer for computer sensibility—a decade or a century, perhaps, but just a moment in the grand march of history.

So, soon enough we'll learn to make computers organize their thoughts. We'll make them learn from us and help teach others, too. We'll give them inhumanly dextrous limbs and uncannily observant senses, and also show them how to build copies of themselves. This could begin a flood of "automatic self-replication"—machines making more machines at very low cost. Then we'll learn to cope with the resulting exponential growth of wealth and productivity.

What will it take to make machines that really think, that solve new problems? It won't suffice just to feed computers a lot of separate facts; each must be linked to other things we know. A mind is merely the web formed by such connections; its quality depends on how well it correlates the scraps of knowledge in that web and when it decides to use those scraps—and when not to. (Common sense, for example, demands knowing the exceptions to the rule. You can put things in your pocket—but not if they're too big to fit, belong to someone else, or bite too hard.) And minds must also know about their own intentions: how and when one should persist, submit, or balance between action and reflection.

How big are they, these human webs of information and belief? I'd guess a billion links would more than match the mind of any sage. A billion seconds stretches 30 years—and no psychologist has ever found a way to make a person learn something new each second for any prolonged period. But a billion bytes of memory may soon be cheap. Today computer memories do single operations at a time; soon they'll do millions simultaneously. But let's face facts. We just don't yet know how to weave our knowledge webs into our new machines. I see this as the most exciting research problem of our time: how to put enough mechanisms together in harmony to form minds of growing competence and breadth. Most people still think such things must be impossible to understand. I think they're only very complicated.

Eventually the day will arrive when human knowledge becomes the domain of the computer. When everything we want is already done for us by thinking machines, how will we then spend our time? Which entertainments will we choose, what custom-programmed mental stimuli? And what of Time itself—how long will we tolerate the meager years our bodies last? Our mortal stay seems fixed by makeshift engineering: Our body cells, "controlled" by programmed

suicide and war, degenerate and die as immune systems fail and misinform us to destroy ourselves.

I'm sick of hearing evolution praised; no self-
respecting programmer would bury software bugs
such dreadful ways! I'd bet we'd do at least as well to
start afresh (without that billion-year accumulated
mess) and try to transfer all we really want from those
vast symbol-process-structure webs we call our selves
into more safe and neat immortal codes.

Then finally we'll have to think of how to treat
minds made to our design. How right will it be to
switch them on and off? How wrong would it be, not
to make all the minds one can? Our present civilization's code of ethics came to us too easily: It assumes
that man has no control over mind. We had to choose
only how far our loyalty need reach, past family and
friend, to a stranger from another land. But when we
really start to make ourselves, why, then we'll really
have to face ourselves.

*Marvin Minsky, former president of the American Association for
Artificial Intelligence, is director of the Artificial Intelligence
Laboratory at M.I.T.*

ROBO-SHOCK!

By Kathleen Stein

Melinda and Kirk and Mike and Mark are making a robot. They call it R202, the name of the building they work in at a company called TRW. "R202's purpose in life will be to move around the office and look at things," says Michael Jamgochian, one of its four systems-engineer creators, "to explore . . . to go from Mark Thomsen's desk to Melinda Sherbring's desk when we tell it to and to avoid obstacles and people." Eventually "it will enter, deliver one-liners, and leave," adds Kirk Moody.

Although the TRW group is trying to keep the design simple and modular, building an adaptive, autonomous robot is an ambitious project—perhaps never really done before—fraught with major problems on every level. The biggest hurdle facing the TRW quartet, however, is not technological. It's financial. Employed by TRW, one of the biggest high-tech companies in the United States, the robot's makers aren't getting a nickel from the firm for

research and development. R202's gestation and bi█
must take place after the working day. Melinda, Kirk,
Mike, and Mark have a bright idea, and they have to
moonlight it.

In a sense, robotics can be seen as a symbol of
American technology today, a bellwether indicating
the direction of industry, employment, electronic intelligence, and the human use of human beings. And
in a sense, the boxlike, rolling R202 is a symbol of
robotics. Its creators, like hopeful parents, want it to
win friends, move freely in high circles, and learn
steadily. But R202 faces growing pains. Although
TRW is supplying some hardware, R202 hasn't yet
been given the dowry of corporate support it needs to
enter the American workforce. Some people, in fact,
are blatantly terrified of such machines.

Robots make news. The silly slave-creatures in the
movies generate a huge new toy industry, while the
giant praying mantis-type assembly-line robot steadily
displaces blue-collar workers in the midlands. When
Isaac Asimov recently quipped, "Robots don't kill
people, robots kill jobs," he was only half right. In
1982 the Japanese disclosed information they'd been
hiding: A robot had fatally crushed a worker who had
strayed into its personal zone. The Japanese supposedly welcome each new robot with a Shinto ceremony
when it is installed. Yet behind the scenes Japanese
labor unions are beginning to express deep concern
about the security of their rank and file.

"Four million Americans out of a job by 1990,"
blares one forecast. And according to Harley Shaiken,
labor and technology analyst at the Massachusetts
Institute of Technology, in the next ten years General

Motors alone will purchase 20,000 robots. These machines could displace another 40,000 to 50,000 auto workers besides the thousands already laid off directly and indirectly by automation.

"The argument is often raised," Shaiken says, "that unless we introduce robots, industries in the United States will not be able to compete, and even more jobs will be lost. But that's half an argument. It doesn't tell us who will lose their jobs. For workers, robots or foreign competition is merely a choice between hanging and the electric chair. And that's the bind we, as a society, have to break out of."

Others argue that the loss of jobs is not the most difficult economic challenge posed by robots. "Retraining is the major social problem created by rapid robotization," says industrial-robot expert Eli Lustgarten, of Paine, Webber, Mitchell, Hutchins, Inc., "not unemployment. Massive retraining programs will be needed to prevent the creation of an oversupply of workers whose skills have become obsolete." And at the moment very little is being done to create retraining programs, much less to draw up strategies such as shorter work hours or longer-range plans for the robotized economy as a whole.

"Robots have an extraordinary potential to be beneficial," Shaiken continues. "Robotics is a technology that could enhance the quality of life. But the technology will not do that automatically. If robots are used without regard for how humans are affected, then their promises will be perverted; to talk about their promise in the abstract tells us very little."

Could robots determine Ronald Reagan's future? Shaiken thinks so. Robots were an issue in the 1984 presidential election, he says, popping up in debates about employment, job security, and the future of American technology.

Robots trigger some odd anxieties. Look at the letters to the Mego Corporation, in New York, which makes a robotlike toy called the Mego 2-XL. "I apologize for nearly denying my son the opportunity to befriend a 2-XL because of my prejudice," one letter says. Another: "I'm sure Wayne would rather have a 2-XL help him with his homework than me." Or, "Our friends play with 2-XL more than with us." Is this the pattern of the future—robots replacing parents, friends, and teachers in people's affections? When homebots are a ubiquitous presence in the social fabric, will they be treated to the whole emotional gamut—love, hate, paranoia, lust—that humans inflict on one another? Probably. And what will it do to us? That remains to be seen. But Tom McLaughlin, an actor renowned for his robot roles (he taught Woody Allen's robot-actors in *Sleeper*), tells us he thinks humans might get a little bored and fatigued with being surrounded by inorganic zombies that are relentlessly precise, logical, and tireless—even in their mistakes—never acting on a hunch, intuition, or impulse of fantasy.

New York psychologist Diane Connors thinks there could be a problem if robots take over too many human endeavors. "Experiencing errors and then fixing them is part of the creative process," she says. "Error sometimes becomes purposefully embedded in objects, and that's often what gives them their richness."

And of course, there are the more primordial fears.

"Some people believe devils could come to dwell in robots, and control them and us," McLaughlin says. Another expert cites apprehension over "robo-terrorism," a scenario in which a mad electrician seizes a centralized computerized control system and marshals all the mechanical rovers into squadrons of killer troops guided by a central processor. And then there's the time-honored *Sorcerer's Apprentice* theme, echoed by the Isley Brothers' "I-turned-you-on-and-now-I-can't-turn-you-off" concept.

But more pervasive today is a kind of mixed anxiety: fear mediated by vague, quasimystical longings for a corporeal machine/man union such as portrayed in *The Demon Seed*. In this grade-B movie, Julie Christie is trapped in her own home by her scientist-husband's intelligent computer. The computer builds itself a robot, which proceeds to rape and impregnate her. Eventually she gives birth to a golden-scaled, metallic baby-thing.

Robo-shock is here today—both for those whose lives are dominated by the intricacies of actually designing the things, and for those in whose imaginations sleek little mechanoids already serve, obey, and mix the drinks. Actor McLaughlin notes that when he plays a 'bot, even a robot dandy in a velvet suit, "people come up to me and ask me if I'm real. Real *what*?" McLaughlin laughs. "They think such robots are already here, and they want to know if I'm impersonating one, or *am* one."

When will shock be surpassed by reality? Not for a decade at least, say most experts, and artificial-intelligence (AI) leaders such as John McCarthy think it will take a conceptual leap beyond our wildest theories to accomplish the creation of truly intelligent machines—devices smart enough to challenge their makers.

"There is this immense contrast between some people's notion of what will happen and the harsh realities of what is actually here now," explains David Grossman, manager of automation research at IBM's Thomas J. Watson Research Center, in Yorktown Heights, New York. "When you're in the area of speculative mobile robots—*androids*—you have left the field of what might go wrong and have entered areas where nothing has gone right yet." Indeed, AI and robotics types don't hide the fact that today, most robots' vision is dim. They can hardly hear and barely use a natural language. They don't have the dexterity of a six-month-old baby.

It is much easier to get a so-called expert system computer to play psychiatrist or diagnose a physical ailment than it is to get a robot to solve the most trivial problem—one that a dog might find simple. Like severely retarded children, who require continuous attention from their parents, today's most advanced robots are doted on, second to second, by their creators. "In a robot the interaction with the real world is very difficult," says Michael Brady, senior research scientist at MIT's Robotics Laboratory. "You can't form artificial models of the real world with all its warts, wrinkles, and bumps. Still, that's what we're trying to do," he says, laughing.

Thomsen of TRW talks about realism backlash: "First everyone had the SF idea that a robot could do anything. Then the industrial-automation people came out saying that's a pipe dream and began cutting back expectations. Right now we're swimming against that. We are at the stage where we can start working on a couple of those pipe dreams."

Marvin Minsky, of MIT's AI lab, has said that robot makers should be designing the flimsiest of automatons—robots that shake, rattle, shudder, experience gear backlash, and droop. And then, he says, we should create sophisticated software to compensate for all the mechanical faults.

The TRW quartet is doing something like that. They will be able—through high-level software and fairly simple hardware—to demonstrate exactly what can be done with the remote sensing rover today. They are in the vanguard. But where is that?

For one thing, even at the forefront of robot research, most machines don't walk. Plans for R202 call for it to roll through an office on three sets of wheels, navigating on its own, past clutter and moving people, at record-breaking speeds of up to one foot per second.

This activity, simple enough for the office gofer—or even a centipede—presents the challenge of a dragon hunt for a robot. The most complex problem facing the creators of R202 is designing a program that will continuously update the information the robot receives on its daily rounds and make predictions based on that constant flow of sensory data. The program will give the machine, among other things, an internal representation of the robot's immediate environment. Without this "internal world" in its memory, the machine couldn't move an inch. "It has to be adaptive," Moody says. Sherbring adds: "Up to now humans would make decisions about where the machines would go. We're trying to give it the capability to make these value judgments by itself."

What will be the robot's biggest problem? "People coming up and staring at it," its designers are quick to say. "It's going to be surrounded by people all the time. It's programmed not to move when it's close to people; so it won't"—a self-protective strategy. The robot is dimly aware of people, having been programmed by its makers to "notice" anything that moves and appears vaguely human-sized.

"Imagine yourself," says Jamgochian, "as a robot. All you can do is find out distance measurements with your little ultrasonic sensor. You know how far you've gone in a certain direction, but you're moving on roller skates; so you don't know where you're going. Your eyes are closed.

"Imagine you have to go down a hallway from room A to room B. People are coming up to you, and jabbing you, and saying, 'Hey, you're going the wrong way.' Or, 'You're starting to get false readings.' We have to put ourselves in the robot's shoes."

Right now the TRW group is integrating the software and hardware, and encountering many additional subtle and complex problems. "If the wheels spin on an uneven surface like a carpet or the joints between rooms, and the program tells the robot to navigate a straight line, it'll have a problem," Thomsen says. "What the robot thinks is a straight line might be something else. The robot will have to correct for that, first by measuring with its sensors the distance from walls. Then it will have to keep track of how far it has deviated from its intended path. You have to be certain everything within the robot's inter-

103

nal programming and hardware is precise, because there will be plenty of external deviations and quirks."

"Here's another problem for you," Moody adds. "Say the robot is to move down the hallway in a straight line, but its orientation is off by half a degree. That doesn't sound like much, does it? But move one hundred feet and see how much half a degree causes your robot to deviate."

R202 will be equipped with three types of sensors, the long-distance one being a set of Polaroid sonic range finders, similar to the ones on the camera. Mounted on the robot, the sensors bounce sound off things to determine their distance from the rover. "A major problem here," explains Thomsen, "Is that flat surfaces produce ricochets and confusing signals, which sometimes don't indicate a true distance to the robot." Also, says Sherbring, "If you expect to perceive a wall five feet away, and the sensors suddenly tell you there's nothing in front for fifty feet, what does the robot do? Do you believe your 'internal world' or your sensors?"

The other two sensors are "curb feelers," which order the robot to stop immediately if they touch anything, and "encoders" on the wheel shafts, which measure the angular distance traveled by the wheels. This figure can be translated into distance moved in a direction. "That's how R202 can figure out how far it's gone," Thomsen says. "Then it double-checks against what its internal map says should be around it, and either updates the map or updates the position, depending on where the error is." If there is an error in the integration of these three sense-data systems, R202 might go spinning away into a deaf, dumb, sightless void of disorientation, or at least bump into somebody's desk.

While the TRW group struggles with these problems of mobile robots, scientists at the MIT Robotics Laboratory are confronting the challenges of the disembodied robotic arms, hands, fingers, and eyes. Scientists at the lab contend with problems crucial to robot development—accuracy, speed, and gripper tactility, among others. Michael Brady, who claims his is the biggest robotic-research enclave in the United States, with about 30 researchers, told us about the current limits of mechanoid limbs.

The standard industrial-robot arm moves about one meter a second, he says, which is only about the speed of an average person reaching from the stove to the refrigerator while cooking dinner at a leisurely pace. The MIT group is working hard to break this speed limit.

"When I say *fast*," Brady says about MIT's arm, "I mean on the order of five meters a second"—faster than a short-order cook. MIT's arm also accelerates and decelerates with great bursts of speed. "That's where all the arms's effort is expended," he explains. "We're developing an arm with about three-g acceleration . . . an arm that can deliver something on the order of fifteen pounds at these speeds and torques. So it wouldn't be a good idea to put your head in the way of this robot."

Velocity alone isn't enough. "You don't just want the arm to move at a hell of a speed," Brady continues.

"I mean, if you're reaching like crazy to pluck a glass of wine from a tray before someone else snatches

105

it, you want to make sure you don't whack all the other glasses off the tray while you're at it."

An even greater challenge is mimicking the vast range of motions that is child's play for human hands. "The human hand has not one, but twenty-two degrees of motion," Brady says. "It's not powered by one motor, but by forty-eight. Can we build a machine that has such dexterity?

"You've only got to look at the structure of the hand tendon to realize how remarkably complex it is," he continues.

"Suppose you construct a multifingered robotic hand: You've got to control the individual tendons; a bunch of tendons acting together to control a single finger; and a bunch of fingers working together to control an entire hand!"

What kind of program would you need to have a robot play something simple like "Chopsticks"? "I wouldn't say as *simple* as 'Chopsticks,' " he responds. "I'd be quite happy if we could get a hand to twirl a baton, or roll a ball around in its fingers, or be able to figure out how to pick up a Coke can as opposed to a tennis ball. That's the level we're hoping to achieve in the next couple of years."

Most contemporary robots are numb. They grope for parts, and if they don't grasp them they happily flap their grippers around in the air anyway. As Brady says, there's no point in having a hand if you don't put tactile sensors on it.

"There is little experience in building good, tactile, sensing materials," he says. "The technology is preliminary and the information it yields is fairly coarse—garbage. Current tactile sensors give you only a limited number of points per square centimeter. Or if they give you lots of points, you can't distinguish the characteristics of one material being sensed from another."

Machine vision is Brady's specialty, and it's an area that has seen some of the most intensive research in the course of a decade. Still, there have been no solid results. Right now industrial-robot optics are so primitive a machine couldn't tell whether a humble kitchen fork was lying prong side up or down. And that's a simple problem. "The key to making robots more flexible is to provide them with some understanding of, say, where to put down the coffee cup," Brady continues. "Not on the edge of the table; not in the soup. We don't want to have to say every time: 'Move the jar to position X equals twenty-seven, Y equals thirty-two, Z equals something else.' We want the robot to know teapots have spouts, and cups have handles."

Removing the scales from a robot's eyes requires extraordinary vision from its creator. If the programmer makes a mistake and the robot's model for "wrenches" isn't complete enough, it will view bad wrenches as good and discard the good one. "If you don't present it with enough information," Brady explains, "it won't understand the concept of 'wrench.' "

Paradoxically, designers must store data about emptiness as well as the hard surfaces of things. For a robot to move a teapot through space and not whack either the wine decanter or your mother-in-law, it has to come fortified with extraordinary amounts of data on the space occupied by that particular teapot and on the swept volume as the robot moves through space. To build such a comprehensive data bank the robot designer must analyze reality on its most primitive geometric level.

"How do I represent free space?" Brady asks. "The space not occupied by things—this particular object that is not an object at all, but is actually full of air? I have to represent that free space and also represent the movement of that much more rarefied object—namely, the robot—through it." Ultimately the designer has to consider every contingency one could encounter anywhere, anytime, in the given space and then integrate the reasoning, the vision, and the movements into one machine. There is a model for such a device. "It's called a human being," Brady says gleefully.

From *Frankenstein* to *The Stepford Wives*, people seem to want to create artificial versions of themselves—to play God. But today complex android-mechanoid creatures exist only in books and movies wherein they tend to exhibit the rankest forms of egotism and idiosyncrasy. It is as if the mechanical-man concept gives a novelist *carte blanche* to twist human traits to new and bizarre configurations. The crab-shaped robot in *Gravity's Rainbow* makes only a cameo appearance. But in that time the boorish machine continuously smacks gum made of a malleable variation on polyvinyl chloride that sends out detachable molecules transmitting a "damn fair imitation of Beeman's licorice flavor, to the robot's crab brain," writes Thomas Pynchon. In the autocities of Philip K. Dick's *Game Players of Titan*, homeostatic maintenance vehicles collect trash and check lawn growth. Twenty-legged mechanical repair vehicles propel themselves through the streets, "hot on the scent of decay."

Today, only in our fantasies do we play out robot soap operas in which the entire household is held hostage when the android maid and the Naugahyde butler mutiny and decide to run the house their way. How can we have a mechanical *Upstairs/Downstairs* when there is nary a robot able to negotiate a single step?

"A robot that does all the work in the house is at least twenty years off," according to Kevin Dowling, a researcher at Carnegie-Mellon University, in Pittsburgh. "The home, figuratively speaking, is a very dirty environment. Objects are complexly arranged and constantly being changed." But an even bigger problem, Dowling says, will be to find enough work to keep the home robot busy. "Since a domestic robot will be expensive, having it lying around idle would not be cost-effective. You'd probably give it every conceivable task, but if you were gone the whole day the machine would finish in about two hours. And of course there are some complicated legal implications. What if the 'bot baby-sitter throws the baby out the window?"

"There's an alternative to having a house-cleaning machine," offers IBM's David Grossman. "It's called 'design for automation.' Instead of having a robot smart enough to run around vacuuming up your wallet with the dust and throwing the baby out with the garbage, build your house so that it looks like McDonald's, where all the tables are attached to the wall and have only one leg, and the chairs are attached to the table. Then it's easy to mop. Maybe you'd have high-pressure hoses along one side of the wall: Everybody out of the room, turn on the hoses, and all the dirt is sprayed automatically to the other side, where it collects and runs off."

The mention of McDonald's reminds Grossman of an incident related to him by a former robotics colleague. A conglomerate we'll call Ramjac Inc. was considering a completely roboticized version of a fast-food restaurant. Customers could order burgers, shakes, fries, fried shrimp, and so on by punching a set of buttons. With each order received, refrigerator doors would swing open deep in the bowels of the earth, and robot arms would grab hamburgers, throw them onto skillets, and grab and move milk shakes. Ramjac built a prototype of this culinary wizardry on Long Island, and Grossman's colleague paid a visit to watch it work.

Everything was indeed roboticized except for the final step—putting the food in the bags. That was—and still is—beyond the capability of robots. So at the end of the process stood a human being—with food chutes aimed at him from all directions, and a giant display board that told him what combinations to put in each bag. Everything went well for a couple of minutes. Then he dropped a chocolate shake. He still needed that chocolate, but the next three milk shakes in the shake line were vanilla. He reached around them to get at a chocolate, and in doing so, knocked some french fries on the floor.

"Within an hour," concluded Grossman, "he was knee-deep in garbage."

The robot-human connection also went awry at a

110

major New York bank. In learning to love their robo-mailcarts, employees at Citicorp, in New York City, were forced to make major psychological adjustments. Previously, human mailpeople had made one-and-a-half-hour pickup circuits. The robo-carts made the round trip in ten minutes. According to computer expert Randolph Long, a former Citicorp employee, the carts conditioned the people to set up "internal clocks" in their minds. "After about nine and a half minutes," he remembers, "you began to steel yourself for it—the incessant warning beeps and the heavy rattling." The human carriers were a great source of interoffice news and gossip, too, and were sorely missed for that reason. The robo-carts followed tracks sprayed on the carpet, and Long remembers he frequently considered getting a can of the spray and laying down an enticing trail leading directly to the stairwell.

For management, psychological disruption was the least of the problems caused by the robo-carts. Without learning the ropes by delivering the mail, "raw" clerical help now required months of training at high pay levels to learn what they previously picked up on the mail routes. Problems like these in the workplace probably indicate that it will be a while before robots win a permanent place in the home. On the domestic-robot scene, some experts predict we will see little more than robot guards for a few years. These will be fairly dumb rovers; they'll have all they can do to figure out where they're going. They will be able to detect the presence of people, but unable to distinguish between friend or foe. One robo-guard offered by Robotics International, Inc., of Jackson, Michigan, is based on the classic "motivated" rover principle. That is, this robot has only one objective—to move down hallways in search of electrical sockets. When it finds one, it recharges itself and trundles on to the next plug. For a sentry, it seems slightly self-preoccupied.

But several other robots today appear equally egocentric—if not hypochondriacal—in monitoring the state of their health. "Diagnosis of robot problems should be the nearest thing to medical diagnosis," Grossman thinks. "Some doctors are good, some bad. The first thing a bad doctor does is run a zillion tests just for a start, when it might be something as simple as your necktie being too tight. It's the same with robot difficulties: The toughest thing is knowing in which subsystem to look for the trouble: electrical, electronic, hydraulic, software, mechanical, sensors." IBM's 7565 "robotics system," he tells us, monitors its entire state every 20 milliseconds. And if the self-examination finds anything abnormal the machine shuts itself down and logs the problem.

Grossman remembers a test robot that fooled everyone for months. It kept turning itself off for no discernible reason. Finally someone received an electrical shock from it and realized there was a clogged hydraulic filter that someone had forgotten to replace. "It was trivial," Grossman says, "but when you pump hydraulic fluid through a filter at high speed it generates static electricity; the static electricity built up a charge and the charge shut off the computer." Robo-shock indeed.

At Battelle Memorial Institute, in Columbus, Ohio, experts specialize in self-diagnostic systems applicable to robots. "Its not as spacey as it sounds," says Barry Brownstein, manager of the digital systems and technology section, "and there's lots of motivation for it." Reports indicate that the average robot has 400 hours mean time between failures. "Some problems are akin to human ills," says Brownstein, "but others are very different. You can't open up a person and implant health monitors everywhere. And you can't put too many of them in robots either, because the reason a lot of machinery goes down is sensor failure." Some robots have sensors for the sensors, a design idea that could, if carried far enough, compound the problems infinitely—loops within loops.

Brownstein and company are designing robot-to-human communication systems so that remote—lunar, undersea, nuclear-plant—robots could report what is wrong with them to the guys back home; and the humans could respond with suggestions for compensating for the robots' problems. This design principle, says Brownstein, is called graceful degradation. In alien environments, most robotics experts believe, the robots will have to be designed with self-repair and compensation components for breakdowns—or they will have to be designed to be thrown away.

"If robots are to expand beyond fairly focused applications," Brownstein continues, "much must be done to improve reliability and to involve relatively unskilled people in care and maintenance. We want these machines suitable for people already in the environment, instead of trying to make a superclass of robot doctors."

When it comes to mechanoid maintenance, John

Hall, of Hall Enterprises, in Pittsburgh, thinks he's got a head start. Although few robots exist in his part of the country, Hall is sure they will proliferate and will need maintenance. "When a robot malfunctions," he says, "the cost is enormous. It can stop your whole system. Preventive maintenance is going to be increasingly important—we anticipate problems with mechanical wear, wiring, dirt, and smoke. In chemical plants there's corrosion. In painting operations paint globulars. In welding, there's smoke, dirt, and oil. The price for breakdown is so high you can afford to spend some portion of it as preventive medicine and beat the cost."

In the long run, the robots that will take over the world will probably not be anything like the tin men we see in the movies. They may not even look much like R202. They'll probably be much like us—but better. Grossman on the future of robots: "I think we're fighting an uphill battle in trying to make computers control robot limbs. I think there's another potential solution: The molecular biologists can find ways of manipulating genes. And they could make biological machines that can do the same thing. In the long run I'd put my money on them, if ethical concerns don't prevent that line of research."

At the Center For Adaptive Systems, at Boston University, a group directed by mathematician and interdisciplinary scientist Stephen Grossberg is studying the neuromechanisms of learning, perception, and motor control—for robotics. "In the course of brain research we are led to mathematical models of a number of neural processes," Grossberg says. "Our goal is to use the designs that come out of our direct study of behavior to suggest designs for new types of machines."

Grossberg thinks a natural counterpoint to computer-based intelligent machines is to use the brain's extraordinary learning properties as a model. One reason there has been such relatively slow progress in questions of machine learning, he tells us, is that the architecture of the brain is so different from that of computers. Since the brain is organized primarily for adaptation to uncertainty, a new artificial intelligence based on the brain's "self-organization," its adaptive nature, should be a major motif of artificial intelligence, "not a peripheral theme you tack on later, as people in AI have done with great ingenuity." But not *enough* ingenuity.

Grossberg gives us an example of self-organization: "How do the eyes react to motions of the head when you're running? Your head is bobbing along—it has nothing to do with your planned motion. How do the eyes know to move in compensatory motion? God doesn't go in and say, 'Eyes, I'm going to tell you all there is to know about the parameters of the head, because they are always changing.' No one ever tells us what the rules of the environment are. In fact, there are probably no rules at all in the traditional sense of that word. And this is the critical dilemma for machine intelligence."

As often, it's a dilemma that won't be resolved without more funding. More money goes into funding research in conventional AI, because the computer companies behind it hope for the big payoff in applications. "These people don't study the brain and its structure," Grossberg points out. "And yet, the study of the brain could lead to new architecture, new computers, new machines, new generations of machines in which the goal is not to mimic a computer. So much is known about these future machines that it is very clear to me they will be built."

The quality of excitement Grossberg feels is common among robotics scientists. "I don't think any of it's easy," says MIT's Michael Brady. "There are thousands of wonderful problems and every time we're arrogant enough to believe we've solved one, what we've really done is created three more. And anyone who has tried to do anything as mundane as get a robot to wave its arm around, a TV camera to see, or a computer to understand a natural language will be filled with awe at the effortless behavior of an average three-year-old child. In working on these automatons, researchers are really discovering everything about the human being."

"There are wonderful stories to be written on every level about the nature of robotics," Grossberg says. "After all, if you take it from the highest point of view, we're talking about self-knowledge."

ROBOT NURSES

By Phoebe Hoban

It is a candlelight dinner for two, but only one person is eating. He is sitting in a wheelchair. Across from him sits his dinner companion: a robotic arm that responds to verbal commands. Its electronic voice echoes each order as the man directs it through the motions to serve him his meal: "Up, right, left, open, close." First it takes a prepared plate of food from the refrigerator and loads it into the microwave oven. When the oven beeper sounds, the arm removes the plate and sets it on the table. As a final touch, it lights the candle.

This futuristic scenario was enacted at the Veterans Administration Medical Center in Palo Alto, California late in 1983, where a team of researchers is developing a new generation of robots. Adapted from industrial assembly units, these robotics aids are no nonsense systems designed to assist an estimated 7 million severely handicapped people in the United States alone.

Although the basic technology used to build the robot nurses is relatively simple, their design principle is quite sophisticated—a radical departure from the robotic state of the art. The key to their effectiveness is a unique partnership between man and machine; rather than being designed to work independently, they are geared to work with people.

"The man-machine interface is the wave of the future," says Stanford University's Stefan Michalowski. "The idea of the robot's replacing a human being has cultural and literary connotations. But complete machine autonomy is not our goal. For actual applications, the important thing is how the human works with the machine, and this relationship has infinite potential to extend man's own abilities."

The V.A.-founded Robotic Aid Project (RAP), at the Rehabilitation Research and Development Center, in Palo Alto, was designed by a group from Stanford University using off-the-shelf components. The heart of the system is a Animation Puma 250 arm typically used on automotive assembly lines. It has six joints and can extend to about 18 inches. The arm is coupled to an eight-bit microcomputer that continuously processes data on its motion and position. The robotic aid is equipped with a voice-recognition unit that understands about 70 vocal commands, and a speech-synthesis system that enables it to repeat the commands for verification.

But instead of the usual robot claw, the robotic aid has a "sensate gripper," a two-fingered hand equipped with optical sensors that tell the robot how far its hand is from an object. The sensors' signals are constantly monitored and analyzed by the microcom-

118

puter to control the arm's motion. Thus the robot arm can hover close to an object without knocking it over, until it is given specific grasping directions.

Say, for instance, the user wants a glass of juice. He gives the arm step-by-step directions for locating the bottle, picking it up, pouring the juice, and moving the cup toward his mouth. Similarly the robot can be navigated through the appropriate moves to play board games, turn the pages of a book, pick up a telephone receiver, punch the keys on a pocket calculator, give someone a shave, or even serve an entire meal.

By the end of 1983, 90 patients at the V.A. Medical Center had been trained to use the robotic aid; that fall the robot went home with one of the patients as the next step in its clinical evaluation. But according to its designers, the current model is just the beginning—the robot's evolution is already under way back in the laboratory at Stanford. Here is what's coming up:

To give it some much-needed mobility, the Puma arm has been mounted on a three-wheeled, cylindrical platform so it looks something like R2-D2 with an antler sprouting from its head. The omnidirectional vehicle has special wheels with circumferences made up of a series of rollers so that it can scoot sideways and rotate freely. The responsive machine also has a vertical track so that the arm can be moved from ground level up to a 30-inch working height.

The robot's hand is being redesigned. In addition to carrying optical sensors, it will be covered with delicate whiskers, electrical sensing coils that will scan objects to determine their position and volume in space. These hairs were developed by researcher John Jameson.

"The optical sensors are just not robust enough," explains project director Larry Leifer. "If you dip them into a wet plate of spaghetti, they'll go blind. But the whiskers can be dunked in pasta and will still be able to tell you when they hit the plate," In conjunction with a sophisticated, force-sensing wrist, these tactile sensors will enable the robot to calculate the best way to grip objects, from tools to doorknobs.

Eventually the hand may have three hydraulically controlled fingers, and the team may also test a variety of thumbnail-size sensors that will act like fingertips. "It's our version of God's work," says Leifer, "a hand with multiple thumbs." While the robot itself will be equipped with vision, a video camera may be mounted on the arm to give the user visual feedback.

But the most significant improvement will not be visible: It will be a database programmed to memorize new facts about the robot's immediate surroundings as the sensors feed them into its computer memory. "Right now," Leifer explains, "you have to identify every object individually, describe where it is, and tell the robot how to get there. In the next generation, you will just have to tell the system what it is you want. For example, 'Bring me that cup over there on your right.' "

To be really useful, the robot must be at least somewhat self-motivating. So the team is now developing software that will enable the robot nurse to plan its own motions to avoid collisions, control its trajectory, and plot grasping strategies.

"Human motion is determined by sensation," says Michalowski, "not by a programmed sequence. People have tried to straitjacket robots into predictable actions, but we are devising control schemes that allow the motion to be adaptable. If the robot bumps into a wall, for instance, it should know better next time. That is the direction robotics has to evolve in—to be data-driven rather than program-driven."

The team expects to have working prototypes of the second-generation robot nurse by 1987 and, if it gets the necessary funding, to build six improved robots. "If we had the money, we could produce these robots commercially by 1985 at a cost comparable to that of a luxury automobile," says Leifer.

Meanwhile several new input devices are in the works. Stanford researchers have developed an oral device, called the palatal splint, that enables severely disabled people to use their tongues to nudge the equivalent of a miniature joystick. The team is also working on a set of ultrasonic sensors that respond to nods of the head.

Research on robot nurses is also under way at many other centers. At Johns Hopkins University, Woodrow Simone has devised a robot/worktable system that couples a mechanical arm to a desk equipped with a typewriter, telephone, reading rack, personal computer, and eating utensils. Rather than voice control, this system uses a chin control and a mouthpiece to send Morse code to the robot's computer.

At the University of Tokyo, Professor Hiroyasu Funakubo and his colleagues have developed a two-armed robot nurse. The pair of manipulators is controlled by an eight-bit microcomputer and is capable of a range of tasks, from picking up a telephone receiver to setting the table. Each arm has nine degrees of freedom.

"In the future the problem of helping the world's aged and severely disabled will become increasingly important," Funakubo believes. But he stresses that mechanical systems are an adjunct to, not a replacement for, human involvement. "The human heart has needs that a machine simply cannot fulfill," he says. "First and foremost, people need to be helped by other people, regardless of how advanced the technology may become."

It will become very advanced, very quickly. "Within the next ten years," predicts Leifer, "robots functioning as nurses and domestic servants will be as common as cars." They will be widely employed for useful household work, in nursing homes to care for the elderly and in hospitals for routine work and intensive care.

Interactive robots may also be used on battlefields as automatic soldiers, undersea as bomb retrievers and offshore-oil explorers, and in nuclear facilities to clean up hazardous wastes. "I think the whole field of man-machine interaction is completely open-ended," says Michalowski. "It is the ultimate engineering goal."

SPACE ROBOTS

By Alcestis R. Oberg

A multimillion-dollar weather satellite has a glitch in its computer. Fixing it, says ground control, would mean replacing just one inexpensive part. Unfortunately, at 22,300 miles up in geosynchronous orbit (GEO), the satellite is far too high for the shuttle's space-suited mechanics to repair it.

The scenario is all too credible to NASA. But soon, through a sophisticated remote-control technique called telepresence, such adjustments will be feasible. An astronaut based at a space station or on a shuttle will send a teleoperated robot. Armed with a sensory-feedback system, the robot will make the repair in concert with its human partner, who will feel as if he is actually at the work site. (A rudimentary form of telepresence, the Canadian arm, assisted the shuttle astronauts in retrieving the crippled *Solar Max* in April 1984.)

Though scientists have debated for years the question of who performs better in space—humans or robots—researchers for a NASA study titled the Human Role in Space (THURIS) now conclude that both will serve important functions.

"Robots won't make people obsolete in space," says Steve Hall, THURIS contract monitor at NASA's Marshall Space Flight Center, in Huntsville, Alabama. "The relationship between them will be symbiotic."

The focus of the THURIS study is to break down space work into a set of 40 or so generic activities, representative of the tasks that eventually will be delegated to automatons, astronauts, or both. Based on performance, cost, and risk, program managers will determine the best man/machine mix for such jobs.

In this partnership, solving problems will initially fall to the humans, while much of the physical labor will become the robots' duty. To enhance the robots' performance, the machines will be given some human characteristics.

For example, two or three mechanical arms and hand segments could perform many jobs involved in the retrieval of a satellite. But the real challenge lies in making a robot operate its arms and grapplers as fluidly as a person moves his own arms and fingers. Delicate work would require robotic arms constructed of wire that bends and extends like mechanical muscles.

Tactile information, such as the strength of a robot's grip, would be relayed to the human operator by means of force sensors or strain gauges. To see his work site, the human operator would wear a helmet equipped with stereoptic vision. Two cameras, serving as the robot's eyes, would move in response to the operator's head position and would provide panoramic and closeup views.

Another NASA-sponsored study, Automation, Robotics, and Machine Intelligence Systems (ARAMIS), in which MIT's Marvin Minsky and David Akin have both participated, examined the use of telepresence for satellite repair. The group concentrated its research on the repair of the Space Telescope and a few other satellites, all of which were originally designed to be repaired by astronauts.

A teleoperated robot would be used where "you can't send astronauts," says Akin. "The market for telepresence is satellite servicing at GEO. When you look at the radiation environment out at GEO, you wind up having to make a lead spaceship. That's not the kind of environment in which you'd care to go EVA [extravehicular activity] for long."

Engineers hope to flight-test a basic telepresence prototype system by 1987, although the design, hardware, and procedures will have to be worked out before then. If the difficulties can be overcome and if telepresence continues to develop, man's partner in space could become even more "human." Endowed with artificial intelligence, the robot could consult with his human co-worker about the source of mechanical failures.

It is unlikely, however, that even the most highly evolved robot will obviate humans in space. "The question is not human or robot," says Georg von Tiesenhausen, ARAMIS contract monitor at Marshall. "The question is how much participation of

125

each. There's no competition. Every machine has to have a human interface somewhere."

PART FOUR:
THE BIOMEDICAL FRONTIER

"Do not try to live forever.
You will not succeed."
— George Bernard Shaw

A WINDOW ON THE LIVING BRAIN

By Douglas Starr

Glowing white numbers flashed across his visual field. As if seeking them, the man's eyes and head swiveled toward the left. Then he blacked out. When he awoke he was blind in precisely the same place where the numbers had been.

Intrigued by the symptoms, doctors at the UCLA Medical Center positioned the patient's head in a metal, doughnut-shaped device. Soon a picture emerged on the video display. A glance told it all: Something had gone drastically wrong in the vision centers of the patient's brain. On the screen the region resembled an exploding nebula of red and white light. Moments later the scan showed that the same area had now been engulfed in darkness, as if the nebula had suddenly gone cold. The images explained both the visions and the temporary blindness.

"He had a tumor that was treated ten to twelve years ago," says Dr. Jerome Engel, neurology professor at UCLA. "The damage it left became an epileptic focus." That healed-over scar had triggered the seizures that periodically short-circuited the brain.

Only postron emission tomography, or PET, could have produced such an image. Unlike most diagnostic technologies, PET does not present a static picture of anatomical structures. This combination of nuclear physics, computer science, and medicine depicts function, not form.

Is one part of the brain more active than another? PET shows it in red or bright white. What about aging, strokes, insanity? PET reveals the metabolic activity that could someday help researchers to understand and deal with them all. "We've always been separated from our brains by hair, skin, and bone," says Dr. Thomas Chase, chief of experimental therapeutics at the National Institute of Neurological and Communicative Disorders and Stroke (NINCDS), in Bethesda, Maryland. "Now we have a window."

Beyond the brain PET is opening new vistas on the chemical workings of the heart, lungs, and liver. Some say there's no field of medicine that won't benefit from the technology. "It's the future," says UCLA PET expert Mike Phelps. "It's the only way to observe the dynamic processes of the living body."

A PET room is a peaceful place, with subdued lighting and the muffled hum of computers at work. The patient lies on a padded, stainless-steel tray. His head is inserted into the "doughnut hole" of the bulky machine. About a half-hour earlier doctors injected into the patient's arm a radioactively labeled liquid, usually a solution of the sugar glucose. The most active regions of the brain consume the highest amounts of sugar, concentrating the telltale radioisotope in the process. Inside the machine hundreds of detectors absorb the radiation and signal a computer. The computer combines thousands of such messages into a video image. Bright spots show where the isotope has accumulated and yield a chemical map of the patient's brain. Afterward, having received little more radiation than with a chest X ray, he walks away, leaving behind in a computer memory a full, three-dimensional representation of his cerebral processes.

PET differs substantially from CAT (computerized axial tomography), its better-known cousin. CAT is a fancy X-ray machine: It shoots a series of X rays through the body, and a computer combines them into an exquisitely clear image. But it's basically a photograph. It has nothing to do with chemical activity. Like X rays, CAT can show only what body parts look like: PET shows what they do.

To illustrate, Phelps holds up a slide that shows two images of a man's brain. One, taken with a CAT scan, portrays the brain's normal creases and folds. The other, a PET scan, is black. "What was the matter with him?" I ask. Replies Phelps, "He had been dead for eight months." The CAT scan indicates that structurally the man was fine, even though biochemically he was, as Phelps put it, "at an all-time low."

The first true PET was built eleven years ago by a team that included Phelps and Dr. Michel Ter-Pogossian, then both at Washington University, in St. Louis. The prototype—a crude device—was produced by fastening radiation detectors around a hole sawed in the center of an old, wooden table. A dog was the contraption's first living subject; they strapped him to a platform and pushed him up through the opening. "The image was a funny, squiggly blur," recalls a team member.

A few months later, with an improved machine, they made the first scans of a living human brain. It belonged to Dr. Ter-Pogossian. "It was the custom," he says, "that a team member went first."

The early machines may have seemed clumsy, but they were based on sophisticated nuclear physics. PET uses an unusual class of isotopes that give off positively charged particles, or positrons. Injected into the body, the positrons collide with the negatively charged electrons in the surrounding tissue. The particles annihilate one another, leaving a brief burst of radioactive rays. It's those fleeting rays that the PET detectors pick up.

Soon other teams built more PET machines, adding detectors to enhance the accuracy of the image. They also began experimenting: One scientist watched the pleasure centers of his brain light up on the PET screen as he listened to his favorite music and ate his favorite food. Phelps, an ex-boxer, has had his head scanned 20 times. "It's just a normal brain," he says nonchalantly. Early results were so promising that NINCDS gave $29 million to boost the fledgling technology. Research took off. The dramatic detail and clarity of the images constructed by the computer surpassed the scientists' expectations.

The first target of investigation was the brain. For centuries scientists have puzzled over this three-pound lump of tissue. With at least 10 billion nerve cells and many times more connections, the organ of intellect has eluded their probes. At best, scientists could study such brain-damaged individuals as victims of stroke or injury to get a rough picture of the brain's inner workings. They would record electrical impulses from the patient's scalp or insert electrodes directly into the brain during surgery. Other researchers tried to gather clues by monitoring chemicals in the blood vessels leading to and from the brain. Some investigators destroyed portions of animal brains, then monitored behavioral changes to try to map sites for memory or desire. But the various approaches were painfully indirect. The quest was like studying a gas pump and exhaust pipe to understand the role of spark plugs in your car.

PET opened the hood. Suddenly scientists could watch the entire brain in action, literally seeing where thought processes occurred. And their investigation could extend to healthy individuals, with no prior history of neurological disorders. "We no longer had to depend on accidents of nature," says Dr. Martin Reivich, a PET pioneer at the University of Pennsylvania. "We got clearer information than ever on the normal functioning of the brain."

In one of Dr. Reivich's first PET studies of healthy volunteers, he shined light patterns into their right visual fields. Later he played tones into their right ears while running a brush across the back of their right hands. The results were graphic. Bands of light in his PET images showed pathways crossing from the subjects' right sensory organs to the left side of the brain. When Reivich stimulated sensory pathways on the left side of the body, he found the exact reverse: This time the right hemisphere was activated. In days he confirmed the crisscrossed, or contralateral, wiring of the body's nervous system. Researchers earlier in this century had spent years amassing convincing evidence of the phenomenon.

At UCLA Phelps and neurologist John Mazziotta filled in other complicated paths. Dr. Mazziotta played a tape of a Sherlock Holmes story to volunteers through headphones. Parts of the left hemisphere, which processes information in an analytical fashion, were found to light up. When he played musical tones, the emotional right hemisphere brightened. "It was the content," says Mazziotta, "that determined where the information was processed." Then he asked subjects to match two different tones. Most listeners processed the information in the right side of the brain. But a trained musician used the left side more. He apparently thought about music in a more analytical way.

Finally Mazziotta scanned several volunteers with their eyes closed and ears stopped. These sensory-deprived brains generally "cooled" from hot white to blue-green. But still the left hemisphere remained more active than the right. Mazziotta theorizes that the right side may act as a "sentinel" for information. Shut off the sensors and the sentinel shuts down.

All this describes an organ that's remarkably complex. Yes, there are crossovers, and yes, the left and right hemispheres do different things. But PET studies have provided scientists with far more precise maps of brain function and with a better idea of how the organ works than ever before. Mazziotta's tone tests, for example, suggest that some people process the same information in entirely different areas. In other words, the brain changes the circuitry with experience or learning. It's infinitely more flexible than the most advanced computer. Indeed, some scientists say that if the brain were a computer, it would cover Texas with a building ten stories tall. Programming the cerebrum would take hundreds of years.

Given the staggering complexity of the brain, it is no easy challenge to unravel how a breakdown in the system gives rise to mental illness. Yet, in this area too, PET is offering fresh insights. At Brookhaven National Laboratory, in New York, scientists scanned a schizophrenic man who had been institutionalized for years. He had been hearing voices telling him he was God, and he regularly got into fights with another patient whose voices insisted *he* was the devil.

When Alfred Wolf and his colleagues scanned the patient, they saw a startling image. While most of the man's brain glowed in bright yellows and blues, the frontal areas showed a far dimmer color. (The frontal areas control foresight, emotions, and abstract ideas—functions over which schizophrenics lose control.) "We knew right away that we'd hit upon something exciting," says Wolf. The team scanned another dozen and then two dozen more schizophrenic patients. In each case the same striking pattern emerged. The frontal areas burned sugar far more slowly than the rest of the brain. The pattern remained even after the patients were treated with drugs. In other words, schizophrenia may be a physical—even genetic—disease.

"No one had looked at what the schizophrenic brain was *doing*," says Wolf. "For the first time, we saw its ability to use glucose was altered."

Soon other conditions revealed their secrets to PET.

134

Scans of manic-depressives showed chemical changes, although none as consistent as those of schizophrenics. Severely depressed patients seemed to have their entire brains burning on low. One study found significant chemical changes in the memory centers of people with mild amnesia.

We'll never replace psychiatrists with PET; mental illness is too complex for the scan to explain. But PET studies add weight to the growing notion that upbringing may have less to do with mental illness than previously believed. "There's something physically wrong with these people," concludes Dr. Mark Raichle, a Washington University neurologist. Adds Wolf: "The big question is, Will we be able to do anything about their conditions?"

In the meantime other researchers are focusing their PET cameras on victims of Alzheimer's disease, the most common form of senility. At the National Institute on Aging, in Maryland, Dr. Ranjin Duara scans a graying, wrinkled woman who has arrived from the Midwest. For months she has been forgetting things: the names of objects or whom she had meant to telephone just a moment before. When an image of her brain appears on the screen an hour later, a small, dark crescent shows up in a memory area. The ominous crescent fits a recognizable pattern for Alzheimer's.

Dr. Dura scanned his first Alzheimer's patient less than two years ago, when the disease was a mystery from beginning to end. You could guess that someone had Alzheimer's when the symptoms began; you were certain when he died. Autopsies show an atrophied brain laced with microscopic tangles of dead nerves.

135

But the progression of the disease that afflicts some 2 million to 3 million Americans was a medical enigma—until PET.

The scans indicate that Alzheimer's disease begins in the roof of the brain, dimming centers of memory and orientation. Then it spreads forward, leaving the patient increasingly confused. Eventually it dims the entire brain. Nerve cells degenerate. The victim becomes bedridden and, in a few years, dies.

"PET really hasn't told us anything about the cause," says Duara, "but by highlighting the specific areas affected by the disease, it should aid us in finding a cure." Duara says researchers will soon test dozens of drugs, using PET to see how they modify the chemistry of the disease. Running regular scans is quicker than waiting for symptoms to change.

The technology may also help doctors distinguish Alzheimer's from other forms of senility. Depressed patients become senile but have strikingly different brain patterns from victims of Alzheimer's. Seeing this, doctors can prescribe counseling and antidepressants rather than custodial care, which some patients find restrictive.

For some diseases there's no hope—only the chance to save future generations. At UCLA scientists are stalking a killer called Huntington's chorea. Victims suffer bizarre writhing, slurred speech, insanity, and—always—death. It killed folksinger Woody Guthrie. His doctors mistook it for alcoholism and shunted him in and out of mental hospitals for years. "There's nothing that can stop it," says Phelps. "It's genetic, clear and pure."

Huntington's destroys parts of the brain; the damage shows up in CAT scans five to ten years after the symptoms begin. Yet PET scans show chemical changes in the brain almost immediately. That's good news: Scientists might someday treat the chemical process before the physical damage begins.

And if carriers could be prevented from passing Huntington's on to their offspring, the disease might be eradicated altogether. Children of an afflicted parent have a frightening 50 percent chance of becoming victims themselves. But symptoms don't generally appear until midlife; so many people reproduce before they are aware that they are sick.

"It's devastating for a parent to realize that his or her baby may suffer the same tragedy," says Phelps.

Here's where the UCLA research may someday help. Phelps and co-worker David E. Kuhl scanned a group of young people whose parents had Huntington's. Although no subjects were yet afflicted, about half the subjects showed the telltale chemical of the disease. Two have since developed the disease. Could PET predict who will get Huntington's?

Phelps insists that's still just a distant possibility. Yet, already he worries about the ethics involved. "Do you know what it does to someone to say, 'You're definitely going to get Huntington's?' Yet the drive to reproduce is so strong in humans that without this kind of information, you can't frighten people away."

While medical researchers work toward a long-term solution to the problem, PET is helping other victims today. Surgeons at UCLA and other centers around the country have used PET scans to guide them in treating dozens of epileptics.

In a brightly lit operating room, a surgeon examines a little girl's brain. Peering through the hole in her skull, he sees the gray tissue glisten in the fluid that cushions it. He inserts a cutting tool and twists. Then, using something that looks like a long, thin metal spoon, he scoops out some tissue. The half-dollar-size chunk does not differ in appearance from normal brain tissue, yet it is the cause of the epilepsy that has plagued the girl for years. Now she'll be free of her strange, recurrent trances.

The operation is performed regularly on patients whose epilepsy is the result of erratic impulses that begin at certain points in the brain. Like dominoes knocking down others beside them, the impulses spread to other sections of brain tissue, causing them to send out impulses of their own. Within minutes whole sections are firing spastically. The electrical overload sends the victim into a seizure or hypnotic trance.

Scientists don't know what triggers the seizures, but they have learned that sometimes it helps to remove the spot where the anarchy starts. In the pre-PET days, finding the trouble spots was a little like hunting for an enemy submarine. For days the patient would wear a crown bristling with half a dozen wires sunk several centimeters into his brain. A machine recorded the electrical waves that each wire picked up. During a seizure doctors would monitor the impulses. By comparing how strongly each wire detected them, the seizure's point of origin could usually be located. It was risky and uncomfortable; on rare occasions surgeons removed the wrong part of the brain. Yet frequently the epileptic was cured by the operation.

Now there's an easier, safer alternative. Doctors

can watch a PET screen. Between seizures trouble spots glow as greenish-blue regions of very low metabolism. During seizures they glow white, using several times more energy. PET provides surgeons with a map that guides them to their target with extraordinary accuracy.

Dozens of these operations have been performed by doctors at UCLA and the National Institutes of Health. "In those cases in which we've removed tissue," says Phelps, "diagnoses based on PET scans have been correct nearly one hundred percent of the time."

UCLA's Mazziotta recalls a particularly bizarre case in which a woman came to the emergency room with inexplicable seizures. "She'd smell horrible things she'd never smelled before. She suffered from continuous nausea and vomiting. Then she'd go into a seizure. Yet all her tests showed nothing was wrong.

"I was a resident then and asked her permission to do a PET scan," he recalls. The scan showed hyperactivity in a small, kidney-shaped brain area associated with smell. Doctors did a biopsy and discovered a tumor. The woman's seizures and the mysterious smells stopped when the tumor was removed.

If all this makes you think you'll soon find a PET at your hospital, critics say you'd better think again. PET's good for research, they argue, but far too expensive for clinical use. The doughtnut-shaped "camera" costs $1 million. Furthermore, because positrons—the radioactive tags—have half-lives of only a few minutes or hours, there must be a cyclotron to produce them. Add several million dollars. For hospitals straining to reduce costs, it seems like an impossible expense.

This argument, however, may not hold true in the future. PET will become cheaper as more people use it, points out Washington University's Ter-Pogossian. And even if PET scans are estimated at $2,000 each (they're free now because they're still experimental), the procedure is worth it. A correct PET diagnosis could save you thousands for the time you don't spend in the hospital. "Doctors waste millions of dollars on unnecessary X rays," says Ter-Pogossian. "It's what you get out of the treatment that counts."

Still other critics charge that PET is a dinosaur, destined to extinction by an upstart called NMR (for nuclear magnetic resonance). This diagnostic technology uses a powerful magnet to rattle chemical bonds in the human body. The energy the NMR units emit is converted into an image by a computer. It's radiation-free—an advantage, some say, over PET.

Ter-Pogossian, who routinely uses both diagnostic techniques, emphasizes that PET occupies a different niche from that of NMR. He notes that certain laws of nuclear physics enable NMR to look at only a few chemicals, including hydrogen and phosphorous. That's great for examining structure but poor for examining chemistry. PET, on the other hand, uses a class of isotopes that bond to almost anything the body uses. It can image anything taken up by the body; radiation exposure is minimal. "NMR will replace the CAT scan," says Ter-Pogossian, "but new insights into disease will all come from PET."

As PET centers start producing ground-breaking results, experts predict that the technology will come to be applied widely in medical diagnostics. At Washington University researchers are scanning the brains of premature infants to learn why so many suffer mysterious, fatal strokes. Researchers at Johns Hopkins are using PET to study the chemical messengers that regulate the brain's thoughts and moods. A team at the University of Texas, in Houston, hopes its PET will someday predict—and help avoid—heart attacks up to ten years in advance.

Already 43 PET centers exist around the world, with 20 in the United States and 7 in Japan. NINCDS and other agencies say they'll support the American effort with millions more dollars. That, researchers say, makes PET less an experimental technology than an unstoppable trend—and vindication for visionaries who once predicted that computers could save lives.

"There's a tremendous force that has been building up very quietly," says Phelps. "The applications will increase. PET will change all of medicine."

BIRTH ON ICE

By Michael Jeffries

Francesca, who is sterile, and her husband, Mark, plan to have a baby in a few years. The child will be five years old at the moment of birth. Infertile women giving birth to five-year-old newborns isn't as paradoxical as it seems. Before disease robbed Francesca of her ability to become naturally pregnant, she had three eggs fertilized by her husband deep-frozen in suspended animation. Now, years later, doctors will reimplant the eggs in her womb, where she can carry them to term. Three successive children, entirely Mark's and her own, will have spent several years in a cryogenic tube before the journey toward birth.

The remarkable possibilities of freeze-drying livestock embryos are well-known. Within two years British researchers will bring the technique to humans. Couples like Francesca and Mark may be having their offspring frozen before birth and saved to begin life in the future.

Cryogenics involves plunging living cells into a bath

of liquid nitrogen, where they exist on the edge of extinction. To prevent ice-crystal formation and death, the cells are drained of their water content. This halts all their biological activity before they are frozen. The "reduced" cells can remain at −196°C for generations and still be reactivated without damage.

Cryogenic cattle breeding actually sprang from U.S. laboratories more than a decade ago. At Rio Vista Laboratories, in Texas, and Jackson Laboratory, in Bar Harbor, Maine, embryonic freezing became fully commercially practical. Several American zoos are experimenting with the technique as a way to save rare or endangered species.

But it is England and Australia where American techniques are finding their most exciting application. Already Australian scientists have frozen a dozen human embryos. When two embryos were thawed in the lab, they resumed normal growth.

"Freezing embryos," says Dr. Carl Wood, leader of the Australian team of Queen Victoria Medical Center, in Sydney, "complicates the concept of reproduction so that I could not sanction the process before appropriate legal review. I am concerned about the ethics of it."

For instance, cryogenics would make it possible for a child's life to begin long after his father had died. Since the father's estate already would have been probated, what inheritance rights would the belated child have. If his mother dies, who becomes the child's legal guardian? What if both would-be parents die before they thaw their cryogenic embryos; should the semi-living ice capsules be destroyed, or be implanted in a surrogate, or be left in the limbo of the deep freeze?

There is more. Scientists are convinced that an embryo conceived today can be held in suspended animation and resurrected hundreds of years hence—after both parents have died. The development of techniques to produce test-tube babies, so that an embryo can be implanted in any mother, not necessarily its biological mother, has cleared the last major obstacle to keeping embryos in suspended animation for as much as 1,000 years before birth. The Rip van Winkle legend is coming true in a modern scientific idiom.

It has just begun to dawn on scientists that cryogenics offers the potential for human survival after nuclear war. A nucleus population of frozen embryos from volunteer couples of healthy genetic stock could survive to inherit an otherwise doomed world. In vaults deep underground, cradled in their lead-lined nitrogen casks, an entire population would sleep safely through the holocaust above. Researchers have yet to consider in any serious manner the creation of a human "population bank" held in suspended animation against such a catastrophe. But they acknowledge that, theoretically at least, the concept is scientifically feasible.

The trick in making cryogenics feasible isn't the freezing—scientists have long known the effects and problems of keeping living material, such as food, fresh and cold—but the thawing. Bringing a cell from such a low temperature back to life is a tricky process.

In the case of a human embryo, temperature in the steel tube where the infant slumbers is raised at a precise rate from —196°C to 37°C, normal body temperature, inside an electronically controlled thawing chamber. Embryologists culture the child in a body-temperature incubator until they are sure its cells are functioning and developing normally. In particular, microscopic checks identify the child's sex and determine whether chromosomes controlling the baby's genetic development are undamaged. Once the embryo's vitality is ensured, it is gently implanted inside its mother's womb with a quick and relatively painless procedure.

The science of applying cryogenics to biology grew unsteadily for 20 years following its birth in 1949, when scientists discovered that certain bird sperm can be deep-frozen, then returned to normal. The big breakthrough came in 1969, as British researchers closed in on the possibility of creating a test-tube baby.

Scientists fertilized human eggs in the lab but were unable to implant them in women successfully. They determined after many failures that the eggs would take only when the mothers' hormone cycles and balances were in perfect harmony. That meant waiting at least a month from the moment biologists removed an egg from the prospective mother for fertilization until they attempted to implant it.

Dr. Patrick Steptoe, leader of the research, felt that it should be possible to freeze embryos for a month until the recipient's next reproductive cycle. He was not the only one with that idea. In 1972 another British scientist, Dr. David Whittingham, reported the first successful freezing of baby mice in embryo form. (Dr. Ian Wilmut, a talented researcher at the

Agricultural Research Council's laboratories at Cambridge, achieved a similar independent success. Unlike Dr. Whittingham, he did not implant his thawed embryo for birth.)

At the time Whittingham was not concerned with human embryos. However, since the reproductive systems of mouse and man are similar in many ways, he soon turned his attention to man. At Whittingham's lab in the Medical Research Council's Mammalian Development Unit at University College, London, pink-eyed white mice scamper around a cage. They live, eat, and mate quite normally after being revived from five years of embryonic suspended animation. "They are perfectly healthy and normal," Whittingham says. Recently some mice frozen for seven years—more than three times their natural life span—have been successfully thawed and have survived birth. This is probably the longest period after which any mammal has been successfully revived from cryogenic storage.

Three days after his mice mate, Whittingham removes the colorless embryos, which by then have grown from one to eight cells, from each mouse's reproductive tract and prepares them for immersion in supercold liquid nitrogen.

For the next few years the churn, with its temperature kept constant, becomes the embryo's artificial womb, though of course the cells cannot grow. The frozen creatures clamp into an unrecognizable grayish mass. "There are about thirty frozen mouse embryos in a test tube," Whittingham's technical Alison Halsey explains. Tapping a container of nitrogen on the floor with her toe, she continues, "We still have mice from the original batch of several hundred frozen in 1973 in here."

Whittingham has achieved an 80 percent survival rate after freezing and thawing more than 10,000 mouse embryos; up to 70 percent of the mice were actually born. Today more than 20 laboratories use this technique, some in modified form, to freeze embryos of rats, rabbits, sheep, goats, and cattle successfully.

So what are the chances for the human race? "If the woman is made to produce extra eggs, they could be fertilized and stored at the eight-cell stage," Whittingham has stated. An embryo could then be reimplanted in a subsequent cycle, say, three months later.

"If the first attempt was not successful, you could easily repeat the process," he notes. "The procedure could also be repeated when the woman wanted a second child without going through the initial process of superovulation. This raises the possibility of egg banks or of having children by donor."

Whittingham recently collaborated with London gynecologists who hope the technique can produce test-tube babies much more reliably. So far he has not reported any success. Of two human embryos frozen, one was "lost" and could not be recovered. The other was dead after thawing.

Many biologists believe success is only a relatively small technical step away. Closest to achieving a viable cryogenic baby is probably Dr. Ian Craft, of the Royal Free Hospital, in London. It is ironic that Dr. Craft's attempts to open a new realm of possibility for women who want babies depends so much on women who want to avoid having children. His lab specimens for artificial fertilization and freezing are human eggs donated by women about to be sterilized. Craft's research program is approved by the hospital's ethics committee.

At present the biologist is perfecting the basic technique of freezing and reviving two-celled human embryos that were fertilized in the lab. These experiments will continue until Craft is satisfied he can safely transfer a defrosted baby into one of his 45 hopeful patients. When is that likely? "I would hope within the next two years to have some success in freezing an embryo and reimplanting it into a mother," he says.

Craft says that he is prepared to use frozen embryos to help sterile patients conceive, but he would stop short of using a surrogate mother.

Eventually, some doctors think, cryogenic techniques may be applied to the extremely difficult problem of storing complete human organs with their many differentiated cells in transplant banks. Once these organs can be safely frozen, the surplus of kidneys, livers, hearts, and other transplantable tissues would enable surgeons to ensure much better matching to prevent rejection by the recipient's immune system.

The potential of human cryobiology is presaged in agriculture's incredibly successful results with "cryobirth." Among farm animals, the success rate for frozen-embryo birth is 50 to 60 percent.

Cattle and sheep grazing contentedly in the emerald pastures of England's Institute of Animal Physiology, in Cambridge, are testimony to this fact. Healthy calves and lambs have been born there after spending up to three years in suspended animation. Visitors are invited to meet the aptly named Frostie, a brown and white cow born after having been frozen for three months.

Animal research biologist Dr. Christopher Polge is collaborating with Craft in adopting similar techniques for humans. Dr. Polge says, "These animals are quite normal and produce healthy offspring of their own after freezing." So reliable is the liquid-nitrogen storage technique that the institute and commercial companies have begun exporting high-grade strains of farm livestock to New Zealand and Poland. Polge asks pointedly, "Why export a cow weighing half a ton when you can send one hundred frozen embryos by airplane in an insulated flask?"

As for the safety of long-term freezing, Polge discloses that he carried out a unique experiment, perhaps the strangest activity to mark the silver jubilee of Queen Elizabeth II. In 1977 he defrosted bull sperm that had been frozen in 1952, the year of her accession. "It was perfectly healthy and produced a normal calf," he says. This quarter-of-a-century survival is regarded as the longest cryogenic storage of living sperm.

Such success augurs well for man's future. A number of scientists agree that once a human embryo is frozen, biological aging becomes irrelevant. "Theoretically, it can exist virtually indefinitely in a state of suspended animation, provided it is capable of withstanding freezing to a temperature at which there is no further biological activity," Polge asserts.

Could there ever be a need to store animals or humans in this way and awaken them 200 or 1,000 years from now? "Who knows? Anthropologists in a thousand years might decide it would be interesting to resuscitate a human being from the present century to see how genetically he would differ from the population of the world in the future," Polge declares. "It is not fictional. In theory it could be done. Farm animals such as Frostie, laboratory mice, and human test-tube births have shown the way."

Scientists, however, shy away from any projection of their research into the arena of surviving nuclear war. And clearly such a use poses extreme problems. One immediate challenge of a nuclear attack is to withstand the cessation of essential services and and the failure of all utilities. "If the embryos were to survive, one would have to ensure that refrigeration equipment would be developed to keep them at the temperature of $-196°C$ for some years," one scientist points out.

They would need developments in low-energy, long-term refrigeration techniques, probably utilizing solar, nuclear, wave, or some other form of energy. Further research may enable embryos to be stored at higher temperatures, reducing power demands. Self-contained power sources that would be safe from nuclear attack are already being researched for use in emergency government bunkers.

But before they can prove that cryogenic embryos can outlast a nuclear attack, scientists have to evaluate the potential damage to frozen animals from the natural radiation to which we are all exposed daily. During cryostorage normal enzyme repair mechanisms of cells do not function. Even so, natural levels of background radiation would be so low that 50 percent of mouse embryos stored between 200 and

1,000 years would be able to survive, Whittingham predicts.

This is based on collaborative work with geneticists Dr. Mary Lyon and Dr. Peter Glenister, at the Medical Research Council's Radiobiology Unit, in Harwell, England. Dr. Lyon bombarded frozen mouse embryos with up to 100 times the natural background dose of radiation for periods of from 6 to 27 months.

At all radiation levels, the embryos were capable of development to the implantation stage. Those transplanted into adult female mice developed into fetuses. Some were allowed to proceed to natural birth, and the resulting mice mated.

Twenty to 30 percent of the 7,000 embryos used in these experiments were born, a figure researchers are confident they can improve with better techniques. Lyon has calculated that about 500 mouse embryos would have to be stored in ice to provide a surviving colony with a good safety margin. "Thus, the preservation of unique genetic stocks of mice by storage as frozen embryos is now a feasible proposition," she has reported.

If this finding proves to be similar in man, then anthropologists in 32,000 years might decide to retrieve one of our contemporaries from suspended animation. By then, if history is anything to go by, the average human could be as different from us as we are from the hairy Neanderthal.

Long before that day the benefits of frozen-embryo storage will be reaped in medicine and agriculture. In research, for instance, the major advantage of using inbred animals is to maintain uniformity. Unfortunately, genetic drift is difficult to control, because of the continual natural mutations that gradually accumulate in lab animals. This can distort the results of similar medical research carried out at different centers. Alternatively, cryogenic animals can remain constant, created specifically for a set of tests

Despite present progress, we are still exploring the foothills of the cryogenic potential for man. Within the next few years cryogenic storage should begin to ameliorate the widespread problems of infertility in marriage, such as those faced by Francesca and Mark. For the future it just might be the closest we'll ever come to attaining immortality.

SOUND SCOPE

By Patrice G. Adcroft

She was a walking time bomb, though neither she nor her doctors knew it. A few years earlier, surgeons had removed a blood clot from the young woman's brain, but the headaches and blackouts continued. She went to five medical centers, searching for an answer. All the tests—X rays of her brain and blood vessels—came back negative.

In the brain there's no chance for a surgeon to finger the furrowed regions the way he can reach in and touch the liver or bowel. Unless brain tumors are extremely large or so close to the surface that they bulge the kid-glove-like dura—the protective covering that drapes the brain—the neurosurgeon operates without eyeing his mark. Guided by CAT scans and angiograms taken before surgery, he tunnels blindly through the delicate tissue to the affected region.

For some patients, including this woman, this procedure could be too risky. Doctors occasionally opt for radiation or drug therapy, with varying degrees of success. Now, however, many doctors are finally seeing into the brain immediately before, and even during, surgery, thanks to a development called ultrasound imaging. By removing a small portion of the skull, sometimes no bigger than a burr hole, and by barely touching the ultrasound instrument to the dura, the neurosurgeon can view the brain's internal structure on a TV screen. This technique allowed doctors at the University of Chicago Medical Center to pinpoint and remove two small bundles of abnormal blood vessels—one the size of a blueberry, the other even smaller—buried like deadly land mines in the young woman's head.

Suddenly the most delicate and complex system on Earth, the human brain, has become far more accessible to the pioneers who try to repair it. Using the eyes of ultrasound, "we have performed surgery we would not have dared to do otherwise," says Dr. George Dohrmann III, associate professor of neurosurgery at the Surgery-Brain Institute, University of Chicago Medical Center. Deep-seated tumors—those rooted in such vulnerable areas as the tissue below the speech center—can now be biopsied or excised. Surgeons can plan their descent through the so-called silent areas, where incisions do not harm the patient's functions later, and monitor the deft maneuvers of catheters and cannulas. Through a darkness ultrasound makes visible, they can watch as they drain abscesses and clip aneurysms.

The image that gives the surgeon so much information—the depth of the tumor or cyst, its general size, and the best angle of approach—would reveal little to the rest of us. The slice of brain being scanned appears on the TV screen as only a fan-shaped shadow.

Ultrasound works on the same principle as sonar, bouncing sound waves off objects to determine their location and size. Only the instrument's scanhead touches the brain. This vibrator-shaped, rather intimidating shaft is sheathed in plastic to keep it sterile. The surgeon holds the scanhead's tip, less than two centimeters in diameter, to the skull's peephole, while dripping a saline solution on the dura to conduct the sound waves into the tissue.

It's actually the scanhead's transducers—three hidden crystals, each with a graduated frequency—that send the sound waves into the cavity. The sound travels from one tissue boundary to the next, echoing back some of the energy at each obstruction. When the sound returns, the energy is converted into electrical signals, which a computer processes and translates into grayish images on a TV screen. Because the echoes fire in rapid sequence, you can watch movements in the brain as they occur, from the pulsing of a blood vessel to the insertion of a needle. After surgery, doctors can pause before closing, using the scanner to spot such dangerous complications as hemorrhaging.

By turning the scanhead slightly, the surgeon can view the gray matter in 90-degree arcs throughout the brain, not merely what lies under the peephole. The image can be a few centimeters deep or can penetrate to the other side of the brain. To peer deeper, the surgeon changes the frequency. There's still a problem with this, however: High frequencies can't scan deep areas effectively; low frequencies can, but they don't deliver sharp images. The difficulty lies in finding the best compromise.

Ultrasound is not new to medicine. In 1950 Dr. Lyle A. French, of the University of Minnesota, found a tumor in an autopsied brain with the aid of an ultrasound detector. A number of unsophisticated scanners have been around for more than 20 years. But older machines were technically limited: Instead of a decipherable image, they simply showed a squiggle on a screen when the sound wave hit an obstruction, such as a cyst. When the CAT scan arrived, ultrasound was relegated to screening cardiac, abdominal, and other problems.

Then in 1979 Drs. George Dohrmann and Jonathan Rubin, now assistant professor of radiology and chief of ultrasound services at the University of Chicago Medical Center, began to use ultrasound imaging during brain surgery. (A few other doctors throughout the country had also renewed their interest in the concept.) Working with a company named Advanced Technology Laboratories, in Bellevue, Washington, they developed an instrument called the Neurosector. A compact ultrasound imager, it has now been used effectively in hundreds of operations, including 250 performed by Dohrmann and Rubin.

"Now it's almost unlimited in the things it can image during surgery," Rubin claims. These images help minimize risks, disclose hidden dangers, prevent needless surgery, and in some cases reduce the number of operations a patient must undergo. For this reason, doctors consider the $44,000 machine cost-effective.

Dohrmann recalls one typical case in which an elderly woman operated on for a brain tumor was probably spared a massive stroke when ultrasound revealed that the cancerous growth had hijacked part of an artery. "Had we entered the tumor, as originally planned," the surgeon says, "we would have gone right into that artery."

Unlike CAT scans or angiograms, which emit radiation, ultrasound poses no health risks, Rubin adds. During studies conducted at the University of Michigan Medical Center and at hospitals in New York, Louisiana, Florida, and even Tokyo, there's been no evidence of infection or brain damage from ultrasound imaging.

In more recent months the technique has been used as a window to the spine during back surgery. An extension of the brain, the spine is also riddled with vulnerabilities; so it's critical that doctors manipulate it as little as possible during surgery. Ultrasound presents vital information on the exact location of the trouble. "An incision one millimeter in the wrong direction can mean loss of motor function and loss of bowel or bladder control. It can affect the sexual organs," says Dr. Barth Green, associate professor of neurological surgery at the University of Miami and attending surgeon at Miami's Jackson Memorial Medical Center and the Veterans Administration Medical Center. "This way, you know exactly where to go to find the pathology. It reduces the chance of error."

This has proved particularly helpful when gunshot victims are to be operated on. Ultrasound easily identifies metal objects; so doctors no longer have to hunt for bullet fragments. "It gives us the X-ray eyes of Superman," says Dr. Green.

At Jackson Memorial, Green has applied ultrasound imaging to disc removal, a fairly common operation. Because the surgeon can scan for stray cartilage (a cause of repeated operations) before finishing, the chances of a successful one-time operation are improved.

Not all brain and spinal surgery requires ultrasound imaging, though. "It's more than a toy, but less than a necessity," according to Dr. Rand Voorhies, assistant professor of surgery at the New York Hospital-Cornell Medical Center. Often tumors are either very large or fairly near the surface, Dr. Voorhies explains. "We bring out the imaging equipment only when we think it's going to make a difference."

Right now neurosurgeons disagree about how often—and in which circumstances—ultrasound imaging can benefit surgeon and patient. Some even contend that the image won't add to their knowledge of the tumor's boundaries. Others retort that ultrasound can often outline a tumor's general limits. "That's not saying it can tell you where every last tumurous cell is. That's impossible. But it can give us a good sense of the borders," Dohrmann says. This information becomes important when a doctor does a biopsy (the best samples are obtained from the tumor's core) or when a surgeon tries to find out whether most of the tumor was removed.

Furthermore, a few surgeons believe that ultrasound imaging will facilitate many other types of surgery. As the resolution sharpens and the scanhead shrinks, doctors may learn to pinpoint problems throughout the body more easily. "We may even be able to use it in corrective surgery, such as shunting hydrocephalus [releasing water on the brain] while the baby is still in the womb," Dr. Green speculates.

Infants' heads are readily scanned with ultrasound (the soft spot means docotrs needn't remove any bone); so for the past several years surgeons have used the technique when placing catheters and shunts in babies' heads. In other areas, ultrasound imaging still meets with some skepticism. One surgeon said, "You know, I can biopsy brain lesions blindly. I don't need your ultrasound. I can just find them."

Dohrmann agrees that in many instances this is so. "But wouldn't you rather be able to see it?" he asks.

ELECTRIC ANESTHESIA

By Brian Goldman

A forty-two-year-old Russian woman was wheeled
into the operating room at the Vishnevsky Surgical
Institute, in Moscow, for surgery to remove her gall-
bladder. Dr. Mikhai Kuzin, her surgeon and the
director of the institute, motioned to the anesthesiolo-
gist to attach electrodes to the woman's forehead and
behind each ear. He then switched on the nearby
Anesthelic-MP02 electroanesthesia device, developed
in France by Aimé Limoge, professor of physiology at
René Descartes University, in Paris. Instantly, the
current began coursing through the woman's brain,
gently placing her into a deep level of anesthesia. The
operation proceeded as scheduled, and the woman
was spared the risk of drug-induced death. In North
America alone, about 1,000 people die from the
effects of anesthesia each year.

Using electricity to anesthetize the brain is not a
new idea. Research abounded on both sides of the
Atlantic during the first half of this century. But

American anesthesiologists lost interest in the early Sixties, when experiments that used a single current produced convulsions, muscle twitching, heart irregularities, and closure of the test animals' air passages.

But Limoge, then a dentist and electrophysiologist, refused to let the idea die. After experimenting with a variety of different currents, he developed a device that combined two currents: The combination, he reported, eliminated the side effects. Still, no one is certain today what effect the current has on the brain. Preliminary studies indicate that the Limoge current stimulates the release of endorphins, which help relieve pain.

At the Vishnevsky Surgical Institute, Kuzin says that surgeons now use Limoge's invention for the whole gamut of surgical procedures. "Patients wake up two or three minutes after the current is stopped," he explains, "and without the usual postanesthetic drowsiness."

Over the past three years, Limoge's company, E3A, has produced and sold more than 200 Anesthelic-MP02 machines, costing $3,500 each, to interested physicians in France, Belgium, Switzerland, Spain, and the Soviet Union. Those physicians have found electroanesthesia to be useful in many situations, including lengthy neurosurgical procedures and open-heart surgery. Dr. Jean-Claude Pire, an anesthesiologist at the Centre Hospital Regionale Robert Debre, in Reims, France, has used the Limoge current on more than 1,000 patients. "The major advantage," says Pire, "is that we can obtain a seventy-five percent reduction in the amount of narcotics required during or after surgery." This, he explains, is beneficial when dealing with elderly people or those with chronic respiratory diseases. In such cases, narcotics can depress the patients' breathing.

Other anesthesiologists have found the Limoge current to be particularly successful in treating postoperative pain in infants (another high-risk group) and in women giving birth.

Despite its popularity in Europe, the Limoge current remains controversial in the United States. In part the skepticism is a result of shoddy experimental evidence. Jean-Pierre Thierry, a public-health technologist with the Center for the Study of Advanced Technology, a French government-funded agency that has tested the device, admits that Limoge "learned to run before he learned to walk," promoting the current for clinical use before extensive animal and human studies had been performed. Only now are large-scale double-blind studies being carried out.

Some American anesthesiologists, though, are greeting the invention more optimistically. Dr. Theodore Stanley, a professor of anesthesiology at the University of Utah, observed Limoge's techniques while he was a visiting fellow in France. He also collaborated with Limoge on two published studies demonstrating the current's effectiveness when combined with other anesthetics. He agrees that more research is needed to convince the North American medical establishment. "It could be an invaluable addition to medical science," he says. "But it has a long way to go."

BORN-AGAIN NERVES

By Richard Wolkomir

When a piece of metal struck his head, injuring his right eye's optic nerve, Gary P. Kase, a rigger at a California shipyard, became blind in that eye. Doctors told him there was no hope for recovery: It has been a medical axiom that nerves of the central nervous system (CNS) do not regenerate.

But Kase's vision gradually returned. What had occurred was a process long sought by scientists— spontaneous regeneration of a part of the CNS.

With spinal-cord injuries paralyzing more than 20,000 Americans each year, and brain disorders such as Alzheimer's disease afflicting millions, learning how to regenerate the neurons in the CNS would be a major medical breakthrough. And within the past few years, research in this area has been progressing rapidly. The discovery of two proteins by researchers at Stanford University, plus a number of animal studies on neurons, are yielding valuable clues to the riddle of nerve regeneration.

Unlike the nerves in our skin and muscles, which belong to the peripheral nervous system, damaged nerves in our CNS—neurons in the skull and spine—do not grow back. Furthermore, scientists have long believed that we are born with all the brain neurons we will ever have.

But in April, 1984, Rockefeller University's Fernando Nottebohm presented findings to the Institute for Child Development Research that question this. Nottebohm discovered that the forebrains of birds produce new neurons into young adulthood.

"We ought to apply ourselves to see if adult neurogenesis occurs in humans," says Nottebohm. "And if it is not found, we should ask, 'Why not?' "

Along similar lines, anatomists John R. Sladek and Carol Phelps, at the University of Rochester, have shown that in certain animals, severed brain-cell axons—which transmit impulses from one nerve cell to the next—repair themselves.

"If we can find out what this growth factor is," says Sladek, "we can then determine whether it will be possible to stimulate the regrowth of brain tissue at will."

Phelps points out the benefits of regeneration. "About twenty percent of the population suffers from a nervous-system disorder. The ability of the brain to repair itself after the onset of such ailments would be of enormous importance," she says.

Recent discoveries by neurobiologists Pate Skene and Eric Shooter, of Stanford University's School of Medicine, may help scientists in their search for the factor that triggers regeneration. They found that when a nerve is injured, its insulating tissues begin manufacturing a protein. In the peripheral nervous system, the levels of this protein build, but in the CNS, this protein tends to dissipate.

In addition, Skene has discovered that certain neurons—as well as tissues—produce a separate protein when starting to regenerate.

"Cells that don't regenerate don't seem to produce this protein, which we call growth-associated protein," says Skene. "We are focusing our research on this. To me, it's the most promising avenue."

Other scientists are looking to apply currently available techniques to stimulate nerve regeneration. British scientists believe that the Diapulse machine, a radio-wave generator used in the United Kingdom and Canada to heal bone fractures, may promote healing of nerves in the CNS. In his latest study, Dr. David H. Wilson, president of England's Association of Accident and Emergency Physicians, used the machine on 40 cats paralyzed by spinal-cord injuries. After treatment, 38 of the cats could walk again.

"We see it now as having enormous potential in the treatment of acute spinal injuries. There are indications that it promotes regeneration of [damaged] nerves once thought to result in lifelong paralysis," he notes. Wilson intends to begin human tests soon.

Electricity may also help heal injured spinal-cord nerves. Dr. Robert O. Becker, an orthopedic surgeon at Upstate Medical Center, in Syracuse, New York, has found that bombarding certain cells with electrically charged silver ions returns them to their embryonic state. Embryonic cells multiply rapidly and have the ability to adapt to different parts of the body.

It's conceivable that these cells could be removed

165

from a patient, treated electrically, and then returned to the injured area. Because the patient would receive his own cells, there is no chance of rejection.

A number of other methods have also shown some promise. Researchers are experimenting with the effects of hormone treatments on damaged nerves, with implanted polyester channels that guide the growth of new axons, and with certain chemicals that may prompt regeneration.

Perhaps the most dramatic work involves transplanting brain cells. Don Marshall Gash, associate professor of anatomy at the University of Rochester Medical School, has placed human brain cells into the brain of a monkey. The cells, which were taken from a brain tumor, were rendered nonmalignant before the operation. The cells have survived in the animal's brain.

Someday, such neutralized tumor cells may be transplanted into the brains of humans with neuron-destroying diseases. In the meantime, this research could shed light on the process of nerve regeneration. By the end of the century, some researchers believe, the mystery will be solved.

ELECTRIC NERVES

By Doug Garr

Dr. Terry Hambrecht flips on the video-cassette recorder, and a young man in a wheelchair appears on the monitor. The man is a quadriplegic—he has no feeling in any limb—but in a few seconds the camera reveals the results of some remarkable research. The man slowly grasps a paper cup with his right hand, gently closes his fist, and raises it to his lips to drink. His gingerly movement could not be called graceful, yet it is not entirely awkward either.

Out of camera range is a PDP-11 computer, which commands a system that is eventually wired to the muscles in the patient's forearm. The system is known as neural prosthesis, and, although it has been tested on only a dozen or so quadriplegics in the United States, researchers are hopeful that more refined, portable devices will someday restore reasonable mobility to paralyzed limbs—even to the point of walking.

The current experiments rely on what will ultimately be regarded as a rather cumbersome, primitive system where the patient remains tethered to a computer and must depend on technicians to start the program. Eventually, however, Dr. Hambrecht plans to replace his PDP-11 standing frame model with a microprocessor worn on a belt. Since most quadriplegics retain shoulder movement, they could use their elbow to flip on the microprocessor. And with further advances, Hambrecht speculates, it may eventually prove possible to design a neural prosthesis that could be voice activated. Then, a very complicated and sophisticated program could carry out the intricate muscular coordination required for decent mobility.

Hambrecht directs the neural-prosthesis program at the National Institute of Neurological and Communicative Disorders and Stroke, a federal agency. His program has existed for only a decade, but he has been dreaming of this kind of work since he was graduated from college in 1959. That year his best friend was incapacitated in an automobile accident. This prompted him to wonder what could be done to help the paralyzed. Hambrecht holds a degree in electrical engineering and is also a medical doctor; his dual qualifications make him a natural leader in this relatively new phase of bioengineering. In fact he did his internship in surgery, thinking that most neural prostheses would eventually need to be surgically implanted, like today's cardiac pacemakers.

Happily, scientists are already past that stage. The actual electrodes, stainless-steel wires only 600 microns thick, are implanted with hypodermic needles in what is a fairly fast and uncomplicated procedure. The physician inserts the syringe and then applies an electrical current to see how the muscles contract. When the wire's in the right spot, he extracts the needle.

The electrodes stay in place because they have a barblike tip that grabs the muscle, much like a fishhook.

Though medical science has known for centuries that muscles contract when electricity is applied, the big mystery was how it could be done in a manageable fashion. The solution appeared to be far in the distance until the advent of the Computer Age. Why not have a microprocessor direct the action—bridge the gap, so to speak—in the disabled nervous system?

"We discovered that the computer could do most of the bookkeeping," Hambrecht says. "It could decide how much to stimulate which muscles and in what order, thereby coordinating the intricate pattern of muscular contraction that underlies even the simplest of movements." The computer gives its directions, sending out a pulse that moves the muscles. Both the duration and the frequency of the pulse determine how much the muscle will contract.

Some of the more advanced neural-prosthesis work is being done at the Rehabilitation Engineering Center at Case Western Reserve University, in Cleveland, Ohio. There Dr. Hunter Peckham, the director, has succeeded in teaching patients two kinds of grips with the system. One is called the key grip, which uses the thumb and forefinger, allowing a user to pick up a key or a coin. The other is called palmar-prehension, in which the thumbs, index fingers, and middle fingers can actually grasp an object, such as a phone receiver. "When you think about opening and closing your hand, that's simple," Peckham notes. "But if a person has no feeling, then it's really complex."

Still another research team, in Yugoslavia, is working on a neural-prosthesis system for the lower extremities, one that might someday eliminate the wheelchair. But that is at least a decade away. Right now Hambrecht and his colleagues would simply like to develop a reliable, totally implantable system that would allow a quadriplegic to perform basic chores unaided. "The biggest clinical problem we face is that we have wires going through the system and into the muscle," Peckham says. "One of the next breakthroughs would be a wireless system." It certainly isn't impossible to envision a transmitter sending the computer's messages to electrodes implanted in the muscles. In fact, Peckham says it has been done already in some animal experiments.

Another phase of neural-prosthesis research involves something that might be called "artificial feeling." How does the patient "know" how hard to grip a paper cup without crushing it? Could such a system sense temperature as well as pressure? Dr. Andrew Schoenberg and his team at the Utah Biomedical Test Lab are developing artificial sensory transducers to measure tissue compression so that the force exerted on an object can be precisely quantified. Current experiments involve the use of a very thin (28 microns thick) polyvinylidine fluoride film with the trade name Kynar (something like Mylar). This material, made into a glove, would bounce pulses off objects much the way bats use ultrasonics to navigate. When the reflected signal hits the surface of the film, it will oscillate at a specific frequency, providing the glove wearer with an artificial sense of touch.

Even this proposal is less than ideal, for someone must put the glove on the patient. And that raises the toughest barrier of all: Technology cannot hope to re-create *real* feeling, only simulate it. When healthy arms are lifted, the brain messages are second nature. For the quadriplegic, the brain must always consciously dictate what it wants the limb to do. As Peckham points out, "The patient has to learn to communicate with his nervous system."

A neural prosthesis may never restore the instantaneous, fine-tuned muscle movement that normal individuals take for granted. But for the 200,000 Americans now confined to wheelchairs—and others all over the world—it could mean greater self-sufficiency and the ability to accomplish tasks once thought impossible.

THE BIONIC LOVER

By Ruth Winter

Priapus, the Greek god of fertility, held sway over women with his penis—always erect and spectacular in size—the envy of every red-blooded male. While most men can emulate Priapus when the need arises, for an estimated 10 million sufferers of impotence in the United States, an erection is the stuff only of myth. Until now. Researchers have recently uncovered information on why impotence happens and have developed techniques that offer these men an erection that might give Priapus pause.

New drugs, hormone additives, silver-wire implants, and anal electronic stimulators are among the treatments designed to restore normal sex lives to the impotent. There's even an apparatus that turns the scrotum into a little pump room for inflating flaccid cylinders implanted in the penis. We'll discuss these later. First, let's take a look at the recent strides researchers have made toward finding the real—and often misunderstood—causes of impotence.

Although not fully understood, an erection is known to occur in response to psychological, neurological, and sensory stimuli. When the physiological and emotional components are in sync, blood engorges the corpora cavernosa, two spongy, tissue-filled cylinders lying on either side of the urethra, and the penis becomes stiff.

As recently as three years ago, health professionals believed that at least 90 percent of all impotence resulted from such psychological problems as depression, anxiety, and fear of hurting the sexual partner. Now doctors have discovered that a large percentage of impotent males have an underlying physiological condition.

"Because of better diagnosis today, it has been found that at least fifty-five percent of all cases of impotence have organic causes, most of which are medically or surgically correctable," says Dr. E. Douglas Whitehead, founding member of the Association for Male Sexual Dysfunction, a New York-based group that diagnoses and treats impotence. He estimates that 75 percent of all men with organic-related impotence can be helped.

A variety of physical problems can bring about impotence. These include vascular problems, hormonal imbalance, nervous-system disorders (like Parkinson's disease), diabetes, drug and alcohol side effects, and the aftereffects of surgery on, or injury to, the penis.

One of the catalysts for the current scientific interest in organic-related impotence occured in 1979, when Dr. Richard Spark and his colleagues at Harvard Medical School reported on a study of 105 impotent men. Of these, researchers found that 37 had endocrine-gland disorders. Once the appropriate therapy was started, potency returned in 33 of the 37.

As a result of these and other findings, doctors now consider several factors when seeking a cause of impotence. A diagnosis starts with the physician's taking a complete medical history and a detailed psychosexual history, which includes some psychological testing. He then does a physical exam—concentrating on the genitals and on the vascular and neurological factors contributing to erection—and evaluates the blood's hormone and sugar levels.

Another variable weighed is the man's ability to have erections during sleep. (Normally, a man has four to seven erections while sleeping.) If erections occur and are firm enough to achieve penetration, then the problem is usually emotional, because the erectile mechanism obviously works.

To assess these erections accurately, a doctor may recommend nocturnal testing in a special sleep lab. There are also two new tests that can help speed the diagnosis.

The first, a cuff that is positioned on the penis with Velcro fasteners, contains three snaps that break at varying degrees of pressure, providing an accurate reading of penile rigidity during sleep. Called The Dacomed Snap Guide, it can be used at home. It doesn't, however, give information about the number of nocturnal erections or their durations, both of which may prove medically significant.

The second device, now in clinical testing, is BIDDS—Biosonics Interface Digital Diagnostic System. This transrectally stimulates the nerves involved in erection. If no automatic response occurs, then a doctor looks for neurological abnormalities.

Other tests that are used in diagnosis:

• Ultrasound, whereby sound waves help in evaluating the adequacy of blood supply to the penis.

• Arteriograms, in which doctors inject dye into the bloodstream and then take X rays of the penis to determine the condition of the blood vessels.

• Sacral nerve reflex testing, which measures the electrical activity of the nerves affecting the function of the penis.

• Skull X rays, which detect problems with the pituitary gland. Located at the base of the brain, the gland sends and receives chemical messages from the sex glands and other endocrine glands.

Once the diagnosis is made, doctors begin considering the appropriate treatments. "If impotence is a side effect of medication," says Dr. Whitehead, "such as an antihypertensive drug or a tranquilizer, an equivalent prescription may be substituted and the problem solved very simply."

In about 5 to 10 percent of all cases, hormonal imbalances cause impotence. They are of two main types: a shortage of the male hormone testosterone or an excess of prolactin, a hormone produced by the pituitary gland. The first condition can be treated by giving testosterone and the second by administering Bromocriptine, which inhibits prolactin production.

When impotence is due to blood-vessel blockage, vascular surgery may increase the flow of blood to the penis. Unfortunately, though, the success rate is low, and the procedure sometimes causes a permanent erection.

If the impotence results from a physical condition that either drug therapy or a change in medication won't remedy, or if the patient suffers a psychological problem that therapy (including marital, family, or sex therapy) can't help, penile implants are an option.

More than 100,000 men have had penile implants. Most of these are young or middle-aged men who are in reasonably good health and have strong sex drives and enthusiastic partners. A surprisingly large number of older men, however, want implants as well, says Whitehead, and they're "frequently pleased with the results."

Two types of implants exist: The first uses a semirigid prosthesis. The early models, which consisted of a pair of rods surgically inserted in the penis, caused a permanent erection, one sometimes detectable through clothes. A newer model, from Dacomed, features a silver wire coated with silicone and Teflon, and wrapped as a coil. Since it's flexible, it can be bent down when an erection is not wanted.

The second type, an inflatable implant, raises the penis by means of a small hydraulic pump. Fluid is stored in a container surgically placed in the abdomen, and the pump is housed in the scrotum. Two inflatable cylinders are implanted in the penis by way of the groin (so no incision is made on the penis itself), and when an erection is desired, the patient presses the pump. He can deflate the prosthesis at will.

"Ejaculation and fertility aren't affected by either type of prosthesis," Whitehead says, "providing the functions were intact before implantation."

There are pros and cons to each of these implants. The semirigid type is relatively inexpensive, costing about $800, and requires only a three-day hospital stay. The pump costs about $5,000 for hospitalization and surgery, and the procedure demands longer hospitalization, says Dr. Robert Davis, assistant professor of urology at the University of Rochester.

But Whitehead, who prefers the inflatable prosthesis, contends that the semirigids don't increase the width or fullness of the penis, sometimes buckle during intercourse, and make it difficult to treat urinary and prostrate problems.

"The inflatable gives a much more natural erection," he says. In fact, it's often undetectable to a woman who doesn't know that her partner has had an implant. Some men prefer to go into the bathroom or inflate the prosthesis in the dark so their partner will remain unaware of the implant. On the other hand, women who know about it often incorporate inflation into their foreplay, Whitehead adds.

No matter which implant a patient chooses, he'll probably be satisfied. "The latest survey shows that more than ninety percent of all couples in which the man has had an implant are happy with the result," says Whitehead.

Soon a prosthesis device that doesn't require surgery may be available. The MEGS (for Male Electronic Genital Stimulator), developed by Biosonics, Inc., is now in clinical trials. It works like this: A bulletlike mechanism that's three inches long, just under an inch in diameter, and encased in plastic is inserted into the rectum. Remotely controlled by a radio-transmitter unit contained in a watch or other piece of jewelry, the MEGS, when activated, stimulates the nerves to the penis and prompts an erection.

177

"Each unit will be custom-made," explains Dr. Henry S. Brenman, research director of Biosonics, "so that the man doesn't end up accidentally opening someone's garage door."

If the human trials now in progress are as successful as those with primates, Dr. Brenman predicts that MEGS will have been made available by prescription in mid-1984.

PLASTIC SURGERY 2000

By Shelley Ross

An operating room, the year 2000. The patient, who is having breast-reduction surgery, lies wide-awake on the table. But she feels no pain; a system of electrical probes that stimulate her brain's natural opiates takes care of that.

Nor does she fear that a scalpel's slip or a surgeon's botched sense of proportion will mar her anatomy. A sophisticated computer program, coupled to a CAT (computerized axial tomography) scan of her breasts, has churned out mathematically precise before and after pictures to guide the transformation. And her surgeon is actually a robot, with unshaking hands and perfect sangfroid.

There's no gore on twenty-first-century doctors' gowns, either. A laser makes bloodless incisions, and a revolutionary biodegradable "glue"—modeled on the natural glue with which a mollusk sticks to the sides of a dock—seals the cut without sutures. (The mollusk's secretion becomes a fibrous protein much like human connective tissue.) Postsurgical infections are just about extinct, too. Instead of scrubbing up, the doctors have passed their hands and instruments through sonication devices that kill germs with sound waves.

This forecast comes from Dr. I. Kelman Cohen, who is no misty visionary but the chairman of the plastic-surgery division of the Medical College of Virginia, in Richmond. The real revolution, however, won't involve an operating table at all. Think you'll be needing a face-lift by 1999? Forget it. If Dr. Cohen is any seer, your fountain of youth will probably come in tablet form. By instructing the cells in your face to repress some genes and amplify others, this pill—or injection or ointment—will actually do what TV face-cream commercials only promise: make your collagen tissue young again.

"Your body produces three kinds of collagen," Cohen explains. "The collagen in your face is a mixture of about eighty percent Type One collagen, the type of collagen in rigid structures like bone and tendon, and twenty percent Type Three collagen, which is more elastic. My hypothesis is that aging skin switches to a different ratio, with more Type Three, and that's why you get sagging and wrinkles." The cure? That will come from the caldrons of molecular biology.

"In cell cultures, pharmacological agents can manipulate that genetic machinery," he notes. "There is no reason we can't tell your collagen cells, 'Make x percent of Type One,' but we have to find a way to do that without hurting the rest of the body. If the very elastic collagen of your blood vessels started making too much Type One, you would be in trouble."

But since specific cells have specific traits—abdominal fat cells transplanted to your hand, for instance, get pudgy when you gain weight—Cohen predicts that rejuvenation drugs will be custom-tailored. By 2000 you won't need any fancy "fat-suction" treatments to eradicate cellulite, either. "I think we'll know so much about the cell's enzyme systems that we'll be able to control where fat is deposited," says the surgeon.

Face-lifts, nose jobs, and tummy-tucks are only the petits fours of plastic surgery; its meat-and-potatoes is reconstructing burned faces, torn limbs, cleft palates, and other congenital deformities.

Here, say the experts, the next frontier is the immunological barrier. You can't willy-nilly wear someone else's nose or arm, because your immune system recognizes it as foreign and rejects it. This explains why organ-transplant recipients are treated with drugs that suppress their bodies' natural defenses. Currently, immunosuppressive drugs are judged too dangerous to use for anything less serious than a vital organ transplant. But what if scientists found a way to trick the immune system?

"Then we'll really be able to talk about spare parts," says Stanford University's Dr. Lars Vistnes, chief of the plastic- and reconstructive-surgery clinic. "We'll have immunosuppressants with fewer side effects, or, better, we'll manipulate the transplanted part biochemically so the body recognizes it as its own." Once cell biologists learn to identify and block the antigen sites that label tissue as foreign—a feat Cohen forecasts for the next decade or two—spare fingers, ears, and skin tissue will be routine.

Sophisticated synthetic materials will mimic Mother Nature more successfully, too, making artificial skin, breast tissue, and other organs amazingly lifelike, says Cohen. And by the turn of the century, cleft palates, skull and face abnormalities, club feet, and other birth defects will be repaired before birth, with intrauterine surgery.

If you're still interested in a garden-variety nose job or other cosmetic procedure by century's close, don't worry. "Gone are the days of the standardized 'Dr. Diamond nose,' " says Cohen. "Today we design a nose that goes with your face." High-tech computer imaging (already used by at least one surgeon for correcting craniofacial defects) and foolproof surgeon-robots will all but guarantee success. "If robots can build cars," says Cohen, "why shouldn't they do the mechanical work of surgery?"

PART FIVE:
THE NEW LASERS

*"The wave of the future is coming,
and there is no fighting it."*
—Anne M. Lindbergh

DAWN OF A NEW RAY

By T. A. Heppenheimer

The shower of molten lead and lithium rains from the top of a reactor chamber nearly eight stories high. A gunlike mechanism fires pea-size pellets of nuclear-fusion fuel through the falling spray. And as the mixture of metals and fuel cascades down the inside of the chamber, the fuel pellets are caught in a cross fire of ultraviolet laser beams emanating from ducts in the walls. The rays make outside layers of the pellets blow off violently, exerting a pressure on the pellets' centers up to ten times the pressure in the middle of the earth.

In a few trillionths of a second under this laser-beam bombardment, the center of each pellet heats to four times the temperature at the center of the sun. The pellet explodes from the inside out.

All of this primordial violence in the reactor is aimed toward a peaceful end. Researchers say that when this chamber is built—sometime before the end of this century—it will provide enough harnessable power to supply electricity to a city of half a million people. But paradoxically, the payoff in fusion energy for home and factory depends on steady progress at the nation's weapons laboratories. In particular, it depends on results from an extensive program already under way to build the world's largest lasers.

Huge laser-beam generators are operating or are under construction today at California's Lawrence Livermore National Laboratory and at New Mexico's Los Alamos National Laboratory, the nation's centers for the development of hydrogen bombs. Lasers built at these labs will first be used to set off the explosions of H-bombs the size of grains of sand. The resulting microexplosions will resemble those of full-size bombs, producing strong bursts of radiation.

But the scientists who are building these lasers don't think of themselves as H-bomb designers. For one thing, each explosion in their labs will be no more powerful than the pop of a firecracker. And many of the researchers are looking ahead to the day when the mass detonation of tiny fusion-fuel targets will be routine and cheap, when their laser devices move quietly into the country's power plants.

For decades many of our most valuable technologies have grown out of military research. Some of today's commercial jetliners were originally designed as Air Force transport and tanker aircraft. The microchip, the heart of any computer, was developed to meet the needs of the Air Force's Minuteman ICBM program. The exploration of space owes a debt to early military work in rockets and missiles. The Air Force has already used airborne lasers experimentally to shoot down small missiles, a step toward the kind of "star wars" technology President Reagan suggested in a speech in March, 1983.

In their preliminary forms, the huge lasers of the

future bear little resemblance to the trim laser guns of science fiction. It's easier to compare today's most advanced lasers to a house of immense halls and chambers with all of its plumbing showing.

The beam is born in one chamber, in a master laser of low power. It produces a pulse of the proper wavelength and duration—a billionth of a second, for instance. The beam has all the characteristics needed to set off the fuel target except one. It is a million or more times weaker than the final laser pulse that will be focused onto the pellet.

This master pulse is then split up into subpulses by using beam splitters, partially transparent mirrors that let half the pulse go through and that reflect the other half in a different direction. Each subpulse then enters an "arm" of the laser, a train of amplifiers. These amplifiers boost the power in the subpulses. But while these subpulses are being amplified, they lose sharpness. Rather than remaining precisely focusable, they flare out like flashlight beams. So after each stage of amplication, the beams are cleaned up, their fuzziness removed and their sharpness restored. To do this, the laser beam in each arm is focused by a lens and passes through a pinhole in a metal plate. The main part of the beam goes through, but the fuzzy smears of light hit the plate surrounding the pinhole and are absorbed. Each laser beam then emerges fresh from its pinhole, ready to be amplified anew.

At Los Alamos the chambers of each amplifier are filled with carbon dioxide and nitrogen gases. When the laser is to be fired, a powerful beam of electrons sweeps through the gas. The electrons collide with the carbon dioxide and store energy in the molecules. Then, when the laser pulse comes through, it triggers the gas molecules into releasing their stored energy, which comes off as additional laser light, amplifying the original pulse.

In Livermore's laser program, the amplifiers use large, dark-purple slabs of glass containing the element neodymium. The slabs are surrounded by flashlamps. Just before the laser fires, the flashlamps blaze with light; the flash stores energy, this time in the neodymium atoms. The laser pulse following the flash causes this energy to be released as additional laser light.

By alternating amplifiers with pinholes and their lenses within the laser arms, researchers can boost the energy in the pulse as high as they want while maintaining a clean, focusable beam. After several such amplify-and-clean cycles, each arm comes to an end. The laser beams in these arms are now at full power, ready for focusing onto the pallet. The rays strike the target from as many different directions as there are arms in the laser.

Such descriptions of the inner workings of lasers don't give much of an idea of what the devices actually look like. The world's largest, at Livermore, is called Nova. Many of its components are in a room the size of a high-school gymnasium three stories high. Within it are two tall frames built from steel beams, reaching nearly to the top and painted a dazzling white. The frames are laden with intricate instruments. Along two of the walls are sets of holes, each more than three feet across, to let the laser beams pass through. All the gear is as clean as the fixtures in a hospital's operating room; visitors wear white booties over their shoes, and they don nylon jackets to keep from bringing in dust. But this isn't the Nova laser itself. It's merely the laser-beam switchyard, where beams are turned and focused to enter the target room. The frames hold a set of mirrors to redirect the beams from the laser and its amplifiers.

The laser, next door, is in a long, open hall nearly large enough to house an indoor football game. Dominating the scene, almost filling the volume of the bay, is a steel lattice the size of a baseball grandstand, its beams and interlaced frames also painted a brilliant white. Along the length of this lattice, engineers today are meticulously assembling Nova's components, blue cylindrical pipes holding amplifiers and filters. The pipes resemble oversize versions of long telephoto lenses for cameras and convey a similar impression of precision and cost. Nova represents nearly $200 million worth of highly precise optical technology, carried out on a massive scale. When construction is completed next year, Nova will be five times more powerful than any laser built before.

The money for Nova comes from the U.S. government, by way of the Department of Energy (DOE). DOE is the manager of our federal energy programs, such as synthetic-fuels development and fusion-energy research. Less well known is DOE's role in the development and production of the nation's nuclear bombs. Nova and the other large lasers will serve for research in both bombs and energy. The boss of Nova, however, is a laser man, pure and simple.

He is John Emmett, widely known among physicists as a maverick. He drives a black Corvette at very high speeds and likes to think of himself as a dashing technologist-about-planet. He concocts rare and exotic liqueurs to try out on friends. He has long been fascinated with high explosives and is a licensed demolitions expert. Occasionally he takes friends on boulder-blasting expeditions, going out into the desert and blowing large rocks apart with dynamite. In his younger days he graduated among the top 10 percent of his class at Caltech. Then he got his Ph.D. at Stanford under Arthur Schawlow, who had shared in the invention of the laser and later won the Nobel Prize for his work with lasers. Emmett went on to the Naval Research Laboratory, near Washington, DC, where he built up a world-class group of laser experts. Since 1972 he has been directing the laser work at Livermore.

Like most large federal science programs, Nova has sprung from a mix of technical considerations and politics. It got its start in 1975. At that time Emmett was building Shiva, the precursor to Nova. It was to be nearly as large in size as Nova, but with about 10 percent as much power.

In the mid-Seventies the laser world was agog over the power and size of Shiva, which would feature 20 arms and would fill a very large bay within its quarters, Livermore's Building 391. But Emmett knew it was already time to begin planning something bigger. His laser builders had succeeded in inventing new types of neodymium glass, which could handle higher power levels with a laser. The researchers had also raised the efficiency of the laser amplifiers and devised means for fabricating particularly large components. Moreover, they had proved that, by using pinholes and lenses, even very powerful laser beams could be kept clean and focusable. So Emmett knew he could build a laser much more energetic than Shiva.

The broad outline of his plan was deceptively simple: He proposed to double the size of Building 391 by constructing a second bay. Within these two bays Nova would also have 20 arms. But two of these arms would have more power and energy than all of Shiva. That was the measure of the advances he had made in building lasers. He sought approval for Nova and won the backing of the director of the federal large-laser program, an Army general named Alfred T. Starbird.

Emmett was working closely with John Nuckolls, an expert on the design of the pellets to be zapped with the laser beams. The design of such pellets is a complex art, and Nuckolls believed he had a pellet concept that would work particularly well. Then, in 1977, Emmett's plans began to go awry. Shiva went into operation and began firing laser pulses at other pellets designed by Nuckolls. With the data from these experiments, Nuckolls went back to work on his Nova pellet and decided it wasn't quite as good as he had thought. For Emmett this was bad news. It undercut his case for building the full-size Nova, with all 20 of its arms. Moreover, pork-barrel politics was raising its head.

Nova would cost $200 million, and within the federal laser program, there was a limited pot of money available. A number of other labs wanted a cut of the Nova cash. In the words of Lowell Wood, a leading laser expert, "There were a lot of people saying, 'For only twenty million dollars I can do thus and such. Wouldn't it be a lot better if you gave Emmett one hundred eighty million and gave me the twenty million?' " Congressmen argued over whether the laser programs in their districts were getting their fair share. Of course, Nova had to have enough to do something significant; otherwise, as Wood explains, "you would just fritter the money away. Like giving one dollar to each citizen and telling him to go support his favorite laser program—unless he'd prefer to spend it on a six-pack."

Another issue facing Emmett was whether Nova should be built merely as a more energetic version of Shiva, or whether it should have an extra degree of usefulness. In laser parlance, Shiva operated "in the red." This had nothing to do with cost overruns; it referred to the wavelength of its light. Shiva operated in the infrared, at long wavelengths. But the pellets did not readily absorb infrared light. They worked much better at short wavelengths.

The way to get these shorter wavelengths is with frequency-multiplying crystals, which look like big slabs of window glass set in frames. The idea is to shine the laser light through a window whose panes are made from the crystals. The infrared goes in, and green laser light comes out at half the wavelength of the original infrared. Or, by tilting and rotating the crystals, it can be arranged that blue light comes out at about 30 percent of the original wavelength. Shiva had been built without these crystals; the question was whether they should go into Nova. They would give Nova greater flexibility for use in experiments but would cost millions.

In Washington such issues are resolved by setting up a high-level commission to take an unbiased look. The commission that would decide the fate of Nova included two former directors of Livermore, as well as Burton Richter, of Stanford, who had won a Nobel Prize in physics. The commission chairman was John Foster, who had been director of Livermore from 1961 to 1965 and who in those days had been an early and enthusiastic leader in pushing for research on large lasers.

From the outset the Foster committee was sharply divided. Each member had a different view of the proper course for the large-laser program. Many of them wanted to use part of the Nova money for an entirely different laser project. After much debate, several committee members favored upgrading Shiva rather than building Nova. To Emmett such a course would have meant disaster.

At that point Foster made the key argument, which dealt with the details of pellet microexplosion. When the laser beams zap a pellet and the pellet core compresses and heats up, the fusion fire begins as a hot spot, a momentary flash in the center of the pellet. If the pellet is sufficiently large, this hot spot can act as a match, which spreads its fire into the surrounding fusion fuel, propagating into this fuel as a flash from a blasting cap spreads into a charge of dynamite. Foster pointed out that even the full-size Nova would not be large enough for such "propagating-burn" pellet experiments. These would have to await the next laser beyond Nova. But the full-size Nova would be *larger* than would be needed to produce that central hot spot in a pellet. Foster suggested that Nova be built but on a smaller scale than Emmett had envisioned. Nova should be only as large as would suffice for experiments with this hot spot, and no larger.

In June 1979 Foster called a gathering of his committee at his home amid the hills south of Los Angeles. It was a sunny day, and the visitors soon gathered around his swimming pool, which faces the Pacific. Naturally the talk was of lasers, and as the discussion proceeded, a compromise bubbled up among the group, a solution to the Nova problem. They would recommend building only half of Nova, with just ten arms. If the experimental results looked good enough, Emmett might get the go-ahead to put in the other ten arms.

Emmett was not happy. He wanted all 20 arms, and he was angry at the entire Foster committee. He also was angry at John Nuckolls, his pellet expert, who had been a consultant to the committee and had endorsed the compromise. As far as Emmett knew, next year Nuckolls might come up with another good idea in pellet design, which would achieve propagating burn when zapped by the full 20-arm Nova.

For his part Nuckolls was painfully aware of the budget limits: "It was like people out in a lifeboat. There's not enough food; somebody's got to go overboard." What went overboard was ten of the arms. But in their place, softening the blow to Emmett, Nova was given the frequency-multiplying crystals. Unlike Shiva, Nova would have short-wavelength laser light, enhancing the performance of its pellets.

Meanwhile, Shiva's success was setting doubts as to whether Nova could be made to work. One of Shiva's big problems had been how to keep all its components in exquisite alignment—its amplifiers, lenses, and pinholes. Emmett's solution had been to build a computer-controlled alignment system, which was something of a shot in the dark. No one had ever built such a computer system before, and Emmett was betting the success of Shiva on its achievement. This alignment system showed its worth in January 1980, when an earthquake hit Livermore.

When the ground started to rumble, Emmett looked up from his desk and saw a big oaken bookcase full of books beginning to sway. He ducked under the desk and probably saved his life. The bookcase crashed right where he had been working.

To Lowell Wood, "the building looked as if a bomb blast had gone off inside. The fluorescent lights in the ceiling fell in. All the partitions in the office were turned over sideways. Emmett and I went in there, and the place looked worse than a building trashed by vandals. The ceilings were strewn all over." The quakes rolled and swayed for more than a minute, and the 200-ton Shiva frame sheared some bolts and rocked out of position. But within a week riggers brought in jacks and wrenched the frame back into place, putting in double-strength bolts for good measure. The computer alignment did the rest. Within two weeks after the quake, Shiva was back in operation.

But sometimes the story of the development of huge lasers appears as mazelike as the pipes and chambers of the devices themselves. Despite its quick recovery, Shiva was shut down in December 1981. And during 1982 Livermore was left without any large laser at all. Moreover, at the time it was shut down, Shiva's potential was still far from wrung out. As Wood puts it, "Up to the week before they started tearing down Shiva, we were doing experiments that were extremely interesting. The day it died it was the highest-power laser-research facility in the world. It was torn down to save money." It was torn down for other reasons as well.

By 1981, with Nova well under way, the laser program badly needed data from high-power experiments using green laser light, a wavelength much shorter than Shiva could provide. The data were needed to show that Nuckolls could overcome pellet problems that had been uncovered using Shiva. There were two ways to get such data: rebuild Shiva for improved performance, or tear it down and cannibalize some of its parts to build another laser. Either move would cost money and leave Livermore without a major laser for some time. But Emmett had to choose.

He chose to cannibalize. From the used components of Shiva and other parts, he fashioned another laser as a stepping-stone to Nova. The new device, called Novette, has just two arms of the same design that will go into Nova's ten. It thus represents only 20 percent of Nova, yet has more power and energy than its parent laser, Shiva. But while Shiva filled a steel scaffolding three stories tall, Novette is almost low enough to see over. Like Nova, Novette features long chains of blue pipes holding optical components, including laser amplifiers 18 inches across. They resemble components in the rocket-drive units of the spaceship *Discovery* in *2001: A Space Odyssey*. The laser is equipped with the long-sought frequency-multiplying crystals. All of this gear—a kind of miniature Nova—stands in a white room that could hold two large movie theaters.

Why didn't Emmett rebuild Shiva? Emmett knew the earlier system would lead nowhere in laser design, but Novette could pave the way for Nova. With only 2 arms compared with Shiva's 20, Novette would be less costly to operate.

But Emmett also had his eye on politics. Any move to upgrade Shiva would give ammunition to his critics, who would ask whether in fact Nova might not be worth delaying while the program went forward with improved versions of Shiva. Emmett still wanted all 20 arms for Nova, and it happened that Shiva was occupying the space in Building 391 in which Emmett proposed to mount Nova's second group of ten arms. He had not been able to win support for his plans within the DOE. But he had the support of Mel Greer, a key staff member of the House Appropriations Committee, and with this support, he hoped to have the clout to get all 20 arms. Emmett's critics have charged that when he tore down Shiva, he was really engaging in a political ploy to make room for the second group of Nova arms. In any case, Greer's help proved unavailing, although the ten-armed Nova was approved.

And what lies beyond Nova? To understand the scenario, consider the energies of high-power lasers. When they are built, their energy will be measured in megajoules, a megajoule being the energy of a half-pound of high explosive. A megajoule laser pulse will be a remarkable phenomenon. If it is delivered within a billionth of a second, and it can hardly be of longer duration, it will be about a foot long. If it is focused by lenses to an inch in diameter, it will amount to a stick of dynamite flying through space at the speed of light. Though it will be made entirely of photons, its length, width, size, shape and energy will be the same as that dynamite stick.

Nova will deliver 0.1 megajoule. By the standards of the future, it will be no more than of medium size. But even now Emmett's designers are drawing up plans for what may well be the king of the lasers. Appropriately this superlaser is to be named Zeus. Emmett hopes it will cost no more than Nova, but he expects it will reach the Olympian energy of five or even ten magajoules, making it brighter than 1,000 Shivas. If Zeus is built and fulfills its promise, it may stand as the most powerful laser that will ever be constructed. Future laser builders then might treat Zeus as a point of departure and work downward, seeking to reduce the laser energy needed for successful microexplosions using the pellet designs of the future.

And what will the country gain from Nova and Zeus? A trip to the offices where Emmett's scientists work demonstrates that much of the research is aimed toward a payoff in new military strength.

The two-story buildings, faced with tinted glass, are not open to visitors off the street. Even to approach the buildings, guests need a badge and official escort. At the end of a small entrance lobby is a closetlike room monitored by a TV camera on the other side of a small plastic window. A door in his booth leads to the inner sanctum of offices, their hallways decorated with temporary signs like CAUTION—UNCLEARED VISITOR UNDER ESCORT and UNCLEARED VISITOR—UNCLASSIFIED DISCUSSIONS ONLY.

The security precautions are evidence of Livermore's long-standing involvement with nuclear weapons. A laser microexplosion amounts to a nuclear fireball on a laboratory scale, a model useful to designers of future bombs.

"We are already doing weapons physics," says Hal Ahlstrom, one of Emmett's close associates. "We can study the behavior of materials within a nuclear explosion, creating the temperatures, the pressures, and densities that are appropriate to nuclear weapons. There are no other laboratory systems that can achieve the conditions we can.

"Then there are the nuclear-weapons effects. To really do significant experiments on weapons effects, we need a laser able to deliver a couple of megajoules to a pellet and have it give off a couple of hundred megajoules of thermonuclear yield." That would be the energy of 100 pounds of TNT. "We would get lots of neutrons and X rays from the explosion. That would be enough energy so that we could put a test chamber with a whole satellite or missile nose cone next to the reaction chamber. Expose the nose cone and determine its response, how its electronics or other components hold up. See how well it would stand up to reentering the atmosphere in the presence of a nuclear blast."

These laser experiments in particular would add a new dimension to our underground nuclear-weapons tests in Nevada. "People think we like to go out in the desert and shoot off bombs, but that isn't true," says

198

one nuclear-weapons expert who has spent many years doing just that. "A test can take a year or more from conception to completion, and they're usually oversubscribed with experiments. It's hot. You get sand in your relays, and things don't always go as planned. Believe me, it's no picnic. Nothing survives in the thermonuclear environment. You do an experiment once and it's done. If the results are not what was expected, it's difficult to repeat. But with laser fusion in the laboratory, you can repeat your experiments at will."

These big lasers could be especially useful to weapons designers if a treaty should ban all nuclear testing, the underground tests as well as the aboveground ones that have been banned since 1963. "We would maintain a cadre of trained thermonuclear designers," says Alexander Glass, president of KMS Fusion Inc., a major pellet-research lab. "You could train people in thermonuclear design, train them to understand thermonuclear physics. If there were no [underground] nuclear-test program, the nuclear-design laboratories—Los Alamos and Livermore—would have a hard time maintaining a cadre of competent designers, because they would have no data to work with." But if the huge lasers work as planned, "researchers could maintain their design capability by working on pellet designs."

The big Livermore lasers will be well suited to this weapons research but will not be suitable for the next development, the use of lasers to generate electric power. Livermore's lasers are built with neodymium glass, which becomes quite hot each time the laser fires. Afterward it takes several hours for its thick rods and disks of glass to cool down. That isn't a problem for weapons work; bomb researchers don't require more than two or three laser firings a day. But for use in a power plant, a laser must fire up to ten times a second, zapping pellets rapidly to produce a continuous flow of energy. Also, a power-plant laser must have higher efficiency than Livermore's lasers of glass.

These requirements can be met with other lasers whose amplifiers are chambers full of gas. Gas lasers also heat up when fired. But they can be cooled much more easily than glass, and they cannot shatter or crack when hot; so researchers can fire them many times a second. Further, such lasers offer higher efficiency than glass can provide.

The center for research on gas lasers is at Los Alamos, and when large lasers come to be taken seriously as electricity producers, Los Alamos will take on even more significance.

The largest of its lasers is called Antares. The star by that name is big and bright-red, radiating copiously in the infrared. The Antares laser also works in the infrared, with a wavelength ten times longer than that planned for Nova. This has put Los Alamos at a disadvantage, since it is the short wavelengths that work best with laser pellets. Still, gas lasers are potentially so important that the $62.5 million Antares has been pushed forward even more rapidly than Livermore's Nova. Antares has only 40 percent of Nova's power, or twice the power of Novette. But the Los Alamos entry went into full operation in October 1983, more than a year ahead of Nova. Until Nova is complete, Antares will hold the title of the world's most powerful laser.

An unusual feature of Antares is the windows through which its laser light passes. Since no type of glass is transparent enough to let light of such a long wavelength pass through, the windows in Antares are made of thick, circular slabs of pure salt, sodium chloride, highly polished. The salt is somewhat foggy to look at. But at infrared laser wavelengths it is perfectly transparent. One such window is on display near the Antares offices. It is kept under a plastic cover, with moisture-absorbing chemicals close by it. The window is more than a foot across and costs $25,000; if you breathed on it, its surface would begin to lose its polish—from the moisture in your breath.

The laser amplifiers are in a large room. Here, however, is none of the whiter-than-whiteness of Nova. This big Los Alamos laser room is colored in green, brown, and red, and suggests a high-tech boiler factory. The laser amplifiers themselves bear an uncanny resemblance to industrial boilers. In fact, the Los Alamos scientists refer to them as "locomotives." There are two amplifiers, heavy steel cylinders 55 feet long, each with a row of portholes along one side. Each weighs 165 tons and is built from flanged sections bolted together, just like a real boiler. But as one of the project leaders says, "Industrial boilers don't have to be optically stable." Thick steel walls ensure that the amplifiers will maintain their careful alignment with the other optical components. Each "locomotive" holds carbon dioxide and nitrogen gases at three atmospheres of pressure. The two of them together cost $6 million. By contrast, when the transcontinental railroad was completed in 1869, the iron horses on the scene cost about $15,000 apiece.

Antares has been a priceless source of experience in building large gas lasers. Yet the long wavelength of its carbon dioxide gas means that Antares itself will soon be a technological dead end. Carbon dioxide was chosen because researchers had had experience in using it for high-power lasers. But the large gas lasers of the future will have to achieve much shorter wavelengths, easily absorbed by fuel pellets. Unfortunately, producing such wavelengths isn't simply a matter of pumping out the carbon dioxide and pumping in some other gas. Everything must be designed anew. What may well be the prototype of this short-wavelength laser of the future already exists at Los Alamos.

It was first tested late in June 1983. Rather than being named for a god or a star, it is called—prosaically—the Krypton Fluoride Laser. The name refers to the mix of gases in the chamber of its laser amplifier. Krypton is an inert gas closely related to xenon, which is used in photographers' flash lamps and strobe lights. Fluorine, by contrast, is highly reactive. To fire the laser, powerful bursts of electrons flash through the chamber, depositing energy and momentarily producing molecules of the compound krypton fluoride. Then when a pulse from a master laser enters the chamber, it makes the molecules break apart and give up their energy, which in turn amplifies the original laser pulse.

The Krypton Fluoride Laser is rated at 20 kilojoules, half the power of Antares but more than that of Shiva and more than Novette can produce at its shortest wavelength. Yet it is much smaller in size. Rather than filling a hall the size of a very large ballroom, it could fit into a fair-size household basement. Its two electron-beam generators are each no larger than a walk-in closet. Their electrons pass down two long pipes each about four feet across and enter a laser chamber the size of a Volkswagen Beetle. Surrounding this chamber are two thick, orange bands—electromagnets that control the flight of the electrons. The laser then gives off a burst of ultraviolet light at a wavelength even shorter than the blue light available with Novette's frequency-multiplying crystals. This short wavelength permits the best possible performance in a laser pellet.

This Los Alamos system is a laser amplifier; it would need much additional optical equipment to qualify as a full-fledged laser. Still, it has a number of features that point the way to the future. It is inexpensive and simple. It was developed in the remarkably short time of 15 months, at a cost of only $3 million. It can be built in large sizes by combining many modules, all incorporating the basic Los Alamos design. It has one of the highest efficiencies yet achieved in a large laser and can be fired many times a second.

Building large lasers isn't quite like building aircraft for dusting crops; so it will be a while before we will really be sure that this Los Alamos design can be scaled up a hundredfold in size to the point of being useful for an electric-power plant. Nevertheless, laser builders are optimistic. They profess few doubts that if they are given enough money—say, $500 million— they can build a krypton fluoride laser big enough to power a small city.

Large krypton fluoride lasers may offer even more. They may well be the key to an entirely new type of rocket engine, with 1,000 times the performance of the engines in the space shuttle. Such rockets have been studied for a number of years by Roderick Hyde, an associate of Lowell Wood's at Livermore. Significantly, Wood's work in advanced lasers formed much of the basis for President Reagan's "star wars" speech. In fact, Wood originated many of the laser-rocket ideas that Hyde then developed further.

These rocket engines would set off fusion microexplosions within a rocket nozzle formed from magnetic fields. Powerful magnets would produce these fields, which would channel the fireballs from the microexplosions and force them to blast out the back, producing thrust. These fireballs would be far hotter than the exhaust from even the best of today's rocket fuels. Such a rocket could fly to Mars in as little as ten days, to Jupiter in a month. Laser spacecraft could power mankind's first missions to the stars.

Because of the close links between this research and continuing work on hydrogen bombs, the news that such long-haul ships can be built may remain classified long after scientists nail down details. But behind the lines of military security, some of today's designers of giant lasers are dreaming about interstellar vessels. At the same time, they're sketching ideas for highly efficient, safe laser-power plants. Long before any general calls the lightswords into battle, researchers are forging plans for the peaceful use of the most powerful beams on earth.

FLASHBLASTER

By Bill Lawren

"Charging!" shouts physicist John Asmus. He pushes a button on a console and waits a few seconds while the transformer builds up electrical energy to 4,000 volts. Dangling from an arm at the other end of what Asmus calls his Rube Goldberg contraption is a nine-inch xenon flash lamp capable of producing 1,000 times the candlepower of a car headlight. Directly underneath the lamp sits a stainless-steel roller that has been coated with a thin film of lipstick-pink Plexiglas. Now Asmus yells "Firing!" and pushes another button. There is a brilliant flash of light and an ear-piercing bang. This is the third "shot" at the steel roller, and as Asmus examines it, he finds that the Plexiglas film has been evaporated while the steel surface below has remained unmarred. In what seems like an act of magic, Asmus has blasted the Plexiglas molecules apart and vaporized them, simply by using light.

The machine that accomplishes this feat is called

the flashblaster. There are seven flashblasters in the world, all of them built by Asmus and all constructed from "whatever salvage and spare parts were available at the time." Indeed, the machine he is using at the moment in a San Diego Laboratory looks like the concoction of a basement inventor: The power source has its functions—ON, OFF, and FIRE—scratched crudely on its surface, and the cradle in which the flashblaster's target rests is a ramshackle wooden box. But despite its Flintstone appearance, the flashblaster is fast becoming one of the most versatile innovations in the arsenal of modern applied physics. Over the past several years, it has been used to strip rust from the sides of ships and to clean paint from metal surfaces. And it is now being tested for what may be its most vital application: the cleaning of toxic chemicals from contaminated surfaces.

Curiously, it was the world of art and art restoration that first put Asmus on the trail of the flashblaster. The superintendent of galleries in Venice, Italy, approached Asmus, a pioneer in laser applications, about using lasers to clean the grime and pollutants from the city's treasured statuary and buildings. Laser light easily cleaned the capitals on Venice's renowned Campanile in the Piazza San Marco, and it helped restore statues in the Como Cathedral and frescoes in Florence. But the time involved in restoring larger works of art proved to be overwhelming. "If you're cleaning an Andrea del Sarto painting, the laser's all right because you're accustomed to spending as much as a day to clean as little as a square inch," Asmus explains. "But when you extrapolate a square inch a day to cleaning the Winchester Cathedral or the

Parthenon—and these were serious suggestions that were made to me—you're starting to talk about a thousand years' worth of job security. Well, I didn't want to stand around pushing the same button for a thousand years, so I started looking for some way to make light work on a grander scale."

White laser light can be used as a cleaner because it is absorbed only by the nonwhite encrustations on an object, which then heat up and disintegrate. When the laser light hits the white material, say marble, underneath the black encrustation, it bounces off harmlessly because the white color will not absorb the white light. Asmus decided that a very bright white light might work as effectively as a pointed laser and would be able to clean larger areas at a time. He began testing a xenon flash lamp, which had been used as the source of raw light for the first ruby lasers in the Sixties. "All we were really doing," says Asmus, "was going back from the laser to something a bit more rudimentary. In that sense, the flashblaster represents both an evolution and a devolution."

As Asmus began to modify the flash lamp to make it more powerful and capable of operating at a wide range of wavelengths, practical applications for the flashblaster began to pop up like so many targets in an enormous shooting gallery. Asmus and his colleagues were soon swamped with requests from art restorers, manufacturers, and military contractors.

In addition, a number of steel mills are considering using flashblasters to clean oil film from their machinery without having to use toxic chemicals. The nuclear-power industry is intrigued by the potential of the flashblaster to clean radioactive corrosion without having to resort to sandblasting, a process that creates more waste in the form of radioactive sand. At California's McClellan Air Force Base, plans are being made to use a robot-drawn group of four flashblasters to strip paint from the wings of fighter planes. "We looked into using lasers," says Manuel Morante, of McClellan's physical-sciences lab, "but the flashblaster does the same job at only a fraction of the cost." (Asmus estimates that the flashblaster can be used for most cleaning applications at a cost of 25 to 35 cents a square foot, as opposed to anywhere from $2.50 to $100 a square foot for the laser.)

But the application that most intrigues Asmus is the cleaning of surfaces that have been contaminated by toxic chemicals. "I'd been reading every day about dioxins and PCBs and yellow rain and the Soviets' work with chemical warfare," Asmus says, "and it all frightened me. I'm *worried* about chemical warfare." During the Califonria medfly scare in the early Eighties, Asmus tried out his flashblaster on malathion, the insecticide that had been used to eradicate the pest. It worked. The malathion molecules were blasted to smithereens.

No one, especially Asmus, maintains that the flashblaster is the magic wand that's going to make all poison disappear. Obviously, one can't shine a light at a vatful of toxic chemicals and make them vanish. But fortunately, that task can often be handled by simple incineration. The job for the flashblaster will be, as it has always been, the cleaning of surfaces. In this case, the unit will be used to decontaminate the incinerators themselves, the ancillary machinery involved, and perhaps most important, the protective clothing worn by humans who handle the chemicals. The U.S. Army has already contracted Asmus to do preliminary testing on detoxification by flashblaster.

In his secluded San Diego laboratory, the physicist examines four scraps of metal that have been dotted with a virulent chemical and then exposed to varying numbers of flash blasts. The last piece, which was "shot" seven times with the xenon lamp, shows no trace of the toxic chemical. Asmus looks up from his work. "If you ask me why I'm an eclectic in an age of specialization," he says, "the answer is fear. I'm afraid of being channeled into something narrow. But if you ask me why I'm doing this particular work"— he looks down again at the inauspicious-looking metal scraps—"I guess I'd have to say that there's a part of me that does what I'm doing just because I'm a patriot."

MARTIAN LASER

By Jeff Hecht

There's a trillion-watt laser sitting in the sky, but don't panic. The USSR didn't put it there. Neither, for that matter, did the United States. Man-made lasers cannot yet produce more than a few million watts and only for a matter of seconds, and nobody on Earth has yet placed such a laser in orbit.

The laser is high in the Martian atmosphere, where nature produces conditions similar to those inside a man-made laser. It may have been operating continuously for millions of years, but it wasn't discovered until 20 years after Theodore H. Maiman built the first laser. Discovery of the Martian laser has earned recognition for NASA astronomer Michael J. Mumma; it's also earned him an invitation to testify in one of the most complex patent cases in history.

That's not the ordinary result of astronomical research, but then the Martian laser isn't exactly ordinary. For one thing, the light it produces isn't channeled into a beam like the light from a man-made laser. To extract energy in a beam from any laser, including the Martian atmosphere, you need a pair of mirrors, one on each side of the laser medium. To do that on Mars, Mumma suggests mounting huge mirrors on two satellites aligned so that part of the sunlit atmosphere always lies between them. He hasn't calculated how much power would be produced. The plan requires some formidable engineering, and Mumma admits it's "not likely in the foreseeable future."

Natural masers (the microwave analogs of lasers) are abundant in interstellar clouds, but Mumma says that the Martian emission is the first *laser* for which there is definite evidence. He also suspects that ammonia molecules near the poles of Jupiter may produce laser light, but that emission is sporadic, and he has been unable to explain convincingly the underlying physics. Other planetary atmospheres may also produce stimulated emission; even Earth's atmosphere may do so. However, the process requires low pressures, which occur only high in the atmosphere, and Mumma says that we would never see laser light from our own atmosphere because it would be absorbed by molecules closer to the surface.

Charles Townes, who shared the Nobel Prize in physics in 1964 for the theoretical work behind the laser, has speculated that earlier discovery of cosmic masers might have helped ground-based physicists develop the laser. It might seem that discovery of a natural laser would have been even more effective. In reality, however, the scientists who found the Martian laser relied on the fact that it emits only a very narrow range of wavelengths. To detect it, in turn, requires a light source that emits a narrow range of wavelengths—a man-made carbon dioxide laser. In short, it takes a laser to find a laser.

The Martian laser turns out to be surprisingly efficient. About 0.003 percent of the sun's energy that reaches Mars is re-emitted as laser light, not bad for a fluke of nature. That's encouraging news for another NASA group trying to develop solar-powered lasers for spacecraft propulsion and power transmission. J. H. Lee, of Vanderbilt University, and W. R. Weaver, of NASA's Langley Research Center, now hope to better the 0.1 percent efficiency of their first solar-pumped laser.

Discovery of the Martian laser was also good news for people fighting a patent on light-powered lasers issued in 1977 to Gordon Gould. A natural phenomenon is generally considered unpatentable. Thus, the Control Laser Corporation, of Orlando, Florida, accused of infringing Gould's patent, has asked Mumma to testify when its case goes to trial. Meanwhile Gould's lawyers contend that the "natural phenomenon" criterion applies only to chemicals known and used in the United States before the patent application.

Like everything else in this tangled affair, the issue is complex. Gould's original patent application was filed in 1959, but it ran into a lengthy series of legal obstacles involving patents filed by Townes and others. It was not until 1973 that the Martian laser was detected on Earth—by Townes, of all people—and it was 1980 when Mumma's group identified the emission as being laser light. By then the patent had been granted.

PART SIX:
THE VIEW
FROM AFAR

*"We are all in the gutter,
but some of us
are looking at the stars."*
—Oscar Wilde

FLY'S-EYE RADAR

By Owen Davies

A new radar-imaging system promises to let air-traffic controllers three years from now see—from as much as 20 miles away—whether an incoming plane has lowered its landing gear. Military surveillance aircraft may use the technique to tell friend from foe at far greater distances than is now possible, and spy satellites could gain remarkably improved vision.

Air-traffic-control systems will be the easiest to develop, says electrical engineer Bernard Steinberg, the University of Pennsylvania professor who devised the imaging method. "Modern airports are three to five kilometers across," he explains, "and much of that space is wasted. If we could put perhaps a thousand antennas into those wasted areas, we could get clear images of the airplanes, not just fuzzy blobs."

The key to Steinberg's technique is to make all those small, separate antennas work like a single, much larger one, just as the new "fly's eye" telescope use multiple mirrors to form a single image. The clarity of radar, he says, varies with the size of the antenna in the same way a telescope image depends on the size of the lens or mirror.

The diameter of a two-inch telescope mirror is 100,000 times the length of a single wave of light. To achieve the same resolution as the little telescope, a conventional radar unit—focusing radio waves roughly a million times as long as light waves—would need an antenna some 20 miles across.

In practice, even if room could be found for such an antenna, its parts would flex so much that it could never be focused. "The position of each point of the antenna must be known to within one tenth of a radio wavelength—as little as half an inch," Steinberg notes.

To get around this, he uses a minicomputer to build a single image from many small antennas, much as radio astronomers create star maps from signals received at many distant observatories. Each antenna has a microchip to calculate its own position.

To keep costs down in his first shoestring experiment in 1982, the inventor used a single antenna, shifting it around periodically and combining the "photographs" later. Yet the results were far better than normal radar could have given, Steinberg reports. In scans of a small town about five miles from the antenna, buildings, streets, and even a truck could be seen. He says greater detail should soon be available.

For military use, the system's promise is clear. America's Airborne Warning and Communications System (AWACS) and Hawkeye surveillance planes are designed to keep track of all aircraft in a battle zone, coordinating friendly forces and warning of approaching enemy craft. Steinberg believes radar-imaging planes could do a far better job. "The AWACS and the Navy's Hawkeye are exquisite designs, but they date back to the Nineteen Fifties," he comments. "This could be the next generation."

Many small antennas, each the size of a dollar bill, would be built into the airplane's skin. Images would be processed in the plane itself by a large, fast minicomputer specially designed for the complex mathematics required.

How soon these predictions will come true depends not on technology, he adds, but on money. "An airport installation would cost about five million dollars for the electronics and considerably more than that for ancillary equipment," he notes. "We are ready to design it today. I don't know what a next-generation AWACS system would cost. Most of it would go to designing an airplane with the antennas built into the skin. That is probably ten years off."

Ironically, the more difficult and costly application seems likely to come first. Steinberg reports that well-heeled Pentagon officials are beginning to take notice of his work, but money for air-traffic safety seems hard to come by.

IRAS EYES

By Thomas O'Toole

NASA Administrator James M. Beggs and Deputy Administrator Hans Mark saved the worst news for last during a two-hour press conference in 1984. Work on the Shuttle Infrared Telescope Facility (SIRTF), which was supposed to have been carried into space by the shuttle in 1986, would not begin as promised this year. In fact, Mark told the press, SIRTF (pronounced *certif*) might not make it into orbit until 1993, when it would be a "very, very strong candidate" to be put aboard one of the space-station platforms. Explained Mark: "That's what we're looking at now. It [SIRTF] is being delayed because the results of the Infrared Astronomical Satellite [IRAS] were so spectacular that they clearly demonstrated the value of having a free-flyer rather than a shuttle-attached payload, which would have a limited lifetime in orbit."

Most astronomers were wildly disappointed. They agree with Mark that the Infrared Astronomical Satellite had been a spectacular success. And, yes, it would be better to make SIRTF a free-flyer, orbiting through space on its own rather than letting it hang out of the shuttle's cargo bay, where its optics could be fogged over by rocket exhaust or the venting of the shuttle's toilet. "The trouble with infrared telescopes is that they don't do well where there are people," says Charles Beichman, of California's Jet Propulsion Laboratory, where the Infrared Astronomical Satellite was hatched and directed. "People bring too much contamination into the picture."

That might help to explain why IRAS, all alone in a polar orbit 900 kilometers high, was such a dramatic success. Its polar orbit took it around the entire Earth 14 times a day, which means that its telescope observed an incredible 98 percent of the sky. It was launched by a Delta rocket on January 26, 1983, from California's Vandenberg Air Force Base, and for all but eight nights, it made spectacular observations of the heavens. On November 22, however, it stopped observing; it had run out of the supercold helium that allowed its beryllium mirrors and silicon detectors to find and photograph celestial objects. The helium, chilling sensors at the focal plane to −455° F, made it possible for IRAS to distinguish between an infrared stellar source and the telescope's own heat.

Six of the nights the IRAS observatory missed in space were the six nights scientists waited to jettison the cover that kept the telescope free of contamination. Even so, a single speck of dust was still blotting the lens when the cover came off, a mishap that cost astronomers two more viewing nights.

How good was IRAS's performance? Cornell University's Carl Sagan calls it the greatest single achievement in astronomical history. The satellite and its discoveries made the cover of *Nature* magazine three times, an unheard-of event in the history of the prestigious British journal.

If nothing else, IRAS proved once and for all the worth of space-based astronomy. Above the atmosphere, away from city lights, and unhampered by rain, sleet, ice, snow, and fog, the infrared observatory in space never stopped seeing things until its helium ran out. "We lose a lot of observing time down here on Earth because of weather and even moonlight," says Gerry (pronounced *Gary*) Neugebauer, IRAS project scientist who also serves the California Institute of Technology as director of the Mount Palomar Observatory, near San Diego. "Looking through IRAS was like having a year-long observing night."

What did IRAS accomplish? In its tireless, 10-month circling of Earth, the 2,249-pound satellite picked up the infrared emissions of more than 290,000 celestial sources, many of them never seen before. It revealed sources hidden by interstellar dust and found galaxies so young and so old that they were too cold to emit the kind of starlight that could have been detected by earthbound telescopes. Nearer to Earth, the infrared telescope identified at least five new comets and found a 1.2-mile-wide "miniplanet" inside the orbit of the planet Mercury. Scientists now believe the tiny object is the burned-out relic of an ancient comet that came too close to the sun. "To me, this was one of the biggest single surprises we had through the entire mission," Neugebauer says.

"It lends a lot of support to the idea that many of

the asteroids we see are the remnants of ancient comets."

Among the brightest payoffs was the satellite's discovery of three bands of fine dust spread over 100 million miles in the asteroid belt between Mars and Jupiter. These bands are almost surely the debris from either a collision between two very small asteroids or from the breakup of a larger single asteroid. The satellite's asteroid count alone made news. IRAS cataloged something like 20,000 asteroids swirling across the solar system, four times as many as had been counted from Earth.

But the biggest surprise was what is now called the Vega phenomenon. IRAS discovered a young solar system forming around Vega, a star just 26 light-years from Earth. There is no longer any doubt of this solar system's existence. "We expected to find rings of debris around dying stars, and we did, like the shell of gas we saw around the star Betelgeuse," Neugebauer says. "But we didn't expect to find anything that looked at all like Vega. The Vega phenomenon is interesting because there's such an excess of large particles around the star that it can only be a solar system in the stage of formation."

Vega is about twice the size of our sun. Further analysis of IRAS data revealed a second star, Fomalhaut, orbited by solid material. Fomalhaut, 22 light-years from Earth, is about one fifth as bright as Vega.

IRAS has brought astronomers across a threshold of discovery. Scientists look to SIRTF to carry them farther into alien realms. SIRTF is designed to be almost twice the size of IRAS. It will have an array of detectors at its focal plane that will make it 1,000 times more sensitive to infrared light than IRAS was. Not only will SIRTF be able to reach much deeper into space than IRAS did, it will be able to spot smaller and fainter objects close to Earth. "I like to compare SIRTF's sensitivity with that of the Space Telescope, which will look at the heavens in the visible light region of the spectrum," NASA's Nancy Boggess says. "But the Space Telescope will not have the sensitivity of SIRTF. In fact, if there were a good-size planet around Vega, the Space Telescope would not see it."

The risks to SIRTF are that its technology will be held back by budget delays and that the astronomers who worked most closely with IRAS will move on to other things and even grow old while SIRTF sits on some shelf in Washington. "We've got a lot of momentum going for us right now," says Beichman. "We're on a roll." Trouble is, if NASA and the Office of Management and Budget prevail, the roll stops here.

REMOTE-CONTROL EYES

By Allan Hendry

Happy is the astronomer who collects his own data. For five consecutive nights Dr. Robert Kirshner, of the University of Michigan, had reason to be happy. He took control of the 2.1-meter (84-inch) telescope at Kitt Peak National Observatory, near Tucson, Arizona. He aimed the huge instrument at some distant galaxies, adjusted the spectrographic equipment, and acquired spectral scans for each of his targets.

All this is perfectly routine at this prominent research facility, of course. As many as 800 professional astronomers visit there each year to use Kitt's 13 telescopes. What made this occasion novel was that Dr. Kirshner was sitting more than 1,600 miles away in his Ann Arbor, Michigan, office! With an off-the-shell Tektronix computer terminal linked to

Kitt Peak by telephone, Kirshner was engaged in the most sophisticated remote-control astronomy to date.

Until now an astronomer unable to visit a distant observatory had to send his instructions to the telescope operator. The resulting data were mailed or phoned to him afterward. With this new system, an astronomer can actually see on a TV screen what the telescope sees while the computer displays the target's spectrum.

Kitt Peak telescope operator Hal Halbedel was on hand in Arizona to make sure the telescope didn't swing blindly into something or suffer other damage. Apart from that, the Michigan-based astronomer was free to do the kind of high-level research that traditionally requires a round-trip ticket and a five-day stay at Kitt Peak's mountaintop dormitory. Working from midnight until 7 A.M., Kirshner obtained from six to ten spectral scans a night, as many as if he had been there.

For the astronomer, the personal advantages are obvious. He is spared the time and cost of traveling several times a year ("It's a real strain," Kirshner notes), and he can teach his classes without interruption. Yet in the long run the real advantage is the money Kitt Peak can save without sacrificing any research. Scientists from all over the world bid for time on the facilities months in advance. Kitt Peak's administrators are being forced to consider a new, million-dollar water system, more dormitories, and a cafeteria expansion. The observatory gets its funding to house and feed all these people from the

National Science Foundation, and severe Reaganomics cutbacks have already forced it to reduce its staff. Practical remote-control astronomy would get people off the mountain and save those costs.

There are still some problems to be solved. Telephone lines carry only one TV picture every 31 seconds, making it difficult to fine-adjust the telescope. And trouble on the line cut into Kirshner's work on one of the five nights. The obvious solution is to use a satellite microwave link, which can transmit a rapidly changing picture. The monthly rent for part of a domestic satellite channel—$2,000—will be saved if only a few astronomers can avoid a visit to the observatory.

Yet remote-control work is clearly in its early stages. Kitt Peak astronomer Paul Schechter says it will be some time before the program pays back the cost of outfitting new instruments and telescopes for remote work. "People in many places are interested in seeing how our experiment works," Schechter says, but with international satellite costs ten times higher than domestic ones, the first work will likely be done in the United States. Kirshner used the terminal again on two other occasions. Eventually Kitt Peak's four-meter telescope will be outfitted with a remotely controlled video camera and a high-resolution Fourier transform spectrometer. Schechter is confident that remote observing will be commonplace by the turn of the century.

On-campus observatories are convenient, but urban air pollution and "light pollution" are making them useless for serious research. Even Kitt Peak is being affected by air and light pollution. By 1986 the most desirable telescope in existence will also be the most distant, placed into orbit by the space shuttle. Remote-control telescopes may destroy some of astronomy's romance, but the future of deep-space research may depend on them.

PART SEVEN:
FUELING THE FUTURE

"Pollution is nothing but resources we're not harvesting."
—*R. Buckminster Fuller*

VIEWPOINT: USING NUCLEAR POWER

By Hans A. Bethe

Two simple facts could end our energy problems: Nuclear power can be produced at least as safely as any other form of energy, and the waste created by nuclear operation can be disposed of without endangering future generations.

Interestingly enough, the United States is the only highly developed nation that has not approved plans to increase greatly its use of nuclear power. Even if nuclear power were abandoned in the United States, other countries would continue to rely on nuclear power. France, the USSR, Japan, and Argentina, for example, are increasing their nuclear-generating capacity substantially. The United States is obviously falling behind in the development of this vital source of energy. This will not make the United States a safer place to live. It means the United States is going to have less energy, fewer job opportunities, and greater economic hardships than those nations now avidly developing nuclear power.

The Age of Oil is nearing its end. The U. S. Department of Energy projects that the price of oil will rise to $100 a barrel in this decade, and some experts predict an even higher figure. But even more important than the high cost of petroleum are the instability characteristic of the major oil-producing countries in the Middle East and those nations' limited oil resources. While for the moment there is a surplus of oil in the world, it will not slow the soaring cost nor avert the inevitable depletion of the world's oil fields.

We might be able to reduce our requirements of imported oil within ten years through a combination of conservation, the manufacture of synthetic fuels, and particularly the substitution of other kinds of energy for oil.

In many cases the substitute for oil will be electricity. There are three ways to produce electricity efficiently: from waterpower, from coal, and from nuclear fission. (I do not include solar power, because it is prohibitively expensive by present technology, nor do I include fusion, which will not be a practical source of energy in this century.)

Of the three power sources, hydroelectricity has been almost fully exploited in the United States and most other industrial nations. Coal is an abundant resource in the United States and in the Soviet Union, but not in other industrialized countries. As far as we are concerned, therefore, electricity will have to come from coal and from nuclear power. The principal worry about nuclear power since the Three Mile Island accident in March 1979 has been the safety of nuclear-power plants. This fear does not seem justified. The presidential commission that investigated the accident, under the chairmanship of Dr. John Kemeny, was in general very critical of the incident's handling. But the commission's report stated, "We conclude that in spite of serious damage to the plant most of the radiation was contained, and the actual release [of the contaminated water and air] will have a negligible effect on the health of individuals."

A significant release of radiation was avoided because the plant's safety mechanisms worked. This incident proved the reliability of multiple barriers against the release of radioactivity: If one barrier fails, the next barrier will take over its job. This principle makes nuclear-power plants very sturdy structures of the sort that can continue to serve the public safety even in the face of repeated errors by the operators. A meltdown didn't occur at Three Mile Island.

Contrary to widespread misconceptions (such as were fostered by the movie *The China Syndrome*), even a meltdown of the fuel in a nuclear reactor would not present a serious danger to the public. The surrounding population would be threatened only if a meltdown were followed by a breach in the big dome that encloses the reactor, the containment building. This is extremely unlikely.

Reactor safety has been further improved since the Three Mile Island accident. The Nuclear Regulatory Commission has tightened its procedures, but the greatest changes have been made by the power industry itself. Of these, the most important is the creation of the Institute for Nuclear Power Operations, to supervise the training programs for nuclear-reactor operators and to inspect directly the operations of the power companies.

People also worry about the disposal of nuclear waste. There is no reason to doubt that waste disposal can be accomplished safely, so that future generations will not suffer damage from the nuclear waste we now generate.

Ultimately nuclear safety is a matter of people, the operators and engineers who operate the machine safely. Not enough young persons enter nuclear engineering and operation. There is a grave peril that antinuclear proponents may have brought about a self-fulfilling prophecy: By claiming that nuclear reactors are unsafe, they may have made a career in nuclear power so unattractive to young people that in the future reactors may really become unsafe.

The energy crisis is real. It has not been fabricated by oil companies or by public-relations experts. The problem of energy is solvable, but not by any single solution. Rather, it will be solved by a combination of partial solutions working together. Nuclear power must be a part of that answer. It is both safe and economically feasible. If civilization is to progress, we must draw upon our ingenuity and harden our resolve to develop all our energy options, including nuclear energy.

NECKLACE IN THE SKY

By G. Harry Stine

Within 25 years we could receive most—and possibly all—of our electricity from a necklace of manmade stars in the sky.

Solar-power satellites (SPS) promise to meet the electrical needs of the next century. Yet a few voices are already urging us to ignore this potentially enormous resource.

One problem is money. To harvest this power requires a huge investment. And considerable manpower. We must build two five-gigawatt SPS units per year, starting in 1990.

Challenging as this is, it can surely be accomplished. And it can be done safely. The Department of Energy has studied the SPS carefully and worked hard to forecast its environmental and social effects. (Contrast this objective study with the biased reporting that currently plagues nuclear power.)

So far these evaluations have been generally favorable. It seems the SPS could solve our energy problems without creating health hazards or social ills. You can find out for yourself: Send for the references cited at the end of this piece.

But first let's look at a few of the most common fears that could delay SPS development.

An SPS might send back its power in the form of a beam of microwaves. For many people, microwaves mean ovens: Anyone blundering into the beam would be cooked in seconds, wouldn't he?

Well, no. The total energy is enormous, but spread over almost 100 square kilometers. At its center, the planned power density is only 23 milliwatts per square centimeter. This is less than one fourth the continuous exposure allowed by federal job-safety regulations.

Then, again, we might use lasers to send SPS power to Earth. And surely lasers are dangerous? After all, we've all seen pictures of lasers slicing through several inches of steel.

Again, it's a question of power density. An SPS laser beam need not be any more powerful than the microwave beam. About a fourth as strong as the desert sun. We would not even see its infrared light.

When it comes to the SPS—or, for that matter, almost any other technical subject—some people simply have not done their homework. Given the price of hand calculators—even specialized scientific models now cost less than $30—this is shocking. The arithmetic needed is simple. Anyone running scared of technology does so out of ignorance and laziness.

Someone once wrote a letter to *Omni Magazine* warning that the SPS would cause terrible environmental damage on Earth because the power satellites would block out the sun. If you can picture the

235

vastness of space, this is obviously ridiculous. But let's look at the numbers, just to show how easily we can answer this kind of question. The basic facts are available in most astronomy books. Our letter writer has no excuse.

The DOE/NASA Baseline SPS Design would use an array of solar batteries ten kilometers long and five wide—an area of 50 square kilometers. (The figure has appeared in most major newspapers and many magazines.)

Geosynchronous orbit (GSO), in which a satellite orbits the earth in exactly 24 hours—thus staying above one spot on the ground—is 35,890 kilometers up. The circumference of the GSO is the amount of room available for an SPS system.

So add 35,890 plus half the diameter of the earth (look it up) to get the GSO's radius. Multiply by 2 for the diameter, and then by π, 3.14159 (the first six digits is plenty), to get the answer. It amounts to 265,515 kilometers.

Let's ring the plant with SPS units. It would take centuries, but think big. We'll allow 15 kilometers for each, leaving them five kilometers apart. Divide the total space available by 15, and it turns out there's room for 17,700 SPS units in GSO. The total area of the SPS system, assuming each unit takes up 50 square kilometers, is 885,000 square kilometers.

However, not all of these SPS units will be between Earth and the sun at one time—only those in a 12,827-kilometer segment of GSO, amounting roughly to the diameter of the earth. Draw a sketch of the planet and see for yourself.

This means that only 855 SPS units will be between

Earth and the sun at any instant. Their area would be 42,750 square kilometers, and that is how much of the planet would be shaded. The total sunlit area of Earth's disk is 129,223,075 square kilometers. The shaded area amounts to 0.0331 percent of that.

The heat energy falling on Earth's sunlit hemisphere is 2.46288×10^{18} calories per minute (246288 and 13 zeroes; if you didn't understand, look up scientific notation in a high-school physics book). The heat energy falling on the solar collectors is 7.68×10^7 calories per minute, or a mere 0.00000000003118 percent.

Earth is a big piece of real estate. Yet most of us think only of the part we see, and most people on Earth have never been more than 25 kilometers from their birthplace. And then there were those beautiful, misleading photos taken by the Apollo astronauts. Earth looks so tiny in them, a fragile blue-and-white marble suspended against the blackness of space. It seems we could hold the planet in our hands.

Unfortunately, many people mistake this illusion for reality when they consider the SPS system, or any other piece of large-scale technology. Ask any pilot how big our planet really is. Or anyone who has had to walk for more than a few days to get from one place to another.

Space is larger by far. It is incredibly vast. Nothing we can build in space in the next century will have any effect on it, not even on Earth itself. The numbers don't lie.

During a NASA study of space industrialization in the early 1980s, a man from one of the nation's largest electrical utilities rose to speak. He remarked that the

SPS is the cleanest, most acceptable source of future energy available. It produces no radioactive waste, it doesn't pollute the air as coal-fired generators do, and it would cost no more than nuclear fuel or coal per kilowatt-hour. Quoting one of the rare rational statements released by the Department of Energy, "Regardless of how the [SPS] system is defined, the net energy ratio is positive." (For those not used to bureaucratese, this means that any SPS system would produce more energy than it would cost.)

The information is available to settle any questions about the safety and practicality of the SPS system. Anyone interested enough can seek it out. It's time for the critics to stop worrying and start learning.

The place to begin is "Satellite Power Systems (SPS) Concept Development and Evaluation Program, Preliminary Assessment," DOE/ER-0041, September 1979. It costs $4 and can be ordered from the National Technical Information Service, 5285 Port Royal Road, Springfield, Virginia 22161. Then read "Some Questions and Answers About the Satellite Power System (SPS)," also from NTIS. The price is $4.50.

POWER ORBITER

By G. Harry Stine

We can totally eliminate the energy crunch if we get busy in the 1980s and work the engineering bugs out of Dr. Peter Glaser's Solar Power Satellite (SPS).

The concept calls for large solar collectors located 36,290 kilometers above the earth's equator, in geosynchronous orbit. Using photovoltaic or thermal converters, the SPS could generate up to ten gigawatts (10 billion watts) of electricity from the constant sunlight of space. It then converts this solar-generated electricity into a microwave beam, which transmits the energy to a large rectifying antenna—a "rectenna"—on Earth. Alternatively, a laser beam might be used.

An SPS would be big—nearly 13 kilometers long by 5 kilometers wide. The rectenna on the ground would cover 16 by 24 kilometers. Its function is to convert space power to the local frequency and voltage, then switch it onto the existing electric-power grid.

There seems to be no technical, economic, health, or environmental reason why an SPS system can't be our cleanest and safest source of electrical power. "The solar-power satellite is probably the most environmentally acceptable power-generating concept we've studied," said a long-range planner for one of the large utility companies.

The power-transmission beam—whichever type is finally chosen—will have such low energy density that it wouldn't even heat water, much less cook a bird that happened to fly through it. We are not talking about the microwave energy density of a household oven or the sort of science-fiction laser cannons of *Star Wars*. Microwaves will transmit the required energy without harming the earth's atmosphere or causing environmental damage. This has been checked out in tests at the Jet Propulsion Laboratory, in Pasadena, California, and with the big radio telescope dish at Arecibo, Puerto Rico.

The SPS concept is more than some far-out dream. The requisite technology either is on hand or can be achieved with a little more refinement. The Department of Energy has completed a series of preliminary studies on the SPS system and is now funding in-depth examinations of specific engineering requirements. You can get copies of the completed studies by writing to the U. S. Department of Energy, Office of Energy Research, Satellite Power System Project Office, Washington, DC 20585.

What remains is to check out critical items in space, using the shuttle to help solve such engineering problems as how to build large structures in space and keep them pointed at the sun without twisting them out of shape. After all, even in zero gravity one moves a structure 100 meters thick and 65 square kilometers on a side gently and slowly, lest it crumple like a sheet of paper.

Expensive? Yes, but so is an equivalent coal-burning power plant on Earth. Preliminary estimates by several groups indicate that an SPS can be built for about the same cost as a coal-fired plant—about $2,000 per kilowatt. The cost of electric power from an SPS system delivered to a home has been estimated from 7 mils per kilowatt-hour to 27 mils per kilowatt-hour—in other words, comparable to, or slightly less than, today's electric rates. If it costs the same, or even nearly the same, to do it in space as on the ground, it should be done in space because this generates a considerable spinoff: the SPS Connection.

First, an SPS system uses a renewable energy source: the sun. A coal plant built on Earth at the same cost within 25 years may face slowdowns because of coal allocations. And the coal plant will pour tons of radioactive carbon-14 into the atmosphere, releasing far more radiation than has ever leaked from any nuclear reactor.

It's true that at current rates of consumption we have enough coal in the United States alone to last 2 million years, but this ignores world needs. As coal exporters, we could look forward to seeing the last of this resource by the year 2250. Humankind requires a more permanent energy supply. And coal and other fossil fuels are far more precious as chemical feed-stocks that can be recycled than as fuels that cannot. Once they've gone up the stack as combustion products, we've lost them forever.

241

To make the SPS system work, we must build at least two generating stations in space every year so that we can begin to shift to the SPS system as our demand for electric power increases between 1990 and 2010. In 1975 the total electric-power capacity in this country was 228 gigawatts; by the year 2000, the demand will rise to 940 gigawatts. But by the year 2000, if we get the SPS program in gear, there could be at least 26 satellites carrying more than one fourth of the load. By the year 2020, there would be more than 100 SPS units on line, and they would then be carrying the bulk of our electrical base load.

Building an SPS system will require space transportation capable of carrying people and cargo into space at reasonable prices—$22 per kilogram or less. This would allow us to do other things in space: take on lots of space research, improve communications facilities, and start relocating heavily polluting industries off this planet and into space because the energy is there, the raw materials are there, and there is no biosphere to pollute with industrial waste.

When we relocate industry into space, an interesting consequence results. About 60 percent of the electric-energy output in the United States is consumed by industrial users; the other 40 percent is consumed by homes, stores, street lighting, office buildings, and so on. Therefore, as we move industry into space, the electrical demand on Earth decreases.

Not only does this mean that we can stop building nukes and fossil-fuel steam plants, but by the year 2020 or before (if we build SPS units faster), we can begin to dismantle the nukes and then the fossil-fuel plants. With industry taken off the planet, there would be electricity for all from the SPS system.

The extensive space-transportation system required to build the first 20 to 25 SPS units provides an additional spinoff: The cost of an SPS unit drops by almost an order of magnitude because its construction material can be obtained from extraterrestrial sources. The first SPS units must be built from materials hauled up from Earth's gravitational pull, and the energy needed to transport the materials costs money. With a space-transportation system paid for in the cost of those first 25 SPS units, however, it becomes possible to get materials from the moon and the Asteroid Belt between Mars and Jupiter—and at far less cost—because far less energy is expended to move materials around the shallow gravity fields of the moon and the asteroids.

Right now the United States, Western Europe, and Japan are energy importers whose industrial systems are based upon petroleum fuels. We face an energy crunch because we made the mistake of letting one end of a trade route get out of our control—in this case, the petroleum sources.

The solution is 36,290 kilometers above our heads. Furthermore, the output of an SPS is marketable. Whoever builds the SPS system will not only solve his energy crunch but become an energy exporter. While high technology is necessary to design, build, and operate the power satellite, the ground rectenna is a low-tech item. It can be fabricated and assembled by local labor, because a rectenna is easier to construct than an office building is.

This is certainly an acceptable space program and potentially a very profitable one. The risks are high, but the up-front capital requirements are no greater than an earthbound alternative. Whoever builds the SPS system will end the energy crisis and in the process cause many of today's problems simply to go away.

MOTHER SUN

By Edward Regis, Jr.

It's A.D. 2600, and the solar system has been gobbled up, plundered. The planets from Mercury to Jupiter, their satellites, even the rings of Saturn have been cannibalized. Humanity has spread itself out across the solar system as if on a vast spider's web, and there are far more people living off Earth than on it. Space settlement is old hat, with people on the moon, on what's left of the planets and their remaining satellites, and in the s'homes—space homes—that have proliferated like splitting bacteria. Sol's entire planetary system has been colonized, and it now harbors a population greater than many Earths could have sustained.

But there's a catch. Although there are hundreds of billions of people spread out from one end of the solar system to the other, planetary materials are nearing exhaustion. A solar system-wide materials crisis looms, something that will make the earthside "energy-crunch" of the 1970s seem like just a ripple.

There's no anxiety, however, no sense of urgency. For the people of 2600 have a plan, a plan that goes way back to 1983 and to a forward-looking space scientist by the name of Dave Criswell.

The plan is to dismantle the sun.

David R. Criswell walks the earth today just like the rest of us. But for most of us, that's where the similarity ends, for Criswell spends a lot of time thinking on immense spatiotemporal scales. He has patent applications pending for lunar power stations; he has an idea for capturing the solar wind. He's president of his own space-applications company, Cis-Lunar, Inc., and when not there he divides his working time between the California Space Institute, at the University of California, San Diego, and the Los Alamos National Laboratory's Institute of Geophysics and Planetary Physics, in New Mexico.

Wtih dark hair and beard and a memorable Texas twang, he looks as if he could make a living riding Brahma bulls or driving steer across the desert. But he doesn't do any of that. He's usually found on the telephone saying things like, "Well, hell, that's just standard plasma physics," or typing into his DEC word processor, or staring out across the Pacific from his office. There, or at his home on the Camino del Sol, in La Jolla, he hatches his ideas for taking the sun apart.

It sounds incredible, outrageous. Even he believes it calls for some explanation. "I think just looking across the ocean stimulates such thoughts," he says. But suspend your disbelief for a moment. Be willing to think long-term and to think big. Criswell's ideas about how to tap into solar power are not for those with weak nerves.

We begin with the notion that in the relatively near future, man's endless search for energy and living space will take him off the earth, first to the space between earth and the moon, then to the moon itself, and finally to the asteroids, the planets, and beyond. We've already begun a small mass movement off the planet. "I spend more time above thirty thousand feet in a jet," says Criswell, "than I do walking about land that is untouched by farming, industry, or residential development. I think this is true for most people."

We've utilized a lot of the earth already. For the last 400 years, from the beginnings of industrialization in Great Britain to the present, human manipulation and use of raw materials—sand and gravel, coal and oil—has increased by an average 6 percent a year. This means that every 12 years the volume of industrial "mass handling" doubles on Earth.

Criswell foresees an even greater rate of increase, maybe 20 percent per year for the next 400 years. Such explosive growth will be a product of space utilization—of our going into space to get our raw materials and to make our homes.

At these rates of expansion, we'll be using planetary resources at a steady clip. Criswell projects that at the 20 percent growth rate, we will have consumed the asteroids by 2140: They will have been made into spacecraft, space stations, s'homes (a word Criswell coined), and macromachines. "At this point," he says, "continued growth will require the disassembly of the moons and the planets. Jupiter processing could start at 2200 and be complete approximately four hundred years later."

So imagine we're to the year 2600 and Jupiter is only a memory. In its place float millions of space habitats supporting billions of people. The remaining planets are of negligible value, and the only source of new raw material is comet influx, approaching Earth at the rate of about 100 billion tons of new working matter per year. While to us this may sound like a lot, to Criswell it's "rather depressing. It's a level comparable with the present world production of primary materials." For a fully industrialized solar system, that's peanuts.

Must human expansion stop in the twenty-seventh century? Will this be the end of growth for good?

Criswell is no pessimist. The richest mine of all is still untapped. Compared with even the largest planet, the sun's resources are immense: 99.86 percent of all the matter in the solar system is in the sun. Against it, planets are tiny fragments, "trivial particles," in Criswell's words, and our processing of them would be mere practice runs for the feat of star lifting.

Star lifting, taking the sun apart bit by bit, doesn't mean extinguishing it. Paradoxically, to remove matter from the sun will be to prolong its life. "It's a well-known fact in astrophysics," Criswell explains, "that the larger a star is, the faster it burns up its supplies of hydrogen, helium, and other fissionable elements."

While our sun's life span sounds plenty long—12 billion years—smaller stars, the white dwarfs, will last 2,000 times longer. "If Sol could be gently unwrapped of its outer layers and converted into white-dwarf form, then the new dwarf would live much longer," Criswell says.

Thinking billions of years ahead is more than many of us can handle. So let's lower our sights and think along with Criswell a modest few millions of years or so into our future to see what his plan would bring.

On such "short" time scales, we'd reap an immediate benefit from skinning the sun: We'd be making truly efficient use of solar energy for the first time. All energy on Earth is—ultimately—converted sunlight. Our stocks of coal, oil, and wood are just remnants of the solar energy that's been falling to Earth for 4 billion years.

"As a race we live in an era of enormous waste of solar energy," says Criswell. "Not only are we failing to use the eighty-one million gigawatts [a gigawatt is a billion watts] per person of power the sun is presently sending irretrievably to cold deep space, but we're also vigorously wasting the inefficiently obtained power that has fallen on Earth over geologic time to produce our fossil fuels and to power our inefficient biosphere."

For Criswell the way to get energy is not to extract it from secondary sources like coal and oil and not to collect sunlight from a distance with solar cells.

The way to do it is to go right to the source, directly to the sun, taking what matter and energy we need and leaving behind a longer-burning star as a reward for our efforts. This is star cultivation, or, as Criswell puts it, "stellar husbandry."

So how do you take a star apart? Easy enough if you have lots of particle accelerators. What we want from the sun is its plasma—the atoms of hydrogen, helium, and heavier elements that make up the atmosphere of our star. These gases are capable of being moved around by magnetic fields, and it will be the job of particle accelerators to create the fields.

Today's accelerators on Earth are minuscule compared with those we'd use for stellar husbandry. America's largest, FermiLab, in Batavia, Illinois, is only six kilometers in circumference. Criswell's mass extractors would be "very large tubes, each perhaps one hundred kilometers in diameter and length," each a portion of a giant accelerator girdling the sun at its equator. The several hundred components of the accelerator would be constructed in space. They'd be made of Mercury. Not the element—the planet.

Solar energy would provide the power to magnets forcing subatomic particles into a circular chase around the sun. In turn, this movement of particles would *generate* a magnetic field, a huge and invisible cylinder of force tangent to the equator and open at the solar poles. "The artificial magnetic field provides openings over the north and south poles of the sun through which plasma can escape," Criswell says. "In effect, they form rocket nozzles over each of the sun's poles."

What forces plasma out the nozzles? Answer: magnetic pumping. The accelerators' orbits will be enlarged and shrunk in cycles, as if a rubber belt were squeezing the sun's middle. These expansions and contractions will create in-and-out pulses of the enveloping cylindrical field, waves of force that will pump solar plasma from around the equator toward the poles, where the pieces of sun will be shot out in gigantic spurts of stellar fire.

Bursting forth at rates of 100,000 times the sun's normal outflow of solar gases, the lifted plasma will radiate heat and light into space. "At great distances from the sun the gases will stream outward as a relatively cool jet." From a temperature of 6000°K at the surface—about 10000°F, or about as hot as an iron welding arc—the expelled matter will cool toward the 3°K level of the interstellar deep.

Finally the cooled hydrogen and helium are collected and formed into great globs of matter held together by their own gravity, just like the mass of the gaseous planets. The result will be a string of man-made planetoids, frozen pearls of stellar stuff awaiting our use.

Criswell presented this scenario at the Los Alamos National Laboratory's Conference on Interstellar Migration, in May 1983. In the clear air, high altitude, and expansive setting of the Jemez Mountains, it's easy to feel that anything's possible. Nevertheless, there were doubts among scientists in the audience about "Dave Criswell's macroengineering project."

What, for example, would keep accelerators from melting? "Mirrors," says Criswell. But don't even mirrors have a melting point? "A mirror with ninety-eight percent reflectivity should be able to keep components behind it to temperatures less than eight hundred degrees Kelvin [about 1000°F] for long periods. A new field of electronics uses components that start to operate only at temperatures in this range. It's very likely that extremely sophisticated, rugged, and efficient devices will be created over the next ten to twenty years that can operate very well on the surface of Mercury or even closer to the sun. On Earth such devices will find applications deep in oil wells, in nuclear reactors, and in the combustion chambers of jet engines."

Well, then, assuming that star lifting will work, what will we do with the material we've lifted? "First we'll construct more oceans. The collected hydrogen could be combined with oxygen extracted from the moon and asteroids to make about 10^{16} tons of water per year.

"Such a cube of water would be larger than two hundred kilometers on a side, a new ocean every ninety years, or over three million four hundred thousand new terrestrial oceans over three-hundred million years of star lifting," Criswell says.

What's more, star lifting will allow the creation of whole new biospheres. Billions of tons of new materials would be available each year to foster the propagation of humans. "A husbanded star could support twenty million times more people than we now support on Earth," Criswell says.

Taking a larger view, by the time human civilization is finished converting the sun into a white dwarf—that is, after about 300 million years—we will be able to transform our star's matter into condensed forms that could power machines of the future. For example, one such machine could harness the force of gravity to propel vehicles at close to the speed of light. At the far reaches of time, when even our own white dwarf burns out, we'll be able to take the excess materials saved from our old sun and recompact them into new white dwarfs. More speculatively still, "perhaps an advanced civilization capable of husbanding a star could convert the original stellar core or a derived core into a suitable black hole. If this could be done for Sol, then the energy release lifetime of the cultured black hole would approach sixteen million times the estimated age of the universe."

Jupiter processing. Industrial stars. Cultured black holes. How much of this can other scientists take seriously? I put the question to Robert W. Bussard, himself no stranger to speculation or to down-to-Earth hard science. Famous for the Bussard Intersteller Ramjet, he's president of INESCO Inc., a fusion-energy research-and-development company.

"I can't take any of this stuff seriously," he says after reading Criswell's Los Alamos paper, "except as a think piece on a galactic scale. It's all too far off in terms of technical developments to yield anything but philosophy—and subjective philosophy at that. Imagine sitting in Florence in 1500 and writing about the future of the world only five hundred years later!"

His comment echoes a point Criswell himself had made when I asked him to estimate how much star lifting would cost. "How much would New York, a Hewlett-Packard calculator, or a B-1 bomber have cost the emperor of Ancient Rome to build?" he replied. "Much more than the value of the entire empire."

But while Bussard and Criswell agree about the difficulty of seeing into the future, neither of them is hesitant about trying to glimpse it, and Bussard acknowledged that "star lifting could probably be done in future times."

When told about Criswell's scenario, nuclear engineer/scientist Theodore B. Taylor was doubtful that we'd ever need to husband stars. "The question is," he says, "Why do you want a sun? Well, one reason is to keep things from flying around. Another is to supply energy, and that energy is accessible without dismantling the sun." How? "With Dyson spheres."

Dyson spheres, the only competitor to Criswell's plan for harnessing the sun's energy, are the brainchildren of physicist Freeman Dyson. In 1960 he wrote in *Science*: "The mass of Jupiter, if distributed in a spherical shell revolving around the sun at twice the earth's distance from it, would have a thickness [of] two to three meters, depending on the density. A shell of this thickness could be made comfortably habitable and could contain all the machinery required for exploiting the solar radiation falling onto it from the inside."

Dyson, one of the world's most famous theoretical physicists, has long dreamed of plans for the "greening of the galaxy." Among other scenarios, he's proposed using the gravitational field of a white-dwarf binary star to serve as a slingshot for interstellar exploratory spacecraft. And he's suggested that an army of self-reproducing robots could mine the ice of Saturn's moons and transport it to Mars to create a new and fertile agricultural planet. So while maintaining impeccable scientific credentials, Dyson has remained open-minded about highly speculative future quests.

At his office at Princeton University's Institute for Advanced Study, Dyson studied Criswell's paper. "The arithmetic as far as I could tell is right," he says. "I didn't find any mistakes. The physics of it is all right. Of course anybody can make up his own scenario of what we might do in the next million years. In some ways Criswell is rather unimaginative:

He assumes more or less that everything continues the way it is now. I would expect much more diversity than he does."

But how does Criswell's star lifting stack up against Dyson spheres? "Oh, it's not very different," he says. "My proposal is open to just the same objections, that it's one possibility among a huge variety. I have no particular reason to say that one or the other is more likely."

Other scientists hope we *won't* do any star lifting. Solar astronomer John Eddy, of Colorado's High Altitude Observatory, and author of *The New Sun: The Solar Results from Skylab* (NASA, 1979), says, "Long before we'll be able to start husbanding the sun, we'll have to know a heck of a lot more about it than we do now. The thought of modifying the outer envelope of the sun scares me; it sounds like someone telling me he's going to take my leg off."

"The problem," Eddy continues, "is that we don't understand, even though Criswell says we do, the basic physics of the energetic-generation process within the sun. Performing critical surgery on a beast that we don't fully understand frightens me."

Worse still, in Eddy's view, are the changes to the earth's climate that tinkering with the sun would produce. "If you alter the sun's radiance by ten percent, you've done a catastrophic thing." We have only one sun, after all, and if our well-intended meddling fouls things up, we won't get another chance.

In Criswell's eyes, however, worrying about climatic changes to Earth will eventually be irrelevant. By the time we're ready to work on the sun, most of mankind will be living elsewhere, in s'homes that can be moved closer to or farther from our new sun in accordance with its radiance. Our current and conservative earthly perspective will have vanished.

It's possible to go beyond even a solar-system perspective. In 1964 the Russian astronomer Nikolai Kardashev postulated three types of civilizations in the universe, which he ranked according to their energy bases. Primitive civilizations like our own are Type I: They live off the decaying fossil fuels of the past. Type II cultures, on the other hand, have harnessed the power of their sun, "for example," he said, "by the successful construction of a Dyson sphere." The most advanced of all, a Type III civilization, has instantaneous access to all the energy in its galaxy.

Criswell has suggested an alternate means to becoming a Type II civilization. And almost as an afterthought, he has suggested a way to detect possible Type III cultures. In fact, he speculates that we may already have detected some.

The key to this is the "missing mass" problem. Astronomers have found that stars in our galaxy move as if under the gravitational spell of a halo of mass encircling it. The problem is, there's nothing optically observable out there. "An intriguing possibility," suggests Criswell, "is that the nonluminous, or missing, mass in the halos of our own galaxy and others is composed of husbanded stars, the associated industrial facilities, s'homes, and stores of hydrogen, helium, and other elements."

Whatever the fate of this or Criswell's other ideas, even his critics acknowledge that his thoughts are inspired. "He's really an impressive mind," says Eddy. "His ideas are wonderful, exciting, heady stuff."

Will any of what he foresees ever happen? I asked Dyson whether Criswell's star-lifting scenario is absurd. "No, on the contrary," he replies. "It's not absurd enough. I mean, what will really happen will be much more surprising."

ANTIMATTER ROCKETS

By Robert L. Forward

An antimatter "factory" in Geneva, Switzerland, is producing millions of antiprotons a second in research that could lead to remarkable new rocket fuels. Barely a thousandth of an ounce—30 milligrams—of this antimatter would be enough to propel a spacecraft to the moon. Ten grams—about the weight of 15 shelled peanuts—could take us to Mars.

Antiprotons are elementary particles with the mass of protons. But, unlike the proton, one of the building blocks of the atom, the antiproton has a negative charge. Collisions between protons and antiprotons result in a 100 percent conversion of particle masses into energy. The high conversion rate means that a tiny amount of fuel can be used to heat a larger amount of plain water to produce a blazing hot rocket exhaust.

The factory for antiprotons is in operation at the European Organization for Nuclear Research (CERN). There, every 2.4 seconds, a pulse of 10 trillion ordinary protons strikes a tungsten target to produce 200 billion antiprotons. Some of these high-speed antiprotons are captured and held in a magnetic racetrack storage ring. Every 2.4 seconds another batch of antiprotons enters the ring, so that 40 hours and 60,000 pulses later there are a trillion antiprotons circling in the magnetic field. Although a trillion antiprotons weigh only about two trillionths of a gram, they contain a measurable amount of energy. If they were used to annihilate a trillion normal protons, 300 joules of energy would be released. That's the equivalent of exploding a tenth of a gram of TNT—approximately the modest "bang" of a cap pistol.

Scientists are looking well beyond mere cap-pistol power. NASA and the Air Force are currently planning studies to explore the concept of antimatter propulsion in detail. The remaining challenge: Although the CERN machine makes lots of antimatter, the process it uses to capture the antiprotons is inefficient. Only 1 in 10,000 of the antiprotons generated makes it to the storage ring. The Air Force and NASA studies will look into how to capture more antiprotons, how to slow and stop them, and how to combine antiprotons with antielectrons (positrons) to make tiny antihydrogen ice pellets. These could be stored, by using magnetic and electric forces, and eventually carried into space in ultracold Thermos jugs, fuel cells for the next generation of rockets.

259

STARSHIP MAKERS

By T. A. Heppenheimer

Forget science-fiction starships. And forget about the British Interplanetary Society's theoretical papers on interstellar travel; their *Daedalus* starcraft probably won't fly, and if it did, would soon explode, according to some advanced computer studies in the United States. The most important starship work in the world takes place at the University of California's Lawrence Livermore Laboratory, where the U.S. government has paid people like Roderick Hyde and Lowell Wood to work on the design of starship engines.

To be fair, the Lawrence Livermore ship has a few features in common with the Britishers' *Daedalus*:

•It is powered by microscopic hydrogen bombs, each less than a millimeter across, each detonating with the modest force of a firecracker.

•These microexplosions will be set off by intense laser beams now being developed at the laboratory for weapons simulation and fusion-power research.

•The hot exhaust that drives the rocket will be expelled from a nozzel formed with magnetic fields, not ordinary metal or ceramic. This approach offers performance vastly better than that of any rocket now in existence.

For years, tight security restrictions kept the details of the work by Hyde, Wood, and their colleagues largely unknown outside Lawrence Livermore itself. In early 1983, news of the starship plans began to leak.

The story begins in 1972. Rod Hyde was just completing the requirements for his B.S. at MIT after little more than two years. He was interested in astrodynamics, the science of orbits and trajectories followed by spacecraft. He wondered whether some advanced, exotic engine might not indeed turn interplanetary flight paths into straight lines.

At the same time, Lowell Wood was one of Livermore's brash young leaders in the new field of laser fusion. His work called for preparing micropellets of fusion fuel, then zapping them with powerful laser beams to produce tiny hydrogen-bomb explosions. In addition, he was a recruiter for a fellowship program; this job took him to MIT, where he and Hyde talked of future engines.

Both scientists agreed that laser microexplosions might be used to propel a starship. Wood arranged for Hyde to get the fellowship and visit Livermore for the summer. Without a security clearance Hyde couldn't work on the real problems, which involved classified questions about the pellets and lasers. But he could study other details, including Wood's notion of using magnetic fields to form a rocket-exhaust nozzle. These fields would allow exploding pellets to blow out the craft's back and produce thrust. Such a rocket could achieve performance a thousand times better than anything yet flown.

Hyde's work—most of it packed into four straight days and nights of calculating and writing so that he could finish in time to attend the world chess championship in Iceland—yielded an amazingly detailed approach to the starship design. He presented his report to the world of aerospace engineering at the Propulsion Specialist Conference, in New Orleans, late in 1972. Hyde laid it all out—the physics, the design concepts, the calculations, and the performance equations.

Almost no one in the audience had the background to follow him. But soon hundreds of requests for copies of his paper started to pour in. Even the National Security Council, under Henry Kissinger, and the office of the President's science adviser at the White House asked for copies. Hyde was nineteen years old.

Back at Livermore, security became even tighter. Laser fusion and its applications represented a highly classified area of work, and Wood and Hyde were forbidden to publish any more in this area. Hyde wrote a very lengthy report giving many more details. This report, UCRL-16556, has been updated since with new material. Quite likely it is the world's most authoritative reference on starship-engine design. It has never been published, but enough is known to give a fairly clear picture of the current state of the Wood-Hyde starship plans.

The most important part of the secret report is the data on fusion micropellets. Like many of today's breakthroughs, work on starship fuel depended on help from a computer. The computer program, called LASNEX, was the creation of another of Wood's young geniuses, George Zimmermann. Zimmermann was newly graduated from Harvey Mudd College, in Claremont, California, and was wondering how to avoid being drafted and sent to Vietnam. Wood hired him, got him a draft deferment, and Zimmermann proceeded to turn out a program that is the world's best at predicting the energy released by micropellets of a specific design when zapped with a laser beam of given characteristics.

At Livermore it is routine to use LASNEX to predict what will happen in laser-fusion experiments, then to run the experiments and find close agreement. Hyde has used LASNEX to test the designs set forth in the British Interplanetary Society's *Project Daedalus* report, proposed as a possible starship design. His conclusion: "Either their pellets won't ignite, or if they do, they'll produce so many neutrons as to burn up their ship." In the LASNEX simulations, by contrast, his lasers and pellets work.

Another thing that's known is Hyde's choice of laser. He prefers a krypton-fluoride excimer device, one of a class of high-performance lasers being studied intensively at Livermore and elsewhere. The same type of unit is now being tested for use in simulating the physics of hydrogen-bomb explosions, as well as the effects of such explosions on missile nose cones.

Hyde has also been simplifying the magnetic rocket nozzle, though he doesn't have a final design yet.

Again, he has sophisticated computer programs to help him. One shows the details of how the magnetic nozzle produced by specific magnetic coils acts in response to a microexplosion. The magnetic field lines blow up like a balloon as the explosion progresses, then bulge rearward, permitting the products of the explosion to escape.

Most important for the future is Livermore's progress in building big lasers. The lab leads the world in this area, which is no small claim. Lowell Wood says: "There are three kinds of liars: liars, damn liars, and laser builders. A guy will build a laser and claim it has fantastic energy in its beam. But then you ask him: Can you produce the energy again, or did you do it only once and blow up your laser in the process?" The Soviets, Wood recalls, once claimed to have the world's most powerful laser. It turned out that the report was based on a single test that burned up all the lenses. At Livermore the claims are legitimate.

And one thing is sure. When starships are built, they will be built according to Rod Hyde's basic designs. Aboard the first ships carrying humans toward the stars, his name will be a household word.

PART EIGHT: SPACE FOR LIVING

*"Stars scribble in our eyes the frosty sagas,
The gleaming cantos of unvanquished space."*
—Hart Crane

VIEWPOINT: OBSERVE THE BEAUTY OF SPACE

By Timothy Ferris

Hubert Reeves, an astrophysicist and director of research at the French National Center for Scientific Research, writes in his new book *Atoms of Silence*: "When someone asks me, 'Of what use is astronomy?' I answer, 'If it had no use other than to reveal such beauty, it would have amply justified its existence.' "

Anyone who has looked at Saturn or the Orion nebula through a telescope will understand what Reeves means. Astronomers and astrophysicists aren't supposed to waste time stargazing—it costs tens of thousands of dollars a night to run a big telescope. Yet I've seen more than one hard-boiled astronomer lose himself gaping at the diamonds-in-ink splendor of the Hercules globular star cluster or the dove-gray draperies of the Tarantula nebula.

The better look we get at the rest of the universe, the more beautiful it turns out to be. Mars through a telescope is enticing, but it wasn't until the Viking orbiters photographed it from less than 1,000 miles overhead that the red planet really came alive: The snow-swept, 84,000-foot-high slopes of the volcano Olympus Mons and the fog-shrouded canyons of Valles Marineris were suddenly transformed from objects of scientific study into *places*, with a wild beauty all their own. The rings of Saturn through a telescope are splendid, but they look incomparably grander in closeup photographs taken by the Voyager spacecraft that resolved them into hundreds of gold and ashen rings, sheet music for gravitational harmonies first heard in the thoughts of Kepler and Newton.

Even the notoriously barren moon drew rave reviews from the otherwise laconic astronauts. The first words spoken by Buzz Aldrin, the second man to set foot on the moon, were, "Beautiful! Beautiful!" When he and Neil Armstrong got back to Earth, they pleaded with NASA to let future moonwalkers have more free time simply to look around at the lunar landscape. Charles Duke, who walked the foothills of the Descartes mountains of the moon during the *Apollo 16* mission, reported, "I just choked up. Tears came. It was the most deeply moving experience of my life."

Aesthetic considerations play little, if any, role in scheduling observing runs on the big telescopes, programming the cameras of interplanetary spacecraft, or determining the missions of lunar astronauts. Yet the startling and literally otherworldly beauty of nature beyond Earth comes tumbling through, all the same.

Why so? *Why* is the universe beautiful?

The Whirlpool galaxy, M51, is an absolutely gorgeous sight, but the Whirlpool galaxy is 35 million light-years away; we see it today as it looked when the first hominids had yet to split away from the anthropoid apes. Why should something so distant in space and time be capable of arousing our sense of beauty?

Perhaps the answer is that the universe really is all of a piece, as mystics have long maintained. The Whirlpool galaxy is made of the same sort of stuff as our eyes and mind, and it obeys the same natural laws. Therefore we resonate with it in various ways. Intellectually, we analyze the Keplerian dynamics of its wheeling stars. Aesthetically, we find it beautiful.

But this explanation raises another question, one that has long troubled philosophers of science: How do the universal laws of nature manage to *be* universal? How does the Whirlpool galaxy "know" that it should obey the same laws that pertain here in the Milky Way?

That riddle, in turn, leads us back to the creation of the universe.

The universe is expanding; of this there is ample proof. If we extrapolate cosmic expansion backward in time, we find that everything in the universe must once have been crowded together, some 20 billion years ago, in the fireball stage that cosmologists waggishly call the Big Bang. The universe, then, really is a *universe*, a single entity, having started out as a seed smaller than the period at the end of this sentence. The atoms comprising the far-flung galaxies all obey the same laws because they got together at the dawn of time and worked out the rules of the game.

The word *beauty* is infamously difficult to define,

but artists and philosophers generally agree that a beautiful object has the power to draw together its disparate elements to form a unified whole and that it tends to draw us into it, making us feel that we are part of its unity. It just may be then, that the beauty we see in planets, stars, and galaxies is itself evidence of the unity of the universe.

This idea detracts from the mystery of neither science nor aesthetics. It may be that the laws of nature were arbitrated during the first moments of the expansion of the universe, but that doesn't explain why there *are* any natural laws or why the human mind is able, however imperfectly, to discern them. Our sense of natural beauty may be one among many cosmic harmonies, but that doesn't explain why nature is to any degree harmonious.

It has been speculated that science will one day arrive at a master equation that will explain everything. I doubt very much that this will ever happen. It seems far more likely that the beauty and the intelligibility of nature will remain to some extent mysterious. Science, as Oliver Wendell Holmes once remarked about life, "is painting a picture, not doing a sum."

Timothy Ferris is the author of Space Shots, *published in October, 1984, by Pantheon Books. His earlier book,* Galaxies *(Sierra Club, 1980), received widespread critical acclaim.*

OMNI'S FUTURE CALENDAR

By Thomas O'Toole

Gerald J. Wasserburg, the man whose analysis of the first moon rocks put the age of the solar system at 4.6 billion years, pushed his notes away from him and sat for a moment, staring out his office window. He paused for effect, then looked straight at his visitor. "We're going to build a house on the moon." Wasserburg declared with total conviction. "We're going to have a mommy and a daddy there, and someone in New Jersey will be able to say to someone else, 'Hey, I've got a cousin living on the moon.' "

Wasserburg is a professor of geology and geophysics at the California Institute of Technology, in Pasadena, and his look into the future is no Aesop's fable. The professor's preview of what lies ahead in space is rooted soundly in what has already happened—and in what can happen in the twenty-first century. Why not build a lunar home for the moon's first family? Or a lunar workpalace where astronomers can set up an observatory that's invulnerable to city lights and electronic pollution? Why not make it possible for geologists to mine the moon for minerals the earth has never had, as well as for any earthbound minerals that are about to be mined into extinction?

"There's no doubt in my mind that people will live off the earth and that the moon is the first logical place to do that," Wasserburg went on. "And if we live off the earth, we'll have children off the earth. When the first child is conceived and born off the earth, it will be a magical moment, an enormously important event in the course of history."

Over the next 50 years, men and their machines will continue to explore every frontier of the solar system, with one exception: Pluto. (Too small, too far, and too uninteresting.) Repairing satellites in space will become routine. So will space industry, which will yield new vaccines, lifesaving pharmaceuticals, genetically engineered drugs, and exotic metals and alloys all for the first time. Man will settle in space aboard space stations, colonize the moon, travel to Mars.

Not all the major missions will involve humans. There will be a robot rendezvous with a comet, spaceflights to asteroids and comets in which robots will dig out samples to return to Earth, and a robot mission to Mars that will bring back a sample from the red planet. Both missions are likely to provide clues about how the cosmos began.

In drawing up a space calendar for the future, *Omni* began with 1986 and looked ahead 50 years, to 2036. It seemed wise to start with 1986. That's when Halley's Comet will appear to Earthlings for the first time since 1910. That's also when *Voyager 2* will encounter Uranus, and when the $1.2 billion *Space*

Telescope will be placed in orbit to begin a ten-year mission that will bring celestial objects closer to us than ever before.

"If Olympus Mons [at 15 miles high, the largest volcano in the solar system] were to erupt on Mars," says Caltech's James Westphal, a principal investigator on the *Space Telescope*, "we'll see it with the *Space Telescope*. It will be an event unparalleled in space-observation history."

Ending our space calendar in 2036 seemed equally appropriate. The world's space scientists have a plan for space exploration that takes us through the next 50 years. Beyond 2036, the vision grows fuzzy.

In drawing up our 50-year calendar, we talked to people in all areas of the space business. People like NASA administrator James M. Beggs; "star wars" General James A. Abrahamson; former astronaut and U.S. Senator Harrison H. ("Jack") Schmitt; Voyager project scientist Edward C. Stone; Jet Propulsion Laboratory scientists Arden Albee and Albert Hibbs; the University of Paris's Jacques Blamont, the world's only scientist allowed to have instruments flown on American and Russian spacecraft; Gerry Neugebauer, director of the Palomar Observatory; and Maarten Schmidt, the discoverer of the quasar and president of the American Astronomical Society. We asked these men to look ahead and tell us what will happen, what could happen, and what should happen. We asked them to be conservative with their budget projections but not with their imaginations.

What they said formed the essence of this space calendar, which we have divided into four epochs. The first might be called the Era of Nuts and Bolts. It starts in 1986, when robot spacecraft will explore Uranus and Neptune for the first time and revisit Jupiter and its four large moons; when other spacecraft will give us our first look at the sun's north and south poles; and when the *Space Telescope* begins its observations of the heavens.

Epoch two starts in 1992, the five hundredth anniversary of Columbus's discovery of America. It will be commemorated with the launch of the first U.S. space station. From it we will launch several missions to the moon, Mars, the outer planets, the comets, and the asteroids. Satellite repair and the commercialization of space will begin in earnest then.

Epoch three is the Age of Space Colonization, an era that will begin when the first American colonists settle the moon. The era will end with the first mission to orbit Mars and return to Earth.

Epoch four is the least easy to forecast, but the experts hope it will culminate in 2036, with the arrival of the first astronaut colonists on the surface of Mars. "If we don't go," warns Wasserburg, "the Russians will go. But if we're all smart, we'll go there together."

Here's a calendar of the next half century in space:

1986. January 24: We'll get our closest look ever at Uranus, a planet that is still a mystery. Currently, scientists don't know even the length of its day. Voyager chief scientist Ed Stone guesses: "It's somewhere between sixteen and twenty-four hours." What does Uranus look like? "The best pictures we have make it look like a tomato," he says. In the first close encounter ever with the seventh planet from the sun, *Voyager 1* will fly by Uranus just beyond it outermost rings, a scant 29,000 kilometers from Miranda, the innermost of its five known moons. So dark are these moons (Miranda, Ariel, Umbriel, Titania, and Oberon) that some experts suspect they are made of the most exotic ices in the solar system. Uranus is circled by nine dazzling rings of dust, within which scientists hope to find the same kinds of tiny satellites that they believe keep the rings from colliding and disappearing.

February 8: Halley's Comet swings around the sun just as it has every 76 years since at least 240 B.C., when it was first chronicled by the Chinese. Waiting out in space to greet the comet will be a Soviet spacecraft carrying French cameras; a European spacecraft named *Giotto;* and a Japanese spacecraft that will follow the comet from a distance and photograph its 100-million-mile-long tail. The U.S. space shuttle will also photograph Halley's Comet on at least two missions, using ultraviolet telescopes developed just for the occasion. The best pictures should be those taken by the Soviet spacecraft, which will come closest to the comet. Explains French scientist Jacques Blamont, developer of the cameras: "We expect to photograph the surface of the nucleus, estimate its size, and understand its nature, all for the first time."

May 15: A German-American spacecraft named *Ulysses* will be released from the cargo bay of America's space shuttle and sent on a curving path toward Jupiter, where it will be caught by the giant planet's gravitational field by July 1987. Then it will zoom back toward the sun. By December 1989, the spacecraft will encounter the sun's north pole. It will overfly the solar equator in July 1990 and the pass over the south pole in October of the same year. The spacecraft will give us our first glimpse of the solar poles, whose magnetic activity complicates the study of the sun. *Ulysses* will also give scientists their first three-dimensional view of the middle latitudes, where more than 90 percent of solar flares occur.

May 21: A silvery spacecraft named *Galileo* will be launched from the payload bay of the space shuttle on a trip to Jupiter. It will reach the planet in August 1988 and orbit Jupiter and its four largest moons in a photographic mission that promises to be the most productive planetary mission every flown. Why the most productive? It will linger near Jupiter for more than 11 months, instead of the few days that were allotted to predecessor spacecraft like *Voyager*. In that time, *Galileo* will pass by Io, Europa, Callisto, and Ganymede at least 11 times before being destroyed by the intense radiation fields around the planet.

Sometime in August, the space shuttle will release the $1.2 billion *Space Telescope* (ST), the most expensive instrument ever sent into orbit. The ST will stay in orbit at least 10, and perhaps as long as 20, years. Space-shuttle astronauts will periodically visit the ST to make repairs and refurbish it. The ST will peer ten times farther into the heavens than any earthbound telescope, meaning it will view cosmic events that happened almost 14 billion years ago. The ST will also be used to study local solar system events. "We're being given an observatory that will allow us to do the meteorology of the whole solar system," James Westphal, of the California Institute of Technology, says. "We'll never fully understand Jupiter's giant red spot, but we will get the longest and closest look ever at that magical region of the solar system with the

Space Telescope."

1988. April: The space shuttle will release from its bay a space robot with an enormous radar dish, three times the size of the spacecraft itself. The craft's name: *Venus Radar Mapper.* By July, it should arrive in orbit around Venus and begin to peer through the sulfuric acid clouds of the planet. Using its radar, capable of "photographing" features as small as one kilometer across, it will generate a global map of almost the entire surface of the torrid (almost 1000°F) planet.

August 24: *Voyager* will encounter Neptune, eighth planet out from the sun and the last to be explored in this century. The spacecraft will make the closest planetary flyby ever attempted in an attempt to solve some long-standing mysteries. Neptune has a puzzling internal-heat engine that radiates twice as much heat as it gets from the sun. Also orbiting it is a moon named Triton, which moves backward around the planet. *Voyager* will have to fly extremely close to Neptune to get a good look at its peculiar moon. Says Stone: "Triton is the only moon in the solar system besides Titan [which belongs to Saturn] with a liquid-nitrogen sea. Also, it's the only moon in the solar system that probably has seasons."

1990. August: A spacecraft with the tongue-twisting name of the *Mars Geochemical Climatology Orbiter* (MGCO) will depart from the space shuttle on its way to the red planet. A year later, in August 1991, it will be in orbit around Mars. Circling what may still be the most mysterious planet in the solar system, this spacecraft will attempt to find out why Mars lost all its water eons ago. The signs of a water-rich planet are evident. Its great canyon, which is three times the size of our own Grand Canyon, was carved out by rushing water, planetologists say. Today it is an arid, red desert.

"The climatic history of Mars presents one of the solar system's most intriguing challenges," says chief mission scientist Michael H. Carr. What the MGCO will try and do is help analyze Martian climate patterns caused by slow changes in the tilt of the planet's axis over millions of years.

Late 1990: *Mariner* spacecraft will be launched from the space shuttle on a long, lonely trajectory that will not take it to its destination until 1994. Its target? A small, faint, young comet named Knopff that swings by the sun every six years. Once it makes its rendezvous with the comet, *Mariner* will accompany it until 1996, when Knopff is closest to the solar surface. Knopff has all the characteristics of an old comet like Halley's. For the first time, a spacecraft will be able to observe a comet as it heats up, as its tail grows, and as the exotic and primeval chemicals in its nucleus boil off during its fiery passage around the sun.

1992. This year will mark the beginning of our second epoch, the Age of the Space Station. Commercialization of space will expand dramatically, and we'll take the first steps toward colonizing the moon and Mars. We'll repair satellites routinely and set up a space-rescue service for marooned astronauts and cosmonauts.

Five hundred years after Columbus discovered America, America will put into orbit elements of the first space station, named after the explorer. Astronauts will assemble the station in space. Its complement is expected to be a crew of three men and three women, who will occupy the $8 million complex. The first crew will stay for six months and be replaced by eight new astronauts—four men and four women. They will set up living quarters, a biological laboratory, a small space factory, and an observatory whose telescopes and instruments can either be turned toward Earth or out at the stars.

1995. Flying the new "transfer vehicle," a kind of space tugboat, three astronauts will venture out from the space station, 200 miles above the earth, to geosynchronous orbit, 22,400 miles up. Once in geosync the astronauts will rendezvous with one of our $100 million communications satellites. Two crew members will don space suits and repair a long-silent satellite. Before the year is out, space-station crews will have repaired six more communications satellites in geosync orbit. The immediate effect of geosync repair, predicts "star wars" Air Force Lieutenant General James A. Abrahamson, former director of the space-shuttle program for NASA, will be to suggest all kinds of new schemes for the kind of satellite repair that saved the *Solar Maximum Observatory* (*Solar Max*) in 1984. Being able to repair communications satellites in orbit will double, perhaps triple, the useful lifetimes of the newest satellites. The *Space Telescope* could be refurbished to extend its lifetime another ten years. Weather satellites could be refitted in orbit with new cameras and electronics, improving the accuracy of weather forecasting by 50 percent. According to Alan L. Parker, president of Ford Aerospace, "By the year 2000, these new satellites will allow you to make a phone call from New York to London for a nickel, and anybody carrying a cordless portable phone will be able to place a call from anywhere in the world—even if you're out in the wilderness—to anywhere else in the world."

1996. In a mission already being planned at California's Jet Propulsion Laboratory, *Galileo II* will leave the space station to depart on a three-year journey to Saturn, still the most dazzling planet in the solar system. Once *Galileo* arrives, a probe will detach from it and fly through the planet's brilliant rings and into Saturn's seething atmosphere, while the *Galileo* mother ship moves in orbit just beyond the planet's outermost ring. A second probe will be launched from the mother ship to the Saturnian moon, Titan. There it will descend into the only moon in the solar system known to possess a nitrogen and methane atmosphere, one that is remarkably like the primitive atmosphere that enshrouded Earth 4 billion years ago.

1997. An instrument-laden spacecraft, the *Lunar Polar Orbiter*, will be sent from the space station to orbit over the moon's north and south poles. Its mission will be to make a geological and geochemical map of the moon; in other words, to tell Earth's geologists what minerals lie beneath the lunar surface. Its secondary mission will be to search for the water most scientists believe exists as ice in the craters at the lunar poles. If the *Polar Orbiter* finds this ice (as many scientists expect it will) astronaut-colonists could plan a trek to the shadowed craters to start their first settlements.

2000. At the start of a new century, two unmanned

missions will leave the space station *Columbus*. The first will be sent on a journey that will take it on two near flybys of Earth-crossing Apollo asteroids, and then on to a rendezvous with either comet Encke, Pennett, or West, whichever is most accessible. Once alongside the comet, the spacecraft will set down on the comet's hard-rock nucleus. Using a drill that resembles a miniature oil rig, the robot explorer will remove a sample of the ice and solids from the comet's nucleus, and then take off, carrying its scientific gems back to Earth. Explains Caltech's Wasserburg: "We need to get a sample of a comet. There are some comets out there that are still primeval representatives of the deep freeze where it all began, 4.6 billion years ago." The second spacecraft will travel to Mars, where it will orbit over the Martian grand canyon, scouting for suitable landing places for future robot spacecraft.

Sometime late in 2000, the shuttle will take its first tourists around the earth, opening an entire new era in space travel. Who will be the first tourists? Most likely they will be heads of state, prominent politicians, Nobel Prize-winners, celebrities, and entertainers, each of whom will pay a princely sum to take the trip. Al Hibbs, of the Jet Propulsion Laboratory says, "That's when we'll know space travel is here to stay, when the tourist trade starts to turn a profit for the space agency."

2005. After a year of travel, the Mars Rover, a mobile robot with tank treads, will land at the bottom of the giant canyon on Mars and begin to move along the dried-out riverbed to dig up soil samples. At least two other Mars Rovers will land in other regions of the red planet, one in an ancient valley and the other in the caldera of the enormous volcano Olympus Mons. Each rover will spend months traveling about 50 kilometers, taking samples of Martian rock along the way. The rovers will then transfer the rock to small spacecraft attached to them. These will blast off from Mars to rendezvous with America's space station. There, space-suited scientists will examine the Martian samples in pristine isolation as a precaution against contamination by extraterrestrial germs. The reason for this mission, says Wasserburg, is obvious: "Mars is a real planet just like Earth, and it has undergone catastrophic climate changes that dried up all its water and left that huge canyon behind. Bringing back Martian rock samples will allow us to date the events that changed Mars forever and tell us why it did not evolve like the earth. Why is there no water or life on Mars? These are major questions that go to the heart of understanding how the cosmos began."

2010. Once the *Lunar Polar Orbiter* locates water in the shadowed craters of the moon's north pole, it will be only a question of time before the first human colonists find their way to those craters. This is the year that four astronauts, two men and two women, will establish the first moon colony, planting the Stars and Stripes on the rim of a shadowed crater near the moon's north pole. Setting up base under the crater's rim and just out of the sun, the astronauts will tap into the ice for their water. And just beyond the rim they will unfold 300-foot-high solar panels to supply their electricity.

The first colonists might be civilian scientists. But don't discount the possibility that they could be astronauts working for NASA and the CIA, or members of the Pentagon's star-wars brigade. A lunar base would be an excellent site for military listening posts. This is no idle scenario. Already, at the University of California at San Diego, there is a study under way to see whether astronauts on the moon, using lunar materials as radiation shields, can protect the settlers from spacebased Soviet particle-beam weapons.

2010—2015. Scaled-down versions of the *Galileo* spacecraft that are to fly to Jupiter and Saturn will land on at least two asteroids and all four large Jovian moons: Io, Ganymede, Europa, and Callisto. These landings will be strictly for science. But the landings on the asteroids could mean the difference between life and death for our planet.

The space agency already has a program called Spacewatch under way. Scientists are keeping a close watch on "Earth-crossers," asteroids that could conceivably move onto a collision course with Earth and destroy much of its life, just as an asteroid may have wiped out the dinosaurs 65 million years ago. NASA's advisory council has already gone on record as saying that the only way to avoid an impending collision would be to anticipate one and to make provisions to deflect the approaching asteroid with a hydrogen bomb.

"The dinosaurs . . . failed to develop the technology to avoid their extinction," the council said, "but *Homo sapiens* has. He can avert any further extinction by asteroid impact. We think he should."

At the same time, a spacecraft protected by the largest heat shield ever constructed will move into orbit around the sun. The ship will fly at the same speed at which the sun rotates, watching a single sunspot through an entire 11-year solar cycle. During the same period, a spacecraft will move out to orbit Mercury and maybe even attempt a landing on its superheated surface, which may be molten enough to swallow any landing spacecraft. Finally, telescopes that see in the X-ray, gamma-ray, and infrared ranges will be put into orbit. And a second-generation space telescope will be launched, this one twice as large and four times as sensitive as the original.

2020. The space station will come of age. Astronauts will be using their space tug to venture far afield in space, where they will erect giant radio telescopes to study the entire Milky Way, and listen for intelligent signals from distant space. The mission will mark the beginning of an intense space-based search for other planets in the Milky Way. The space station will be expanded to accommodate as many as 16 astronauts at a time and will become a full space-manufacturing enterprise, making pharmaceuticals, exotic metals, and electronic parts in an abundance not even dreamed of today.

Four American astronauts will set out from the space station *Columbus* (tripled in size since 1992) on a historic flight to orbit Mars. They'll be scouts for the pioneers who will colonize Mars in the subsequent two decades. After circling Mars, the astronauts will fly down as close as 50,000 feet above the planet's surface in a search for the best settlement sites for a colony. Back on earth, humanity may be deeply divided by the question of whether human beings should colonize another planet.

2035. The Martian colonists will set sail for the red planet, landing there a year later to set up permanent housekeeping. "The technology to make the long journey to Mars already exists," former astronaut (*Apollo 17*) and U.S. Senator (New Mexico) Harrison "Jack" Schmitt tells *Omni*. "The only thing missing is the commitment, which I believe will come early in the twenty-first century." When that happens, the Age of Planetary Exploration will have arrived.

THE BIRTH
OF A STATION

By Dava Sobel

I have heard it described in visionary dreams since I was a child, with its international—even interplanetary—community of brave pioneers, its floating gardens, emerald towers, and high-domed cities of perfect cleanliness orbiting majestically above the obsolete Earth.

The space station was a brazen fantasy when I was young, when the only way to fly was aboard a turboprop and no one had walked on the moon. Aloft beyond reality, where everything was new, anything was possible. Whatever happened up there would be better than what had been down here. And it *would* happen. I remember Fred Freeman's cutaway painting for *Collier's* in the Fifties, with dozens of khaki-clad men swarming through the pipes and chambers of a circular space station 250 feet in diameter. This vehicle, like a huge bicycle wheel, could be spinning overhead by 1963, *Collier's* assured me.

Now that the planning of a real space station is a line item in NASA's budget, more of the grand illusions have disappeared. In their place, the agency is wheeling a workhorse toward the gates of space. It promises to be an utterly utilitarian creature, devoted to meeting the needs of science, industry, and national defense. Yet, this spare, economical space station embodies America's best hope for leadership on the high frontier.

No one on NASA's Space Station Task Force can tell you precisely what the station will look like, only that it will start out small (and relatively cheap) and be capable of evolving into something grander over the decades. Whatever it is, it will fly in low Earth orbit—roughly 400 kilometers up—where the space shuttle can build it, service it, and be serviced in turn.

The embryonic station will provide modest living quarters. From this base, crew members on tethers will tend one or more nearby unmanned platforms. These unattached subsidiary stations will carry gear—such as telescopes—that could be thrown off by an astronaut's flinch or sneeze. But the substations would be close enough to the mother station so that crew members could repoint or adjust equipment when necessary, guaranteeing a steady flow of useful data back to the ground. And the astronauts, even when they sleep or sit idle, will flutter the national pulse with memories of Apollo's glory and the dizzy excitement of having left Earth behind.

The paramount question before the task force right now, however, does not involve the appearance of the space station or the size of its crew; it is, What could or should such a facility *do*? The 25 members of the task force, drawn from NASA headquarters and the agency's eight field centers, are looking to themselves, their contradictors in the aerospace industry, their foreign counterparts, the corporate world at large, the scientific community, and branches of the armed forces for answers.

A space station might, for example, provide a gravity-free environment for superior execution of any number of commercial processes. Some see it as a construction site in space where enormous communications antennas, too fragile to be launched from Earth, are assembled, then boosted into higher orbits almost effortlessly. Others envision it as an outpost where astronauts retrieve and repair malfunctioning scientific satellites. It could become the hub of a multinational exploratory venture, combining instruments that look down at Earth's resources and out to the distant stars with an operations base for manned missions to the moon and planets. Or it could turn into a desolate platform for space-based lasers and particle-beam weapons. Any one of these outcomes is at least possible, NASA learns, as it polls the potential users of the space station for their ideas.

The could-be functions of the space station will dictate its architecture. And by *architecture*, NASA people do not mean construction details. They mean such basic concepts as manned versus unmanned and whether a high-inclination orbit over the poles or a low-inclination orbit close to the equator is the most useful path to accomplish specific mission goals. Only after NASA researchers choose from such options can the detailed design work begin—and then only if the President and Congress are convinced of the need for a permanent American presence in space, and they put money into the idea.

How much money would it take to build one? That depends on answers to more than 300 technical questions already identified. What's the best option for powering such a spacecraft? (Fuel cells? Solar panels? Nuclear sources?) What's the ideal way to navigate and stabilize it? The top choices in every category have to be played against one another to see whether they function together, and if not, to see what trade-offs can be made. But even in the face of all these complex preparations, it is reasonable to consider a launch date of 1990 or 1991, says task-force spokesman Terence T. Finn, and a price tag of about $6 billion should cover all of the expenses from here to there.

"That's a real number," Finn maintains, and he compares it favorably to past expenditures in space. "Apollo cost twenty-five billion dollars in so-called constant dollars, but it would take eighty-two billion to repeat the project in 1984 dollars. The shuttle was somewhere between ten and fifteen billion dollars, depending on how you count, and the two unmanned Viking landers and orbiters together cost one billion dollars."

Finn is bullish on the possibility for success because, for one thing, Americans built a space station before. That was *Skylab*, and it served long and well before disintegrating embarrassingly over Australia.

This time the building job should be easier because the station will be launched in pieces aboard the shuttle and assembled in orbit. It does not have to be designed to rocket beyond Earth's gravitational pull by itself. And thanks to a new, improved capacity for reboosting to higher orbit, it should never be enticed back into the atmosphere by gravity, as *Skylab* was.

At the same time, Finn is well aware that loose talk in a tight economy could kill the space station before it ever progresses beyond the planning stage. He is especially cautious about pictures of possible space-station designs, and he works to keep them away from the public eye. ("We don't know what the damn thing's gonna look like," he wails. "Don't think of it as a couple of cans with some men in them. Or some women.") But there are some 400 engineers on the project, including about 250 NASA employees, Air Force personnel, and the interested parties at the eight corporations under contract to NASA—Boeing, General Dynamics, Grumman, Lockheed, Martin Marietta, McDonnell Douglas, Rockwell International, and TRW. Many of these people are not merely accustomed to picturing machinery in orbit, they are unable to resist the temptation to do so. And that is why numerous extreme, unauthorized designs have sprung up and leaked out into public view.

The grandest of these is the multimodule deluxe Space Operations Center, a busy place where a dozen astronauts are living and working, as conceived by the Johnson Space Center, in Houston. The astronauts in this vision are builders, biologists, and big-business representatives. They man construction booms, and they build and test new species of spacecraft and antennas. They assemble communications satellites, delivered to them by the shuttle, and load the satellites aboard an orbital-transfer vehicle that whisks them into geosynchronous orbit, 35,900 kilometers up, and then flies back to the astronauts like a homing pigeon. In their laboratory, they run dozens of experiments designed by earthbound scientists. The weightless researchers make important minute-to-minute decisions and phone home when they encounter major hurdles. In spare moments, they propel themselves to the free-flying scientific installations clustered around their living quarters and replace the cryogenic liquids that cool the space telescopes. They manage the extraterrestrial manufacturing plants of half a dozen industrial entrepreneurs. They have turkey tetrazzini and other freeze-dried fare for dinner and strap themselves into mesh cradles for zero-g sleep.

Almost diametrically opposed is the stark space platform suggested by another part of NASA, the Marshall Space Flight Center, in Huntsville, Alabama. It is an unmanned utility pole providing power, data management, and attitude and thermal control for instrument modules that snap onto it like pieces of a giant's Erector set. Shuttle crews arrive intermittently, staying just long enough to deliver their cargo and perform a hasty inspection tour. The rest of the time, the platform hums quietly to itself.

Finn supposes that the ultimate design will incorporate a little of both approaches: the Johnson concept of working in space, tempered by the Marshall austerity. Above all, it will be "user friendly."

Whereas in the past NASA tended to design first and worry about use and users later, it will design the space station to be the child of the users' needs. There is a slavish devotion to providing a service that, according to task-force director John Hodge, "represents almost a cultural change" for the space agency and the aerospace industry.

"We engineers tend to invent an answer before we've closed in on the question," Hodge says. "But what we're really driving toward here is suitability for the users. That's why it's up to them to tell us what the design requirements are." To that end, he continues, aerospace contractors have been asked to help identify potential users, particularly those who have not operated in space before, and whisper in their ears of the wonders made possible by zero gravity and zero pressure.

"Part of the contractors' job," Hodge says, "is to tell the commercial world that it's not that tricky to get into space, to change their attitude about space from the gee-whiz to something more routine."

Bob Sharples, who manages the space-station study project at TRW, says his group wrote to the heads of many large corporations, asking, in effect, "Did you guys ever think of doing what you do in space?"

"The answers we got," Sharples reports, "ranged from 'no, and don't bother me!' to 'Hey, that sounds like a terrific idea! Tell me more.' "

Such matchmaking efforts may lead to happy marriages, like the existing relationship between McDonnell Douglas Astronautics and the Ortho Pharmaceuticals Corporation division of Johnson &

Johnson. The two companies have invested enormous energy, not to mention enormous amounts of money, in the hope of manufacturing insulin, interferon, and dozens of other vital substances in space. An experiment they mounted on the shuttle in 1982 showed that their technique was 400 times more productive in zero gravity than in an Earth-based medical laboratory and that the materials produced in space were of far greater purity.

Space-station planners are looking far beyond the traditional user community to get ideas for possible missions. X-ray astronomer Stephen S. Holt, who balances membership on the task force with research duties at the Goddard Space Flight Center, in Greenbelt, Maryland, heads a program specifically designed to plumb previously neglected sources for suggestions about space-station uses.

"NASA's attempt is really exhaustive," Holt says. "We didn't quit after rounding up all the usual suspects."

The program, called Innovative Utilization of the Space Station, didn't quite reach out to the man on the street, Holt says, although it inadvertently attracted proposals from housewives in Pittsburgh and numerous groups of schoolchildren.

"NASA public-affairs people let it be known to selected professional journals," Holt explains, "that we had four hundred thousand dollars to award in study contracts for investigating innovative ideas. Anyone interested was to submit a brief statement of purpose, plus credentials, and then we would select several of the best proposals; these would receive grants of about twenty-five thousand dollars each. Somehow this got picked up in the popular press as a NASA-sponsored contest, offering a twenty-five thousand dollar prize for the best twenty-five word description on the back of a postcard."

Despite that setback, Holt says with good humor, the agency did receive some 300 credible suggestions, properly presented, and announced the 18 worthiest ones in March. The grantees will investigate everything from managing trauma and emergency surgery in space to the effects of zero gravity on reproduction and development in rats and worms. One grant went to a sculptor who proposed to explore the artistic potential of the space station. His plan involves polling his colleagues in the art community to see what kinds of extraterrestrial aesthetics a station might support or inspire.

In the traditional scientific arena, the space station would of course provide improved opportunities in Holt's own field of X-ray astronomy, which cannot be done from the ground.

"I don't want to imply that we've decided we have to have a space station to do better astronomy," Holt says. "We use satellites now, and we could continue to do so. We could also design other instruments like the Space Telescope, which will be launched in 1986 and will be serviced intermittently by shuttle crews." Without humans aboard to aim the instrument, the telescope will look deeper into space than optical gear has ever peered before.

"Of course, it would be nice to have men in space all the time to take care of emergencies," Holt adds, "but it's not essential. The only two areas of science that could not proceed without a space station are the life-science studies of space medicine and space biology, and laboratory investigations of materials processing that require some guy in zero g to switch samples and make decisions. In every other field, work could continue in some fashion, although a space station would make a difference in terms of magnitude."

Meanwhile, informal invitations for participation in planning the American space station have been sent to the European Space Agency (ESA), Canada, and Japan. Task-force director Hodge concedes there is no firm policy yet on the appropriate way to collaborate with foreign groups, but he hopes that an international flavor will suffuse the whole enterprise. He cited the South Pole as a good model, where several countries maintain independent scientific research facilities under the peaceful terms of an international agreement signed in 1959.

"We've got a long history of cooperating with NASA," says John E. Harrison, science counselor at the Canadian Embassy, in Washington, D.C. "Usually it takes the form of, You make your half and we'll make our half, and then we'll bolt them together to see if they fly."

According to Ian Pryke, assistant director of ESA's Washington office, Europeans are looking into various technical areas where they might be able to make important contributions.

"There's no possibility of an ESA-built station," Pryke said. "We could not do this ourselves. But if the

United States decides to go ahead, we'll know which areas could allow our involvement."

Pryke also said that ESA's convention prohibits the agency from taking part in any military programs. Should the final American plans include the presence of the Defense Department, in other words, ESA would have to turn away, although any of its member states would be free to negotiate individual agreements with NASA.

Military spokesmen had little to say about the space station. A senior Air Force official offered a piece of military minimalism: "The Air Force is studying with NASA the potential utility of a space station. Currently there are no firm plans for development or use—pending additional evaluation." But it is interesting to note that Lieutenant Colonel Robert Filo, of the Air Force's new Space Command, joined the Space Station Task Force in February, 1983.

A military presence belongs on America's permanent installation in space, many Washingtonians feel, since there seem to be some martial stirrings aboard the one space station now in the sky: the closely watched Soviet *Salyut* 7.

"It's clear from press reports that the Russians are well ahead of us in the duration of individual manned flights," notes Philip E. Culbertson, NASA's associate deputy administrator. "They apparently have a good research program, and it's probably not just for scientific research. We don't know what they're doing on the military side. But the stories I hear make me think there has to be something there—a new, larger space station, perhaps."

Culbertson is not just keeping up with the Russians, however, when he talks about the need for an American station. As far as he can tell, the space station is "the logical precursor for anything of any great significance in space in the first part of the next century." Without one, NASA would continue its research programs, he thinks, but the country would be the less.

Director Hodge agrees. "What do you see when you look a long, long way ahead at what might be happening in space fifty years or one hundred years from now?" he asks. "Whatever you see out there—men exploring the planets, some kind of permanent base on the moon—you have to assume a space station came first."

Hodge isn't implying that we need the experience of mastering a space station before we can progress to more audacious achievements—like needing to crawl before you can walk. He is speaking of the practical necessity of a space station to be our way station. There we would build our future transports from as-yet-unknown materials that do not—could not—exist in the leaden atmosphere of Earth, under the crushing force of one g, assailed by the wind, the rain, and the burning desire of oxygen to combine with everything it touches. The climate of space is comparatively benign. There is no fire in the places between stars. Nothing rusts. In space, our outsized, outlandish creations of infinite delicacy will seem as invulnerable as battleships. Someday it may strike our successors that the dreams and drawings of the Fifties—as extravagant as they seem to us—were not nearly complex enough to capture the spirit of actual spacecraft.

That is, of course, if the station itself materializes. Not everyone in Washington—where countdowns for space missions really begin—is enthusiastic. With the recession as a recent memory, some federal planners speak as if they are inhibited by the weight of economic gravity.

"We're not ready to commit ourselves to the need for a station," says Victor Reis, assistant director for national security and space in the President's Office of Science and Technology. "We're waiting to see what one could get from it. And the evidence is just coming in."

The future of the station now depends on a series of mundane discussions and decisions. Industry contractors presented their final reports to NASA in a series of briefings held April 5 through 9, 1983. The members of the task force sequestered themselves for two weeks in May at Langley Research Center, in Hampton, Virginia, for a "mission synthesis workshop." They were to translate all the information they'd received into hypothetical plans for three sets of missions—those that have to do with science and applications, those that are mostly commercial in nature, and those that involve new technologies. With this first rough draft of mission priorities, they felt that they could begin to talk seriously about space-station architecture, specific cost figures, and actual capabilities. They have already come up with their first consensus about what the space station might look like and do.

Final decisions and engineering choices should take them to the summer of 1985 to complete, and then they think they will know just what to build. When that time comes, will we be ready to pay the bills?

ROPE TRICKS

By James E. Oberg

A hot-air balloon floated peacefully between the dark-blue sky and the thick, yellow-tinged cloud bank below. Underneath the inflated sphere a small gondola dangled motionless over Venus.

The gondola was packed with samples of the surface and subsurface rock snatched by a computerized scooper from the hellish planet below. Now a small unmanned vehicle plunged from the sky to retrieve the samples.

Trailing behind the arrow-shaped vehicle was a nearly invisible but sinewy filament, a line connected to the mother ship orbiting above.

The arrowhead angled directly toward the balloon and was preceded by a sharp sonic boom. Tension on the line increased, slowing the plummeting vehicle. Small fins guided it toward its target with

the help of an on-board computer designed origi-
nally for precision reentries of thermonuclear war-
heads. The arrowhead homed in on the balloon and
tore through it amidships. As the balloon collapsed,
hooks extended from the arrowhead, converting it
instantly into a grappling iron. The spiky probe
reversed its motion and began moving upward under
the force of the line. The hooks caught onto the skin
of the balloon and pulled it, along with the still-
attached gondola, higher and higher. . .

Standard scenarios of twenty-first-century spaceflight generally depict bigger, faster, and more
efficient spaceships—extensions of the technologies
already familiar today. Too many spaceflight
prophets fail to take into account the likely advent
and radical effect of completely new ideas.

One such idea, slowly gaining recognition, may
revolutionize space-station architecture, Earth-space-
Earth transportation techniques, space propulsion
and power systems, and—as in this imaginative
vignette—interplanetary probes. The idea is space
tethers.

As applied to space missions, *tether* means simply
a long line connecting two or more space vehicles.
The line can be tens or hundreds of kilometers in
length. Current materials—such as Kevlar—can be
applied to building tethers, with potentially revolutionary applications to space operations in the near
future.

In 1983, NASA and Italy's space agency signed
an agreement to fly a joint mission in 1987 involving
an Italian spacecraft and an American tether sys-

tem. The spacecraft is to be reeled out 100 kilometers from the shuttle, like bait at the end of a fishing line. The "bait" will be cast upward to investigate ionospheric physics, and downward to make long-term measurements of the earth's upper atmosphere.

The TSS, or tethered-satellite system, consists of the deployed payload, a boom extending upward like a fishing rod out of the shuttle's payload bay, and a reel assembly with tens of kilometers of cable. During the initial deployment from the mother ship and during the final minutes of retrieval, small jets on the payload keep it in the proper position.

Suppose the payload now hangs beneath the shuttle, closer to the earth. The tether in this case does not bear the subsatellite's entire weight. In fact, the line provides only a small fraction of the force keeping the subsatellite up. The reason is that the payload is "almost" in orbit—that is, it is going only a little bit more slowly than a free-flying satellite would be going at that same altitude. The tension on the space tether provides only enough force to compensate for this small energy deficit.

In general, two tethered objects may be in a stable orbit, but the lower object is flying slightly more slowly than a stable free-flying satellite would, and the upper object is flying slightly more rapidly. The center of mass of the tethered system, located somewhere along the cable between them, is flying at precisely the correct velocity for a satellite at that altitude, whether it's a point mass or an extended structure.

Now imagine that the tether is suddenly cut. In

an instant the lower satellite becomes a free-flying object without sufficient speed to maintain its orbit. So it falls into an orbit closer to Earth. But the upper object has an excess of energy over that needed merely to maintain a circular orbit at its altitude. So its orbit rises somewhat. The physics of the situation make possible an amazing array of applications for space tethers.

Here is one. A space shuttle today burns substantial amounts of rocket propellants to perform its "de-orbit burn" at the end of a mission. A decade from now an American space station will need to carry a significant amount of rocket propellant to boost its altitude against the slow orbital decay caused by aerodynamic drag. If a space station were tethered to a shuttle, both loads of propellant would be unnecessary. In orbit, the station would unreel the shuttle toward Earth. The winged vehicle would hang there until the end of the mission. Then, unlatching the tether would drop the shuttle toward home. At the same time, the space station would rise to higher orbit—all for free.

From a physicist's perspective, this spectacular payoff is the result of a simple trade. While momentum of the entire system is conserved, the tether allows some momentum to be transferred from the space shuttle (which then falls out of orbit without needing rocket fuel) to the space station (which then receives a routine orbital boost without using any fuel either). There is a cost, of course: the weight and complexity of the tether system. But recent studies have clearly demonstrated the cost-effectiveness of this strategy.

Another interesting possibility arises if a long tether is made of an electrical conductor. It then becomes a wire moving through a magnetic field (Earth's). The movement makes it an electrical generator if a closed circuit can be established. As described by NASA futurist Ivan Bekey, "If electrons are collected by a metallized film balloon at the upper end and ejected at the lower end by an electron gun, a current will flow downward through the wire." For a 100-kilometer cable, the current will be about 15,000 volts at 5 amps, producing a net power to the payload of 70 kilowatts.

But such concepts pale to insignificance next to the notion of dropping a tether from a satellite to Earth's surface. If the "anchor" in space were in a synchronous 24-hour orbit, 40,000 kilometers above the equator, the cable would be attached to a spot on the surface—perhaps Mount Kilimanjaro, or somewhere in Sri Lanka (à la Arthur C. Clarke's novel *Fountains of Paradise*), or in the city limits of Quito, Ecuador, or Singapore. Since the cable would have to support its own weight, it would have to be tapered, thin at the bottom and thick at the top. The required material strength is far beyond anything yet available.

The idea for such a skyhook has been around for decades. Yuri Artsutanov first mentioned it in print, in a Soviet magazine in 1960, and it has subsequently been independently reinvented several times. It's also been called a space elevator (transportation would be by "funicular railway" up the line) or, more in keeping with the semilegendary nature of the structure, a beanstalk. And for the foreseeable future, it cannot be built on Earth.

There are still other variations on the idea. Amazingly, they are entirely feasible with such modern materials as Kevlar.

Many military pilots owe their lives to a simple skyhook device that plucked them out of enemy territory when their planes had been shot down. Downed fliers released a helium balloon attached to a long cable that was hooked at the other end to a harness around their bodies. A rescue aircraft with a pronged fork extending below and ahead of it made passes at the balloon, and once the aircraft caught hold of the balloon, the pilots were pulled off the ground and to safety.

In the Arctic, bush pilots have perfected a trick for dropping off and picking up mail, supplies, and other cargoes for isolated settlements. The aircraft lets out a bucket on a long line, then begins flying a tight circle around the bucket, which drops to a target area. While the bucket bounces around, ground personnel grab it, retrieve its contents, and load any return cargo. The exchange complete, the aircraft flies off straight and reels in the bucket.

These operations are feasible with space-based tethers. Some are difficult on Earth, with its deep gravity well—the deepest of any world in the solar system on whose surface humans will ever walk. But such techniques are extremely attractive for smaller worlds such as Mars.

For bigger worlds a "rolling skyhook" may be one

answer. This approach, originated by John McCarthy, of Stanford, and elaborated by Hans Moravec, involves a long free-flying tether orbiting the earth (or any planet) while also tumbling end over end. Its motion resembles that of a diameter on a rolling wheel, its center point remaining a fixed distance from the surface while each end arcs through a full circle. Whenever the tether is aligned exactly vertically, one end is touching the surface of the planet. The tumble rate is adjusted so that the tip of the tether appears to descend from the sky nearly vertically, come to a stop, and then accelerate back up into the sky. But the skyhook doesn't have to go all the way to the surface. It could pick up an airborne vehicle in midflight, whip it up into space, then release it.

A similar pickup-and-delivery system could help future planetary explorers retrieve soil samples from other planets. An interplanetary probe orbiting a target world reels out a long tether with a weighted "sample tube" at the far end. The tethered sampler device—perhaps containing a small, expendable guidance computer to guarantee a precise impact point—descends to the planet's surface, scoops up material, and is pulled back into space.

The sampler's descent and ascent must occur rapidly, as the mother ship holding the end of the tether passes overhead. For target planets with thick atmospheres, this presents a serious problem, because the atmosphere will slow the sampler or burn it up before it can reach the surface.

One solution is balloons. A short-lived robot

dropped untethered to the surface grabs the samples and loads them into a balloon gondola that is quickly dispatched to the upper levels of the atmosphere. There the package is snared by the descending skyhook and yanked out into space.

For target worlds such as Venus, the technological challenge of recovering surface samples has been awesome and intimidating, as long as mere rocket propulsion was considered. But as space engineers are learning, rockets aren't the only way to move mass through the solar system and to and from planetary surfaces: The success of future missions may hang by a tether.

KIDS IN ORBIT

By Barbara Rowes

Someday it could be the ultimate class trip. With little lunch pails in hand and parental permissions reluctantly signed, five-year-old future astronauts would actually ride the action course of the space shuttle *Challenger* for the first-grade space odyssey. "Since there are only seven seats aboard the shuttle and a couple of astronauts and mission specialists are bound to go along, we couldn't fly a whole first-grade class," says William O'Donnell, spokesman for the National Aeronautics and Space Administration. "I guess we'd have to carry one kid at a time."

Since June 21, when a NASA advisory council recommended sending civilians—including educators—into space at least one key issue has remained unresolved. Will the United States be the first to shoot kids into orbit? Well, muses O'Donnell, "we haven't said we're not taking kids. We've not set any age limits."

Far away in Mountain View, California, at NASA's

Ames Research Center, at least one key visionary in the space agency has long been dreaming of flying kids in space. It isn't a Steven Spielberg-style fantasy or the framework for a great new video game, but a creative approach to exploration by one of NASA's most imaginative administrators. "The idea is to start them off very young in space and maybe twenty years later send them up again," projects Joseph Sharp, deputy director of life sciences at Ames. "If you actually launch a four- or five-year-old aboard the space shuttle and tell him there's a good chance he will be going up when he gets older, you will create the time and inspiration to develop sensitive perceptions and a more meaningful understanding of the world. By nature, kids are inquisitive and receptive to new experiences. They may come up with refreshing insights more worldly adults have never even thought of. To discover totally the human dimensions of space, we need to fly not only people at the age of thirty-five but the little people of this planet at the age of five."

While Sharp has long been convinced of the invaluable contribution children could make to space exploration, NASA is not yet ready to lift the recent graduates of *Sesame Street*. "Eventually kids are bound to go," O'Donnell predicts, "but I don't think you'll see a five-year-old up there flying solo for at least the next one hundred years."

Still, at Ames, space scientists are slowly gearing up for the children's flights of tomorrow. A first major step in this direction has been taken by research scientist Emily Morey-Holton, who has investigated the effects of weightlessness on the bone formation of young rats. Zero g is potentially dangerous for immature animals, because weightlessness might disrupt growth patterns, she says.

"We don't really know the effect on young human beings, since we haven't done spaceflight simulations on children yet," observes Dr. Danielle Goldwater, NASA physician. On missions of long duration there is some evidence raising concern about the sustained health of the young. "Long-term exposure to weightlessness might lead to a decrease in cardiac output, decrease in muscle mass and muscle strength, and even possibly cessation of bone formation," observes Dr. Goldwater.

For brief space trips, Goldwater says, "children should adapt quickly to new environments such as weightlessness. And at least from a neurological perspective they should be able to readapt quickly to Earth after a shuttle flight."

But not every child watching the reruns of *Star Trek* will be eligible to follow the footsteps of Captain Kirk into space. "We're going to interview potential candidates to make sure they are mature enough," O'Donnell promises. "You will have to undergo psychological or mental testing whether you are a kid or not. We don't want to take anybody along who will get too excited under stress."

According to Sharp, a psychologist, some children four and five years old appear to be born astronauts. "They are naturally cool in crisis, sensitive to new experiences, and capable of integrating their strange encounters in a dynamic context. And I think we will be able to identify these children out of a classroom. It is like discovering young Arthur Clarkes." In fact, many kids of this breed are already rising to the surface.

Over the years, kids have written thousands of letters to NASA. The majority want only the kid stuff—photographs and printed information. "But a few have really impressed me," admits Sharp, who is notoriously cool himself. "They have written again and again over the years asking probing questions and offering suggestions that reflect an intense involvement in the space program."

Children aren't the only crusaders for putting children in orbit. A young mother from Palo Alto, California, recently wrote NASA: "I have a three-year-old son who is determined to become an astronaut. . . . What I would like to find out is what information or material you have available for grammar-school children and what activities you have available for kids at your center.

"I realize three sounds awfully young, but I am planning ahead to the day when kids blast off." So is NASA.

SPACE AGING

By Bernard Dixon

Space exploration seems to have little in common with geriatrics, the study of diseases that afflict the elderly. While the human race devotes its attention to one set of challenges, however, other, seemingly unrelated areas reap unexpected benefits. An unpopular and neglected specialty, geriatrics could profit immensely from yet another spinoff of man's newest frontier science.

When Spacelab went into action aboard the space shuttle, the crew was monitored intensively for signs of bone deterioration. Since the earlier Gemini flights, we have known that astronauts' bones become thin and brittle after prolonged weightlessness. These changes are similar to what occurs in old persons suffering from osteoporosis.

This syndrome is caused by gradual loss of both the

organic framework of bone and the calcium and phosphorus that bond it together. Osteoporosis makes the elderly much more prone to fractures, particularly in their hipbones. Immobilization of a limb during healing of a fracture is yet another cause of osteoporosis. But "softening of the bone" is merely one of the degenerative changes that accompany aging.

"Picturesque but inappropriate" is the phrase the *British Medical Journal* (1980, *1*, 1288) used recently to describe man's body in space. Floating around weightless inside a spacecraft, a human being simply doesn't need appendages. The physiological changes that have been observed under these conditions indicate a steady reduction in limb size. The legs of space dwellers, for example, might well evolve into purposeless masses of protuberant fibers.

The Gemini and Apollo pioneers did not, of course, suffer such a fate. But x-ray studies made on these astronauts, and on those in Soviet Soyuz missions, show a definite loss of bone structure. The effect is apparent even during short periods away from Earth's gravity. According to the *British Medical Journal* report, this loss amounts to about four grams of calcium per month. This represents 0.3 percent to 0.4 percent of the body's total calcium. Even more alarming, the loss is most marked in those vital long bones that support the human frame. Small wonder that this problem will be closely studied during the forthcoming shuttle flights.

Some of the most disturbing evidence obtained so far came from the 84-day *Skylab 4* mission. The heel bones of two of the three crewmen decreased in density, and tactics designed to prevent the disappearance of calcium were ineffective. Neither vigorous exercise nor a special diet had any effect on the rate at which the heel bones deteriorated. Moreover, measurements of the hormones that control bone-producing cells indicated no changes, affording no clues toward possible preventive measures.

But this problem *will* be solved. When it is, the new knowledge should prove invaluable to clinicians on Earth treating victims of osteoporosis. Already observations on the reversibility of bone changes in astronauts who have returned to Earth have encouraged doctors to make gradual increases in the amount of weight they put upon such patients. Longitudinal stress is apparently important for bones to retain their vitality.

To complicate matters, bone also responds to forces imposed by its muscular attachments. This was why NASA physiologists devised exercise programs for the *Skylab 4* team. But in zero gravity the nerves that control these muscles appear to change, too. This means that the muscular forces applied to an astronaut's bones, even during a vigorous workout, are less than they would be on Earth. The subtle relationship among exercise, nervous activity, and the loss of minerals from bone is highly relevant to the management of osteoporosis in old people.

Even if the space program were nonexistent, a solution to osteoporosis would undoubtedly be found—probably later, rather than sooner. There is nothing like a new and unprecedented challenge to spur the human intellect on to greater feats. Such is the nature of progress that we must send man into space in order to conquer one of the most common causes of immobility in old people.

RETURN TO THE MOON

By James E. Oberg

Late in 1972, the last man on the moon promised to return. "I take man's last steps from the surface for some time to come, but we believe not too long into the future," astronaut Gene Cernan mused out loud as he paused before climbing his spacecraft's ladder. "We leave the moon as we came, and, God willing, as we shall return, with peace and hope for all mankind. Godspeed from the crew of *Apollo Seventeen!*"

Because of continuing shortages of funds, imagination, and boldness, the thought of sending human beings back to the moon has receded further and further since that moment. Ironically earthmen are probably further from landing on the moon now than they were when the first *Sputnik* was launched more than a quarter-century ago. Then it took less than 12 years to accomplish the first landing mission. Now the idea that astronauts might return to the moon within 12 years, by 1995, is generally considered absurd and unrealistic.

Do not despair, however. Many historians of exploration, who tend to take the long views of things, believe that lunar development may follow the Antarctic model. In this view, the Apollo landings were the equivalent of the Roald Amundsen/Robert Scott South Pole races of the early 1900s. They were followed by flights over the pole a few decades later. But it was not until 1947 that Operation Deep Freeze began to set up permanent scientific stations on the coast of Antarctica and, in 1957, at the South Pole itself.

The moon may also be explored in progressive phases spread over three or four decades. New, unmanned orbital missions may complete mapping and geochemical surveys within the next ten years. They could be followed near the turn of the century by one or more permanent scientific stations.

By then the space shuttle and shuttle-derived vehicles, together with upper stages developed for use near Earth (the orbital transfer vehicles), will make the expeditions feasible and cheap; a fraction of the original price of Apollo—which cost about $24 billion—should buy a huge expansion of capability.

The foundations for such a lunar program are now being laid by half a dozen groups of specialists and space enthusiasts. In Houston in early 1983, while the fourteenth Lunar and Planetary Science Conference convened to analyze recent results from interplanetary studies, the first meetings to organize these efforts were held.

In what they called the Lunar Initiative, space scientists at the NASA Johnson Space Center, in Houston, recommended in 1982 that a permanent lunar base be established during the first decade of the next century. To help work out by 1990 where and how such a facility should be built—and what its purpose would be—the scientists further suggested that a series of unmanned lunar missions be prepared. The first step, which should occur as soon as possible, would put a half-ton survey satellite into lunar orbit; it would be followed by remote-controlled rovers on the lunar surface.

Support for a moon base has appeared from a number of unexpected places. In May, 1982, two physicists from the Los Alamos National Laboratory issued their own independent plan. According to Drs. Paul Keaton and Eric Gelfand, a 24-person facility could be built by the end of the century for considerably less than was spent on the entire Apollo program in the 1960s. Keaton and Gelfand called for "a national commitment for an International Research Laboratory on the moon," adding that "a vigorous civilian program like that proposed here is our best guarantee that outer space will be used to strengthen our economy and address basic problems on Earth." This advocacy by scientists with no traditional ties to space research seemed to take on additional significance because the White House science adviser is a former Los Alamos official. (He reportedly gave a "positive response" to the proposal—"so long as no money was involved.") Other nuclear scientists throughout the nation, particularly Dr. Edward Teller (who is best known for his work on the hydrogen bomb), subsequently voiced their support for such a proposal.

A research base on the moon, the Johnson Space

Center scientists foresaw, offers major benefits both to astronomy, particularly radio astronomy and solar physics, and to planetary geology. But they cited more far-reaching, and at the same time more immediate, potential benefits in the moon's natural resources and in its promise for national security.

One critical resource the moon might provide is water to support operations in space. Because the moon's axis of rotation is nearly perpendicular to its path around the sun, there should be deep craters in the polar regions; sunlight undoubtedly has not penetrated them for billions of years. Water in the form of "dirty ice" should have gathered there from passing comets or outbursts from the moon's interior.

It is to find this water that scientists have long urged the launch of an unmanned prospecting satellite to orbit around the lunar poles. "Its scientific value is not questioned, and its relatively low cost is well-known," Dr. Wendell W. Mendell, of NASA, points out. Launching the probe would require only one quarter of the cargo capacity of a space shuttle mission, and it could be sent aloft as early as 1989—if NASA persuades the government to fund it.

Astronauts could use lunar water instead of carrying a full supply all the way from Earth. The presence of water would also make it possible to make rocket propellant—liquid hydrogen and oxygen—on the moon, which would further halve the operational costs of lunar missions.

Some scientists have also cited the benefits of a moon base for national security. "We see the moon as the ultimate high ground to protect near-Earth space for the benefit of the nation," says NASA geochemist

Jeffrey Warner, in Houston. Lunar facilities could be heavily shielded and attached to bedrock foundations, making them much less vulnerable to attack and easier to control than military reconnaissance and communications satellites.

Because it is so far from Earth, the moon makes much less sense as a weapons platform, except perhaps for the defense of equipment in space. Nonetheless, Soviet propagandists have accused American researchers at the Redstone Arsenal, in Huntsville, Alabama, and at Strategic Air Command headquarters, at Offutt Field, Nebraska, of plotting to base laser weapons there in violation of international treaties. Spokesmen for both agencies have denied the Soviet allegations.

Transportation to and from the moon is not a particularly difficult undertaking. Manned voyages to the moon 20 years hence will almost certainly use space shuttle-type technology. By then the American space fleet should include two new boosters: a "heavy-lift vehicle," built of shuttle engines and tanks and able to haul up to 180,000 pounds into orbit, and a high-energy upper stage, which may be based on the liquid-fuel technology of the Centaur rocket.

To get to the moon, several orbital-transfer stages could be lifted for assembly in parking orbit, either by several shuttle missions or by one launch of the unmanned heavy-lift vehicle. Another shuttle launch would carry the lunar landing stage itself—probably a modified transfer vehicle——and the crew cabin. Two orbital-transfer stages would push the core vehicle toward the moon, then return to Earth orbit for reuse. The core unit would park itself above the moon while the lunar crew made the round trip to the surface. The entire craft would then return to Earth.

By then, "aerobraking" probably will have been perfected to ease the return to a parking orbit. The technique will use a balloon to act as a "drag brake" in Earth's upper atmosphere. This will slow the returning space vehicle enough to let it enter a stable orbit—but not so much that it will fall back to Earth. This would allow the lunar ship to travel without a heavy heat shield; a space shuttle could pick the vehicle up in parking orbit and protect it in the payload bay for the fiery reentry.

Manned lunar flight may depend heavily on a permanent refueling station near the moon. A research platform in its own right, it would orbit a few hundred miles from the lunar surface, according to most American proposals. It appears that the Soviet Union may erect such a way station by the end of this decade: Soviet studies suggest that the best location is at the so-called first Lagrange [L-1] point—one of five sites where a space platform will remain permanently in the same position with respect to both Earth and the moon. In theory, a platform at L-1 would wander a bit, but a recent Soviet report claims that the platform could be held in place by burning only a little rocket propellant.

Wherever it is placed, it will make lunar exploration much easier and cheaper. Because the stages are reusable, and because their original development expenses have been absorbed by earlier missions, such a program would be very inexpensive. Apollo costs were comparatively high because an entire space transportation system had to be built from scratch. Returning to the moon will be relatively inexpensive because most of the equipment will already have been bought and paid for.

"We won't go back to the moon until it's easy to go," one top space official noted as the Apollo program drew to a close. Twenty years from now it will have become easy. Political decisions in the next ten years will determine whether the Apollo program was merely a brief interlude in the long, dead history of the moon or a prelude to a lively, profitable, and permanent colonization at the turn of the century.

RETURN TO EARTH

By Nick Engler

In April 1980, when cosmonaut Valeri Ryumin entered outer space for the second time in as many years, his body immediately began to change. The transition from a one-gravity environment to zero gravity affected every part of the cosmonaut's metabolism, but Ryumin remained healthy, comfortable, and unconcerned. As he adjusted to the tedious routine of another half year aboard *Salyut 6*, he radioed mission control at Yuri Gagarin Space Center, in Zvezdnyi Gorodok (Stellar City), that he had "hardly noticed the changes."

Ryumin's favorable physiological reaction echoed the experience of his first six-month mission a year earlier, which set a record for the longest time anyone had ever spent in space. This second trip was the much-hoped-for duplication of space acclimatization data. "It [was evident that the success of the previous flight] was not just an accident or good luck," Dr. Gerald A. Soffen, director of life sciences at NASA, said. "It really proves that humans are engineered quite well for spaceflight."

The major aim of the Salyut program has been to monitor and control the cosmonauts' adaptation process. Physicians are experimenting with regimens of diet and exercise calculated to keep a person fit on Earth without interfering with his adaptation to space. "Our basic goal is to retain the adaptability to both environments," says academician Oleg Georgievich Gazenko, who designed and monitored the biomedical experiments aboard *Salyut*. "During spaceflight our cosmonauts take countermeasures to remind [their metabolic systems] of the typical features of life on Earth.

"Upon leaving Earth, the spaceman is helpless," Gazenko says. "He loses his reactions and responses to his native environment. In a word, once man becomes adapted to space, he loses his ability to return to Earth." Although Ryumin remained vigorous and in fine condition during both spaceflights, he could neither stand nor walk when he touched down.

The space experience alters almost the entire human physiology, from the shape of a man's face to the density of the cartilage in his heel. Most of these changes are subtle, but they are so pervasive that the overall effect is amazingly complex. Because spaceflights of long duration are still new to human experience, no one knows what the potential hazards of moving from Earth into outer space and back are.

The changes in the body that accompany spaceflight are not pathological. Dr. Stanley R. Mohler, director of the Aerospace Medicine Training Program at Wright State University, in Dayton, Ohio, believes everything that happens to the human body in space is as it should be. "The normal adaptation process takes over," says Dr. Mohler. "We're looking at a continuous spectrum of environments with Earth somewhere in the middle. In space we simply adapt to a different level along this continuum." The return to Earth, however, necessitates readaptation.

The considerable environmental shifts that a space traveler encounters on the way up are an increase in radiation and a decrease in gravity. Of the two, the less troublesome, for our consideration, is radiation. Astronauts can simply return home if their space vehicles become too hot. When missions stretch out to one or more years, moderate doses of the amino acid methionine may be used to control the effects of exposure to higher-than-normal radiation. Future space stations will probably incorporate storm cellars, heavily shielded areas where the inhabitants can wait out radiation storms produced by sudden bursts of solar activity.

Weightlessness, however, is another matter. On Earth human beings expend one third of their total energy in overcoming gravity. In zero gravity muscles shrink and metabolism slows down. The heart does less work and becomes smaller. The gravity-compensating curve of the spine unbends and human bodies lengthen appreciably. Body fluids and minerals adjust to lower levels. Some of these changes occur quickly; others occur over several months. And some, such as demineralization, which begin immediately, continue for more than half a year.

Most space biologists believe the human body eventually reaches homeostasis, a stable physiological balance with the space environment. But this condition may not be as desirable as it would sound. If the skeletal, muscular, and cardiovascular systems become completely homeostatic, they could easily degenerate to a point where Soviet cosmonauts and American astronauts may not be able to return home safely. "Our Earthman," says Gazenko, "should not become completely a spaceman."

As each Salyut mission generates a better understanding of space biology and space physiology, each crew returns from orbit in better condition than the one preceding. After the first 96-day mission, cosmonauts found it hard to lift a teacup or to turn a radio dial. The second crew fared better, even after 140 days in space, by keeping in shape with rigorous exercise and vacuum suits that forced their blood to circulate at Earth pressure.

But the two long-duration flights, lasting 175 and 185 days, respectively, suggest that Soviet space scientists are following the right track. Both cosmonaut crews were able to adapt quickly and work comfortably in the *Salyut* environment and return to Earth with no lingering problems. Within a few days of touching down, they could stand and walk normally. Ryumin, who has accumulated almost a year of time in space, appears to have suffered no ill effects. His ability to adapt more easily during his second six-month space tour indicates that adaptation can be a learned response, like any other activity.

But as these pioneers go blazing trails back and forth between Earth and orbit, what will happen to succeeding generations of space colonists? Will children born and raised in space be able to return to

Earth? Though our understanding of the matter is far from perfect, the data we have gleaned from *Salyut* spaceflights allow space physicians to speculate.

According to Mohler and his colleagues, these children probably won't be born into an environment resembling that on Earth. There is a good chance they will grow up in high background radiation and total or near weightlessness. The radiation of space can be diminished with substantial shielding, but it cannot be completely screened. There always will be secondary radiation from the shield itself.

As for weightlessness, Mohler says, "There is a consensus among space physicians that it's doubtful space inhabitants would want to reintroduce anything as debilitating as gravity after adapting to life without it. Under these conditions, children will develop along radically different lines compared to their Earth ancestors. Radiation will increase the likelihood of mutations, and some of these could be passed on to future generations." He suggests that *Homo cosmos* may eventually become a species distinct from *Homo sapiens*.

Even without radiation, the biological disparity will be enormous. Mohler predicts that children born in zero gravity will have elongated bodies and spindly limbs. Their skulls might have a different shape; their faces will be rounder. All their organs and bones will be smaller. Upon reaching adulthood, these individuals will have extremely fine muscle control and excellent coordination, but they will seem frail in comparison to the weakest Earthlings.

While the Russians are actively searching for a solution to facilitate cosmonauts in the readaptation process, NASA at present, has no funding for permanently manned space stations. When NASA is financially able to build a space center, it can use the information already obtained by *Salyut* to bring back to Earth those human beings who have spent long periods in outer space and those people who were born out there. One proposal to help space-bred colonists who have to travel between Earth and its outposts is the halfway house, where people's adaptive reflexes will be stimulated and directed by methods we are just beginning to develop. But first funding must come from Congress to further the study on the ways Earthlings can return comfortably to their home planet.

PART NINE: INDUSTRY ON HIGH

"Hitch your wagon to a star."
—Ralph Waldo Emerson

CONQUEST OF SPACE

By Gerard K. O'Neill

Trends that cannot be reversed make the decades ahead very dangerous—potentially catastrophic—here on our planet. Our land area and mineral resources are limited and can never be extended. They are being pressed more and more severely by a world population that will double in 40 years and rise to three times today's population 30 years after that.

We human beings are problem solvers by nature, and our response to those threats should not be a wringing of hands but an exploration of the ways to solve serious resource and environmental problems. We must find unlimited low-cost energy and make it available to everyone, not just the nations favored with large fuel reserves. And we must tap mineral resources to sustain new industries without damaging Earth's environment. There are limited short-term solutions to some of the world's major problems. But the only viable long-term solution is to begin using the energy and material resources that lie beyond our finite planet—in space itself. That will be a healthy development for another reason: It will draw us outward, encouraging the human settlement of space. For those who already look toward the space colonies that will result from space industry, the immediate question is, What form will that industry take?

If research under way continues to meet its goals, we could establish a substantial industry in high orbit, 200,000 miles above Earth, before the end of this century. Within decades the products of space industry could exceed 1 million tons per year—small compared to the great industries of Earth but worth more than $100 billion annually. The raw materials to feed that industry would come from the surface of the moon. Lunar materials would be separated into pure elements in high orbit, where constant sunlight would supply the energy for extracting metals and fabricating them into finished products. At first many of the workers for that industry would remain on Earth, monitoring and controlling robotic machines through radio and television links. A few, mainly highly skilled troubleshooters, would live in orbit for duty tours of six months or more.

The initial products of industry in space will be solar-power satellites, giant arrays that collect the bountiful sunlight of high orbit and convert it to radio energy. That radio energy will then be sent to Earth for conversion to electricity, ultimately providing our civilization with all the electrical power we need, *without* polluting planet Earth's biosphere.

Up until now, of course, there has been just one valuable product of commercial activities in space: information. Satellites equipped with sensors produce data on large-scale weather patterns, including tropical storms. And satellites orbiting just above Earth's atmosphere use sensitive television cameras to take pictures of the land. From that detailed imagery computers can pick out subtle color changes, which indicate the presence of oil, metals, and fresh or salt water beneath the earth's surface. Satellites also relay information from one ground location to another or to entire continents. There are now more than 100 of these satellites, and more of them rocket into orbit every month.

The success of information satellites—and the dearth of any other space industry—can be explained by a fundamental fact. Information has great value, but it weighs nothing. The cost of launching a satellite from the earth to geostationary orbit (an orbit in which a satellite stays at a fixed point in the sky as seen from Earth) is currently about $18,000 per pound of satellite weight. But once a satellite is up there, it can produce or relay information for virtually nothing. For such established information products as telephone messages or TV program time, a relay satellite can pay back its entire cost of manufacture and launch in a year or less.

As soon as we look beyond the area of information, though, commercial opportunities in space become far more limited because we are up against the costs of lifting raw materials into orbit. Rates to low-Earth orbit for shuttle cargo range from $1,250 per pound to $11,000 per pound. The low figure is for high-density cargo in bulk. The high figure is more typical of shuttle payloads so far and applies to complex low-density objects, of which satellites are the prime example. Any product made of materials that must be brought from Earth on the shuttle, processed in orbit, and returned to Earth for sale must include that high price of lift as an item in its production cost. Pharmaceuticals, which NASA has targeted for early commercial production, are among the few products on Earth that sell for such rarefied prices.

If the industrialization of space is to play a significant role in the total economic picture, it must compete in one of the major markets on Earth. It cannot do so in most of the new, high-technology markets, including electronics and robotics, because such products couldn't be manufactured more efficiently in the space environment than in factories on Earth.

Yet there is one large-scale market for which space industry makes sense: energy, which, like information, can be transmitted without the flow of materials. More than five years ago power at a level of 100 kilowatts was transmitted by radio waves over a distance of one mile in tests at Goldstone, California. While that transmission would have to be scaled up by 10,000 to 100,000 times to reach the power level of a typical electric-generating station, the feat would require no new physics. The energy beam would be larger in area but would not have to be more intense.

In the late 1960s Peter Glaser, of the Arthur D. Little international consulting company, in Cambridge, Massachusetts, suggested transmitting energy from space. Large satellites fitted with slow cells could be located in geostationary orbit. There they would convert sunlight to radio waves, which could be beamed back to the earth. The idea made sense. Sunlight is an intense, reliable resource in high orbit, available 24 hours per day during most of the year. Only in the spring and autumn is a geostationary array eclipsed and then only for predictable periods of less than 40 minutes each midnight.

Unfortunately, Glaser's good idea never gained acceptance, and the problem lies with its friends as well as its enemies. NASA and its aerospace contractors latched on to the Glaser plan as a wonderful reason for a massive new space program. Engineers drew up designs for monster versions of the shuttle—wholly reusable space planes that could carry payloads of several hundred tons. The giant rocket planes were to weigh 20,000 tons at liftoff—ten times as much as today's shuttle.

Companies working on NASA study contracts drew up plans for solar-power satellites that would be as light as possible. Their components could be lifted from Earth in those giant supershuttles and assembled in orbit. The program planners worked up a schedule of several flights per day for the huge rocket planes. That schedule would have had to be maintained for a year if even one power satellite were to be installed.

During the Seventies many studies of solar-power satellites were carried out. In the most comprehensive investigation, the Department of Energy (DOE) spent three years and about $15 million to explore the concept. About two thirds of the funding went into environmental-impact studies. Somewhat to its own surprise the DOE found no serious environmental impact from the transmission of energy by radio beams. There are two reasons for the clean bill of health. First, the intensity of the radio beam was only about the same as the intensity of sunlight. Second, at the frequency of the radio waves, the packets of energy in the beam—in physics terms, the quanta—were only 0.001 percent as strong as those of sunlight and therefore much too weak to damage living tissue. There had never been a question of danger to humans, because the receiving antenna would be mounted on posts above ground level and inside a fenced enclosure. But no one could prevent birds or insects from flying through the beam. The DOE-sponsored experiments found that the radio waves had no effect on birds. And in another experiment no effect was found on even so subtle a natural phenomenon as the dancing pattern of bees.

Despite the fundamental attractiveness of the solar-power satellite, it was shot down by the National Research Council (NRC) of the National Academy of Sciences. The NRC's negative conclusion resulted from its analysis of economics. With evidence of escalating shuttle-flight costs fresh in mind, the reviewers concluded that the supershuttles could never operate as inexpensively as the people at NASA hoped. They also refused to believe that solar cells, the basic energy-conversion mechanisms for power satellites, could ever be made cheaply enough. The NRC study concluded that power satellites could probably be built and would probably be acceptable environmentally, but that they could never compete economically with coal or nuclear electric power.

In my view, that entire sad history, played out over more than a decade, was a classic example of asking the wrong question and getting a useless answer. Although I believe the power-satellite concept is fun-

335

damentally sound, NASA's approach to making it happen collided head-on with basic physics. The energy cost of lifting a power satellite into geostationary orbit is huge because we on Earth are at the bottom of a gravity well that is 4,000 miles deep. Fighting gravity forced NASA's designers into two traps, One, the direct cost of lift, was obvious. The other was a little less apparent. Because the designers had to fight those high lift costs, they proposed lightening the satellites by using complex, costly designs and exotic, equally costly materials. For example, in converting solar energy to electricity, they had to use lightweight but extremely expensive pure-crystal silicon solar cells. They could not use the much less expensive amorphous-silicon solar cells, because those would have been heavier per watt of power. Nor could they use heavy turbogenerators, producing electricity from sunlight concentrated by mirrors, though that would have been a relatively simple, low-technology solution to the energy-conversion problem. But if NASA got the wrong answer by asking the wrong question, what is the right question?

The right question, I suspect, is, What is the simplest, lowest-risk design for a solar-power satellite that could be made out of materials already at the top of Earth's gravity well? We have a large mine of materials up there, and it has already been assayed more carefully than all but a few mines on Earth. The mine is the surface of the moon. From the Apollo project, we know that the material of the lunar surface is about 30 percent metals by weight, 20 percent silicon, and 40 percent oxygen. The metals and silicon are just right for building a solar-power satellite, and oxygen is the "gasoline of space," constituting about 86 percent of the weight of rocket propellant. Continuing to ask what we hope are right questions, we should explore methods for building solar-power satellites from lunar materials within the limitations of the space-shuttle transportation system.

In the past five years one organization has been working quietly and effectively to ask those right questions and to arrive at sensible answers. The organization, which I founded in 1977, with the help of some friends, is the Space Studies Institute (SSI), a nonprofit corporation located in Princeton, New Jersey, just outside the Princeton University campus. The institute is supported by donations from thousands of members; it neither asks for nor accepts government money. Unlike most space-related organizations, SSI does not agitate for governmental action. Instead, it has taken on the responsibility for directly funding basic scientific and engineering research. That has kept SSI in a relatively low profile compared with most other space-related private groups, but it has also made it effective and consistent. Our organization's purpose: to find a practical approach to satellite power and the more general goal of space industry, beginning the peaceful human conquest of the high frontier.

Soon after SSI's formation, we held a series of workshops to develop a cost-effective plan for the development of space industry. The workshop ground rules included staying within the limitations of the shuttle, which can lift only about 29 tons of cargo to orbit on each flight. We developed a scenario for space industry through those workshops.

Pilot plants, remote-controlled and small enough to be transported by today's rockets, would carry out the key industrial functions: material transport, extraction of pure elements, and fabrication of finished products. The pilot plants would be of several kinds. One would scoop up lunar-surface soil and sinter it with heat and pressure into solid, durable spheres. The second would transport the spheres of lunar soil to a point in high orbit above the moon. A third would process the lunar soil into pure elements, alloys, and composites. And the fourth would fabricate those industrial materials into finished products. The products would be the heavier, simpler components of more pilot plants identical to the first. In that way space industry could grow geometrically, 1, 2, 4, 8 . . . , through eight doublings, until 256 pilot plants would have been built. That scheme would provide us with sufficient industrial capacity to build solar-power satellites.

The results of the SSI workshops were published in two articles in the journal *Astronautics and Aeronautics*. According to those articles an investment of $7 billion or $8 billion over a five-year period, comparable to the investment that built the Alaska pipeline, would be enough to produce about one power satellite per year. Each power satellite could be sold to a nation or a utility for about $10 billion. And each could supply the earth with continuous electric power equal to the output of ten nuclear plants. The potential world market for power satellites that undersell coal and nuclear-power plants is well over $200 billion a year. During the course of our workshops, we also reasoned that two other products, less complex than power satellites, could be marketed in the short term: liquid oxygen, for use as rocket propellant, and raw lunar soil, excellent for shielding orbital space stations and factories from cosmic radiation.

In a separate research effort, Hannes Alfven, an adviser to SSI, suggested that there might be asteroidal material trapped in the earth's orbit around the sun by the combined gravitational forces of those two bodies. It was easy to calculate the energy cost of retrieving that material, and it was very low—about 0.05 percent of the energy cost for lifting materials out of Earth's gravity well to the same high orbit. It was far more difficult to decide whether asteroids in that orbit could have remained trapped since the formation of the solar system, given the perturbations of all the other planets. Under an SSI grant to Princeton University, Scott Dunbar studied the problem mathematically and concluded that despite all perturbations, asteroidal materials could very probably still be within Earth's orbit. Dunbar received his Ph.D. from Princeton on the basis of that research. Then he received an NRC fellowship to work with Eugene Shoemaker and Eleanor Helin, at Caltech, in part to search for that material with the large Schmidt telescope at Mount Palomar.

Whether the raw materials for space industry come from the moon or from trapped asteroids, they must be separated into pure elements for most industrial uses. In 1981 SSI made a substantial grant to Rockwell International, the builders of the space shuttle. Under that grant Rockwell's Robert Waldron measured the key reactions for separation of lunar minerals into pure aluminum, iron, titanium, silicon,

339

oxygen, and other elements. Waldron's results indicate that a processing plant in space or on the moon could process roughly 100 times its own weight in soil each year and that very few chemical materials would have to be brought from the earth to keep such a processing plant running.

Although our energy cost for bringing materials from the moon to an orbital industrial site would be only 5 percent of the cost of bringing them from Earth, we would still need a machine to carry out that transport. For the past several years SSI has funded development of the "mass-driver," an electromagnetic catapult. In a mass-driver, electric current is pulsed through coils of aluminum wire, generating a magnetic field. This field accelerates a moving coil of wire, called a "bucket," which carries a sphere of sintered lunar material that's about the size and weight of a baseball. The material then leaves the bucket and accelerates toward its destination, a precise point in high orbit above the moon. There the sintered lunar material enters a very simple collector that has a closed cylindrical tube at one end.

The mass-driver work took a big step forward in May 1983, when Les Snively, of Princeton, completed the newest model—Mass-Driver III—according to a computer-design program that I had written. Mass-Driver III models the first half-meter of a fully operational lunar machine, which would be about 160 meters long. It is a simple device consisting of 20 circular drive coils, each 40 centimeters in diameter and about as thick as a bicycle tire. Stacked against one another, they form a hollow cylinder. Inside the cylinder the bucket coil is free to move. When currents are discharged through the drive coils in a precise time sequence, they produce strong magnetic fields that accelerate the bucket and also guide it on the centerline of the cylinder. Functioning at a fraction of full power, Mass-Driver III gave its payload carrier an acceleration of 1,100 g, enough to go from a standstill to 250 miles per hour in 0.01 second. Full-power tests should see the machine accelerate a payload to its design goal of 1,800 g. That acceleration will bring the payload carrier from a standstill to 300 miles per hour in 0.007 second.

Building on its successful track record, SSI will be funding second-generation development in key research areas during the next several years. Now that Mass-Driver III has proven the accuracy of the computer program by which it was designed, the program will be used to extend the design to the full length of the lunar machine, or 160 meters. The acceleration of Mass-Driver III is enough to bring payloads to a speed of 5,400 miles per hour, the escape speed from the moon, within just 160 meters. In addition, chemical-separation technology will be brought to the pilot-plant state. And SSI will soon be requesting proposals from aerospace companies for solar-power satellites that can be built from lunar materials. If we at SSI maintain our research schedule, by 1987 we'll be ready to publish a consistent, logical overall plan for establishing large-scale industry in space.

When the road to productive, high-volume space industry has been paved by research of that kind, it will be time for action. Nations or groups of corporations are among the possible players at that stage. In order to minimize risks, they will choose products that

341

the marketplace will still want five to ten years after investment begins. Given the pace of change in our technological society, only the most general products—energy, rocket propellants, and lunar soil for shielding space stations and colonies—will satisfy that condition. That is why SSI has targeted these three as the most viable products of space industry. On the fastest time scale, a nation or a consortium of industries could pick up the SSI plan and run with it in 1987. That would result in productivity in space at the 100,000-ton-per-year level by 1992. If events go more slowly SSI will broaden, deepen, and buttress its plan by constructing larger-scale demonstration experiments, until finally the investment opportunity becomes so tempting that a major investment source will commit itself to the development of space industry.

I cannot be sure who will be the first to create wealth out of the constant solar energy and the abundant materials waiting for us at the top of Earth's gravity well. But I am sure that the first group that succeeds will soon have its imitators. Whether the first program is led by Americans, Japanese, Europeans, or Russians, within a few short years all the major space powers will compete in production. When the scale of industry in space becomes large enough to demand the presence of thousands of people in high orbit for long periods, it will pay to devote some of the productivity to the building of space colonies for workers and their families. Those colonies, in the form of spheres one mile in circumference, will rotate slowly to provide Earth-normal gravity for their residents. The space colonists will grow their own food and derive all the energy they need from the sea of constant sunlight. By the middle years of the next century the first beachhead in space will have grown to include thousands of such colonies, each with a language and a cultural heritage drawn from a nation of Earth. Travel between Earth and its colonies will be as common by then as international travel is today. It will be a happy development for our tired and fragile planet when humanity's drive toward production and conquest is redirected outward onto that high frontier.

MADE IN SPACE

By Mark R. Chartrand III

Have you ever tried to pound a nail or lift a heavy object underwater? Some prospective engineers and factory workers are now doing just that, training to carry out similar tasks in a new industry a few hundred miles from your home—straight up!

Right now a water tank is as close as we can come to simulating the working conditions of space. Water adds a drag on movement that would not occur in space, but at least weight and inertia, so commonly confused on Earth, can be separated in a water tank. In space, objects, be they screwdrivers or space stations, have no weight. They still have mass and the inertia that accompanies it. It takes energy to start something moving and more energy to stop it again. You quite literally can't "throw your weight on the wrench" up there, and you don't have terra firma to brace you.

Working in space is different: You must cope with the disadvantages of no atmosphere, no gravity, no temperature. Conversely, there are the advantages of no atmosphere, no gravity, and no temperature. You have a choice. Many industrial processes on Earth are carried out in such a vacuum. Much energy goes into just getting rid of the air. Nature may abhor a vacuum on some planetary surfaces, but the rest of the universe is a pretty good vacuum. No need to waste energy to pump out air. Just open a valve.

Some things just can't be done in air. Aluminum, for instance, can't be welded in an oxygen atmosphere, and so on Earth we go to great lengths to immerse the area being welded in a nonoxidizing gas. That costs. Large structures in space, including the factories themselves, are likely to be made of aluminum because of its weight and strength. In orbit, you can do away with a lot of the paraphernalia of earthbound welding.

With no gravity, you can produce things without using containers. A big problem in growing superpure crystals for semiconductors and in "doping" them with precise amounts of known impurities to elicit their special properties is to keep the alloys from being contaminated by the containers that hold the crystals. In space, a molten blob of silicon or one of gallium can be suspended in midair—I mean midspace—by electromagnetic forces. This feat of prestidigitation will result in semiconductors much purer than those produced in mundane factories and probably will lead to some new type of semiconductor.

However, if you want some gravity, you can simulate it with a centrifuge and vary it to order. You can tailor-make your industrial environment.

The industrious astronaut will work in a very

345

different environment than his earthly counterpart. He may be in shirt-sleeves in Spacelab—the European-built, shuttle-launched experimental factory and laboratory—while a colleague is "outside," deploying a large antenna.

For such outside work, he will use a manned maneuvering unit now being developed for NASA by Martin Marietta. The prototype was recently delivered for testing. This bulky and massive backpack (Earth mass = 109 kilograms; Earth weight = 1,068 newtons; space mass = 109 kilograms; space weight = 0) will enable the astronaut-engineer to fly around and orient himself as needed and to use specialized tools for a variety of tasks.

What tasks?

When Europeans began to discover the rest of the world, the first products taken home were those with a very high value-to-weight ratio, such as gold and spices. So it will be with the first space industry.

The product with the highest value-to-weight ratio is information. It was important to those early explorers and is even more important to us. To be useful, however, information must be communicated.

Communication is the most advanced of the space industries so far. "Brought to you via satellite" is so common today that this once-ballyhooed phrase is no longer flashed on your television screen. By satellite relay, *The Wall Street Journal* prints 90,000 copies a day at its Orlando, Florida plant with only ten people. Soon building-to-building communication will be available anywhere in the world, linking offices of governments, businesses, and private citizens. Such innovations will make it unnecessary for developing countries to invest huge sums in national telecommunications systems: Put an antenna on the roof and your switchboard is in space.

The satellite revolution that will make this possible is a change in how we build the satellites themselves. Instead of making them heavy, with redundant circuitry, we can cram into them more power, larger antennas, more circuits. We no longer have to make them failure-proof: We can send a technician to fix satellites that go haywire. Because of this, The Dick Tracy wrist radio may be a reality by the end of the 1980s.

Information about Earth is another valuable commodity. The business of sensing Earth resources is big and getting bigger. Accurate worldwide crop predictions could avert such miscalculations as the Russian grain deal a few years ago.

Holding second place in the space industry, but gaining ground quickly, is materials processing. NASA and its counterparts around the world have active programs to study what can be done in Earth orbit. For instance, alloys that won't mix under gravity will mix in zero g. Radioactive processes too dangerous for Earth can be performed in space without posing any hazard to our environment. Some pharmaceuticals may cost less by orders of magnitude if produced in space.

As more and more people work in space, even more will have space-related jobs on Earth. Banks and industry will look for investments beyond the atmosphere. Insurance companies—which already insure rocket launches against failure—will cover entire space factories. Medical and training personnel will be needed. Lawyers and statesmen will, as usual, do well in settling the legal and diplomatic questions that arise in any commercial enterprise.

Our first fledgling space factory, the space shuttle, will fly this year. Its manifest is fully booked through 1984. In a few more years there will be permanently manned space factories. Other processing plants will be left on their own, tended periodically by visiting workers. All these endeavors will turn out highly specialized products for consumption here on Earth.

Then the government—that's you and I collectively—will begin to recoup its investment from taxes on space products and services, while we—that's you and I individually—will benefit from goods stamped MADE IN SPACE.

ASTEROID AGRICULTURE

By Brian O'Leary

"The world hunger problem is getting worse rather than better," said the report of the Presidential Commission on World Hunger. "A major crisis of global food supply—of even more serious dimensions than the present energy crisis—appears likely within the next 20 years, unless steps are taken now. . . . Moral obligation alone would justify giving highest priority to the task of overcoming hunger."

This assessment is neither new nor uncorroborated. For years, agricultural scientists have been warning us of some ominous trends: The food supply is dwindling as the world's population grows. Water resources are becoming even scarcer in potential crop areas. The use of fertilizers is creating environmental damage, including possible ozone depletion in the atmosphere. Drought and severe climatic conditions continue to cause fluctuations in food production.

The increasing genetic uniformity of crops also creates problems. By developing fewer strains of food plants, we make them more vulnerable to disease. This could cause widespread shortages and famine.

Terrestrial solutions of the world food problem are elusive. The development of modern agriculture—the so-called Green Revolution (efforts over the last 20 years to grow more food per acre in poor countries)—bought some time but appears to have reached its limits. Nobody seems interested in meeting the high capital costs of intensified, controlled-environment agriculture in greenhouses. And agronomists believe that U.S. food production, once regarded as mankind's ultimate ace in the hole, has now plateaued. "The rate of growth of agriculture production has slowed down," says Anson Bertrand, of the U.S. Department of Agriculture. "We see this leveling off not only in the United States but globally as well."

What are our chances of growing food in space? The Soviet Union is well on its way to proving that space agriculture is feasible. The Russians have isolated people for up to six months in closed environments, where they have successfully grown wheat and made bread. They've done experiments in space, too, preparing for long-term, agriculturally self-supporting, orbiting settlements.

A number of scientists in the United States have investigated the feasibility of carrying on intensive agriculture in space to supply food for the inhabitants of space settlements. Grains, bread, poultry, and pigs could be raised in closed agricultural areas adjacent to orbiting colonies, where light, temperature, and moisture can be varied according to the requirements of a particular crop.

Space inhabitants could develop the full complement of crops and livestock instead of resorting to the dullness of dehydrated foods and Tang, about which the astronauts have complained. Droughts, pests, and pervasive disease—even the passage of seasons—could be eliminated. Fertilizer could be produced in space by using solar heat to combine nitrogen and oxygen from the asteroids. The supply of materials available for agricultural facilities would grow exponentially as colonies were completed; so it would be possible to construct huge areas for growing food in space. Although the workability of closed agricultural ecologies has not yet been conclusively verified, it appears likely that, sooner or later, food will be grown successfully in space.

Recent engineering studies suggest that our most cost-effective means of supplying electricity could be to build satellite solar-power stations and send their output to Earth via microwave links. The stations would be built in space of materials retrieved from the shallow gravity wells of the moon and asteroids. One study showed that a lunar mining and launching facility and a space chemical-processing plant could be built for between $5 million and $10 million. The first satellite power station would be completed only two years later.

Even if satellite power does not turn out to be the primary incentive for developing the resources of space, the study concluded that lunar materials could be economically used to support the projects planned by NASA for the 1980s and 1990s. Lunar oxygen could be used as rocket fuel and for life-support systems in space; lunar silicon could be fabricated into solar collectors for satellites; and lunar metals could form the supports and hulls of large space structures. The door to large-scale space manufacturing and agronomy in space is likely to open sometime during the 1980s after the space shuttle starts routine flights.

Recent engineering studies have examined the possibility of retrieving Earth-approaching asteroids for space manufacturing. This resource is vast. There are probably more than 100,000 such objects with diameters greater than 100 meters and masses around 1 million metric tons. The unit cost to retrieve asteroids may be many times less than the $1,000 per kilogram lift cost of earthly materials using the shuttle or $1 to $2 for lunar materials. The small asteroids have nearly zero-gravity fields. So the prospect of costly landings is avoided. Solar energy for processing and propulsion is continuously available on the asteroid.

The favorable economics of asteroid retrieval, combined with the apparent attractiveness of space agronomy, raise the possibility that food could be grown more cheaply and more reliably in space than on Earth, given a highly developed program of space manufacturing. Large quantities of dehydrated crops could be dropped out of orbit (possibly by an electromagnetic mass-driver device), enter the earth's atmosphere aboard a metal-foam reentry body, land in the ocean near potential consumers, and be towed ashore for use. Astronomers Michael Gaffey and Thomas McCord have explored similar techniques for recovering asteroidal metals on Earth.

A three-kilometer carbonaceous asteroid towed earthward by a solar-powered mass driver (most of the mass-driver mass and expense would go into the power plant and its radiators) could provide enough growing area to support 6 billion people—the projected world population for the year 2000. In the interim smaller asteroids could be turned into smaller growing areas as famine insurance.

A retrieval system would cost in the range of $100 billion to $200 billion, spread over the next 20 to 30 years. This investment compares favorably with the $700 billion it would cost between now and the year 2000 to provide irrigation and to modernize agriculture in the Third World. Given a potential market of $200 billion to $500 billion a year, the payoff would be rapid.

Food production in the United States totals approximately $100 billion; 20 percent of this is exported. Given reasonable productivity in self-supporting space colonies and low-cost transport to Earth, the cost of food production on Earth may be rivaled by the economical breadbaskets of space.

SEEDS IN SPACE

By Thomas Christopher

George B. Park, Jr., is sending his seeds into outer space. As vice president of the Park Seed Company, of Greenwood, South Carolina, and grandson of the firm's founder, Park is proud of the leadership his company has always shown in discovering new ways to market seeds. In 1962, for example, Park Seed was the first seed company to begin packaging products in aluminum-foil envelopes, ensuring that the seeds would stay fresh until planting time. But now George feels he is on to something really big: He is testing the effect that exposure to the hostile environment of space will have on seeds. This project, whose results may have important implications for plant growth on Earth as well as for the future of space exploration, is just one of the many plant-related projects made possible by the unique facilities of NASA's space shuttles. The cultivation of plants in space is finally becoming commonplace.

NASA itself is funding most of this research as a

part of its dynamic space-biology program. Not surprisingly, initial projects are emphasizing questions about terrestrial botany. For instance, gravity, an inescapable force on Earth, is known to play a critical role in shaping plant growth and development. But just how it interacts with the plants is not entirely clear. By using the cargo bays of the shuttles as laboratories, scientists can now observe plants growing in the near-total absence of gravity. The data they have collected may radically redefine gravity's role.

A leader in this research, Allan Brown is the head of a team of University of Pennsylvania scientists who were the first to germinate and grow plants on the space shuttles. Brown has been investigating the effect of gravity on circumnutation (the spiral, twisting movements plants make as they grow). Charles Darwin, who believed that circumnutation was generated by some internal plant mechanism, studied the phenomenon in the 1870s. Since then, however, most plant physiologists have come to believe that circumnutation is a response to gravity. Following a series of preliminary tests, Brown sent a complex environmental laboratory aloft in Spacelab 1 in November 1983. And through time-lapse photography, he proved that common sunflower seedlings circumnutated even when raised in conditions of weightlessness, suggesting that Darwin, despite his ignorance of biochemistry, was probably on the right track.

Another insight into gravity's effect on plants has been provided by the work of Joe Cowles, a botanist at the University of Houston whose research has focused on the lignification of seedlings. Lignin is a polymer that adds stiffness to plant-cell walls. Its production is also thought to be stimulated by the force of gravity. Cowles planted 32 four-day-old pine seedlings and 64 oat and mung-bean seeds in a suitcase-size plant-growth unit and sent it into orbit for 194 hours in March of 1983. The results were inconclusive: A substantial reduction of lignification occurred in the mung-bean seedlings but, curiously, not among the pines or oats. Cowles, however, thinks that if the flight had been longer, lignification might also have been reduced in the other seedlings. And he is sending more pine and mung-bean seedlings into orbit on Spacelab 2, scheduled for the spring of 1985, to see whether the longer flight will result in lignification.

In contrast to these high-tech experiments in which the plants are nurtured and monitored by sophisticated electronic gear, Park's project has, as he notes, "the virtue of being completely simple." Samples of Park products, such as Park's Whopper Tomato seeds, were packed in metal canisters and placed aboard the shuttles to assess the effect that cosmic radiation and the vacuum of space would have on them. "I wanted to use the environment of the cargo bay itself as the laboratory, not to try to create a miniature laboratory inside that two-foot can," Park says. The first shipment of 44 varieties of seed went up in the maiden voyage of the *Challenger* on April 4, 1983, and the seeds returned to Earth five days later with no significant loss of vitality. Indeed, the globe-circling seeds subsequently germinated normally and grew to maturity in the special "space garden" the company planted in Greenwood the following summer. Currently, Park has 1.9 billion seeds, representing 120 varieties of plants, in orbit aboard NASA's Long Duration Exposure Facility, an 11-ton satellite the size of a Greyhound bus, which was deployed from the *Challenger* on April 7 of 1984. These seeds, which are orbiting at an altitude of 297 miles, will be exposed to the space environment for almost a year before they are retrieved.

Jim Alston, Park Seed's research director, is primarily interested in the valuable mutations that may result from the seeds' exposure to massive doses of cosmic radiation. Park, on the other hand, is fascinated by the possibilities of long-term storage of seeds in space.

"The data we've collected so far," says Park, "indicate we could have taken seeds up in a burlap sack and floated them around, for five days anyway, with no significant damage." Exposure to vacuum seems to induce a very deep dormancy in seeds, and Park speculates that they could float in space almost indefinitely without losing their viability. If he's right, our nation's seed banks may one day find a permanent home in space.

PART TEN:
ALL QUIET ON THE SPACE FRONTIER?

*"I think the most optimistic thing
is that we are still here!
We have attained the capacity
to destroy the planet
and haven't done it.
The longer we don't do it,
the better chance we have."*
—Margaret Mead

WORLD UNITY IN SPACE

By Senator Spark M. Matsunaga

The holiday season, with its eternal theme of peace on Earth and goodwill among all people, is profoundly relevant to our dawning Space Age.

I first learned about such values from my father, a Shinto priest, and had them reinforced when I later embraced the Christian faith. The follower of any other tradition—Jew, Moslem, Hindu, Buddhist— would recognize these beliefs as well. For they are embodied in the universal story of the divine birth— the joyously received entry into the world of a child destined to bring salvation to a suffering humanity.

The divinely conceived child personifies a uniquely human capacity for spiritual transcendence. Other species accept and live out their Darwin fates. But humanity constantly transcends its condition by inspired feats of the imagination that the reasoning mind translates into working reality. Thus, although we lack wings, we fly in space; although we lack gills, we swim to the bottom of the sea; when our hearts fail, we revive them or even replace them.

But if science is an active participant in the human quest for transcendence, it is the spiritual impulse that defines the goal, the purpose of human striving, and the ultimate promise of salvation.

The one goal that inspires humanity's greatest achievements is, to my mind, unity. From Einstein's search for a unified-field theory, to Mozart's sublime harmonies, to the exquisitely balanced architecture of the Parthenon, humanity's most inspired achievements have always evoked transcendent unity. By contrast, our Darwinian "real world" continually succumbs to primitive impulses for dominance, divisiveness, and war, which we helplessly rationalize and romanticize.

So two antithetical impulses struggle for ascendancy within each individual, each culture. One, deterministic and bestial, drives us to disunity; the other, transcendent and spiritual, inspires us to unity.

And now, I believe, the age-old struggle between these two forces enters what may be its final chapter. The setting is the cosmos itself. Here on our tiny microbe of a planet, humanity stands poised to launch a new age of limitless discovery. But we cannot hope to populate the cosmos as long as we carry within us the seed of dominance, divisiveness, and self-destruction. Unless we first transcend our worser selves we are doomed.

That is the context in which currently fashionable visions of the future need to be examined. Any suggestions that our greatest scientific minds should be mobilized in a national effort dedicated to finding newer and jazzier outlets for base, primitive fantasies, rationalized in a thousand ways, denies the noblest aspirations of American intelligence and imagination. Such thinking strikes at the very essence of our religious ideals. We cannot attain transcendent unity with a video-game vision of the future.

Already, the greatest visionaries of the Space Age have rejected man's baser instincts. Arthur C. Clarke, for example, has written that we must replace the "technological obscenities" of a star-wars defense with the "technological decency" of an international space effort. In the same vein, Isaac Asimov calls for globalism rather than tribalism in the Space Age. These literary prophets know that even as fantasy, the star-wars program is a second-rate production, a perversion of the uniquely human capacity to create transcendent forms that unify.

It is the task of political leaders to translate such visions into policies that will set this nation on a new and more promising course. It should be a course that future generations, *endless* future generations, can pursue with wonder and zeal.

In that spirit, I introduced legislation proposing a joint U.S.–Soviet program consisting of space missions of gradually increasing complexity, linked to a moratorium on space-weapons testing. These ventures would build toward an international manned mission to Mars in the twenty-first century. The program would unfold in the same time frame as star wars but at far less cost and with far more promise. In contrast to star wars, which polarizes scientific inquiry on the frontier of space, an international Mars mission—a 16-month voyage into space—would enlist the world's best scientists and engineers in a united enterprise, the most stirring undertaking in human history. Indeed, while pursuing this new path of exploration and discovery, Americans and Soviets might even rediscover their common humanity.

No doubt the administrators and custodians of our self-absorbed "real world" will be tempted to dismiss an international Mars mission proposal as naive; but I hope they will pause first, set their legal pads and briefing papers aside, and recall the universal story of the newborn child.

What was it that brought the three wise men to Bethlehem on Christmas Day? Was it to hear yet another lecture on the self-perpetuating complexities of the "real world"? Of course not. They came to behold the *promise* of something new and divinely inspired, a new wisdom that offered rebirth for a multitude of people.

Similarly, we need to ask, Does this new idea fit the need? Is it what our nascent Space Age requires? If the answer is yes, then we should have the courage to take the necessary initiatives in the policy sphere.

As international Mars mission would herald the birth of a new, transcendent age, Mankind's highest aspirations in art, science, and religion would be finally realized. The beast of divisiveness would be securely caged as humanity began a journey into the cosmos, unified at last.

Spark M. Matsunaga, Democratic senator from Hawaii, introduced a bill in 1984 calling for renewal of the U.S. Soviet space-oooperation agreement that was allowed to lapse in 1982, following the declaration of martial law in Poland.

SOVIET SPACE OFFENSIVE

By Ben Bova

The year is 1983. The U.S. space shuttle *Challenger* is in orbit on its first test flight. Its sister ship, *Columbia*, is being checked out at Kennedy Space Flight Center in preparation for its sixth mission.

Disaster strikes without warning: A pair of explosions rip through *Challenger*, destroying the rocket engines at its tail and blowing off the barn-door hatches of the payload bay. The ship tumbles wildly until its two-man crew grimly brings it back under control. The astronauts are alive and unharmed except for some bruises. But *Challenger* is crippled and unable to return safely to Earth.

Suddenly Moscow broadcasts an electrifying message: "In keeping with the terms of the 1972 Convention on Rescue of Cosmonauts, the Soviet Union has dispatched a rescue mission to the damaged American pirate spacecraft *Challenger*."

The world watches worriedly as cosmonauts in two *Soyus-T* spacecraft reach *Challenger* and return the Americans safely to Earth. Inside the Soviet Union.

The media are already buzzing with stories leaked from Washington that *Challenger* was destroyed not by an accident but by Soviet missiles fired from a satellite.

Then Moscow makes a new announcement: The American astronauts are safe, but they will not be returned to the United States until some comprehensive agreements about outer space are signed. After all, Moscow asserts, everyone knows that these astronauts are military officers whose mission in space was to spy on the USSR and steal Soviet reconnaissance satellites.

The military calls it "taking the high ground." Diplomats refer to it as "seizing the initiative." Whichever you prefer, the Soviet Union has launched a major diplomatic and military offensive against the American space program, and particularly against the space shuttles. The foregoing scenario could soon come true. Two critical elements of such a crisis are already falling into place:

The more obvious is a dramatic advance in Soviet space weaponry. The U.S. government has not officially confirmed reports that the Soviet satellite *Cosmos 1267* carries missiles capable of destroying other satellites. But privately some Reagan Administration sources concede that stories leaded in *Aviation Week* magazine in the autumn of 1981 are true: *Cosmos 1267* is an orbital battle station that might well down an American shuttle.

The other element, no less dangerous, is diplomatic. Next month (August 9-22, 1982) the United Nations will convene its Unispace 82 conference in Vienna. It promises to turn the city of political intrigue into the site of a propaganda circus.

The Russians, it seems, hope to convince the Third World, and as much of Europe and the Western Hemisphere as possible, that the U.S. space program is no more than a tool of Pentagon strategy and that the space shuttle is exclusively a military vehicle. If they can accomplish that, they may force the United States to limit its space explorations drastically. At the very least the Russians can then justify their own systematic militarization of space.

Soviet engineers have been working on space weaponry for years. The 1963 Nuclear Test Ban Treaty prohibits placing nuclear weapons in space, and the 1967 Outer Space Treaty bars placing "weapons of mass destruction" in orbit and building military bases on the moon. Both the United States and the Soviet Union have ratified these treaties. But, as James Oberg, a frequent contributor to *Omni* and the author of *Red Star in Orbit* (Random House), says, "Ten years ago Soviet space engineers . . . flight-tested a vehicle for carrying nuclear warheads into orbit and back. Western observers called it the FOBS [fractional-orbit-bombardment system]. . . . Since the system *as tested* never made a complete pass around the Earth, some U.S. Government space lawyers haggled that the payload was not really 'in orbit' and hence was not a violation of the . . . Outer Space Treaty."

For the past 15 years the Russians also have been testing a "hunter-killer" antisatellite system. It consists of a simple bomb maneuvered into orbit alongside its intended victim. When the bomb explodes, shrapnel riddles its target like a shotgun blast. This hunter-killer system was the first active weapon ever put in orbit. So far as is known, it has been used to date only in tests against Soviet target satellites. Some observers have theorized, however, that the Soviet A-sat may have been responsible for the mysterious disappearance of an RCA communications satellite in early December 1979.

No treaty prohibits placing such weapons of *pinpoint* destruction in orbit. In fact, spurred by the Soviet threat, the U.S. Air Force is developing an antisatellite weapon to be carried by an F-15 fighter and fired into space like an antiaircraft missile. Both the USSR and the United States are working on such high-energy-beam weapons as lasers and particle-beam accelerators.

Beam weapons and missiles such as those reportedly carried by *Cosmos 1267* are ostensibly designed to attack only other satellites or rocket boosters. But such weapons might eventually become powerful and accurate enough to attack targets on the ground.

While the Russians' work on space weapons is well established, their political campaign is relatively new. It required a rapid about-face in Soviet policy. When President Carter's representatives at the SALT II talks in the late Seventies proposed to ban all weapons from space, the Soviet negotiators refused even to consider the idea. They quickly abandoned this stance when they realized that the shuttle would be a success.

Soviet news coverage of *Columbia*'s first flight, in April 1981, reflected the tactical change. Soviet news reports never mentioned the shuttle's size, weight, and orbit. Instead, article after article drummed on the military nature of the shuttle and its planned missions.

Red Star, the official newspaper of the Red Army declared that "Pentagon [officials] are gleefully rubbing their hands. After all . . . the Pentagon sees the shuttle in the role of an omnipotent and insatiable space pirate."

A few days after *Columbia*'s first flight, Soviet President Leonid Brezhnev piously prayed, "May the shoreless cosmic ocean be pure and free of weapons of any kind."

And in May 1981 General Alexei A. Leonov, chief of the Soviet cosmonaut corps, declared in a speech in Ulan Bator, Outer Mongolia, that a satellite has the right to fly over the territory of another nation only for peaceful purposes. Leonov, the first man to walk in space and the commander of the Russian half of the joint Apollo-Soyuz mission in 1975, implied that military satellites are fair game for Soviet antisatellite weapons.

The new Soviet line became clear in August 1981, when the Soviet delegation to the United Nations called for a total ban on all weapons in space. They referred specifically to the American antisatellite system as a violation of the principle that space should be free of all weapons. They also described the space shuttle as a weapon.

Soviet diplomacy scored heavily at the September 1981 meeting of the International Astronautical Federation, in Rome. At the sessions sponsored by the International Institute of Space Law, the Soviet delegation gave a series of papers outlining their policies and characterizing the U.S. space program as strictly a military operation.

B. G. Dudakov, a ranking Soviet space lawyer, prepared a paper that spelled out his country's position:

"American strategists' plans as regards handling other states' satellites in orbit can be characterized as piratic in essence. It seems as though some people are striving for the 'laurels' of such notorious sea-pirates of the past as John Hawkins, Francis Drake, and Walter Railey [sic]."

Dudakov himself missed the meeting, a fate that often befalls Russians who wish to travel outside the Soviet Union. But his paper carried on for him: "Without the consent of the state holding jurisdiction over the space object in orbit, not a single state is permitted either to investigate using its own spacecraft the satellites of other states, or to get too close to them, violating a certain distance limit. . . ."

The Russians had drawn a line: No one could touch their satellites, inspect them, or even get within an unspecified distance of them. They apparently feared—or wanted others to believe—that the space shuttle would be used to inspect or dismantle their satellites, or even to snatch them from orbit.

The Russians underscored this line with several other fascinating points. At the same meeting Dr. Vladlen S. Vereshchetin, a member of the Soviet Academy of Sciences' branch on law, called for a program to strengthen and codify international space law. Among the new issues that Vereshchetin raised was the idea of setting up an international agency to oversee the rescue of astronauts and cosmonauts in distress and their return to their home countries. Ominously he also said that military astronauts might not be returned as quickly as civilians.

Arthur M. Dula, a Houston attorney who specializes in space law and who is the chairman of the American Bar Association's Section of Science and Technology, notes that it was the Russians who originally insisted that rescued cosmonauts be returned immediately—even if they ask for political asylum in the rescuers' nation. This provision at the Russians' insistence was written into the 1972 accord on the rescue and return of astronauts.

The new position suggests that a military astronaut might not be treated as a civilian would, that he might even be detained. On the surface this hardly seems to the Soviet Union's advantage. Their cosmonauts are military officers; there are far fewer civilians in the cosmonaut corps than among American astronauts. But in the wonderland of international politics and Soviet propaganda, the Russians can picture space ventures in any way that suits them. Their flights, manned by members of the Red Army, can be defined as peaceful and nonmilitary, while any American space mission, even those flown solely by civilian astronauts, can be designated military in purpose.

"The consistent Russian theme," Dula says, "has been either to forbid or to impede private enterprise in space." Now, he worries, after defining the shuttle as a dangerous weapon, the Russians "are ready to justify the use of military force against the shuttle."

How much of a military threat *is* the shuttle? According to astronaut John Young, not much. "The space shuttle is not a military weapon, any more than a truck is a military weapon," says *Columbia*'s first command pilot. "The shuttle is a truck. You can put lots of different things into it."

About one third of all shuttle flights planned through 1986 will carry Defense Department payloads. Most are communications and reconnaissance satellites; the Department of Defense has no plans to launch armed satellites. Congress and the White House are debating whether to begin work on a laser "battle station" in orbit—an idea recently endorsed by the General Accounting Office—but such exotic weaponry seems to be at least a full decade away.

Yet astronaut Young is convinced that space will eventually become a military arena. Men in a space station, he points out, could watch earthly battles and make decisions without delay. Ground-based planners must have vast amounts of satellite data relayed to the ground, then send their orders back to communications satellites for transmission—a slow and difficult process.

This possibility alone is enough to spur the Soviet campaign against the shuttle. The next round will come at Unispace 82. As usual, the United States is far behind in its preparations—in this case because it was not until the last moment that our government decided to attend the conference at all.

The purpose of the conference is to promote the use of space technology, primarily for the benefit of the Third World. Those nations have already pushed the Moon Treaty, the Law of the Sea Treaty, and other preparations for "a new world economic order." Their goal is to gain the benefits of technology developed in the industrialized nations—by international fiat rather than free trade. Unispace 82 is just one further step in this direction.

One Third World aim is to establish a U.N. agency to monitor—and govern—all space activities. At the Vienna conference the Third World countries want to explore such political issues as the militarization of space, ownership of the geosynchronous orbit, and control of data from Landsats and other observation satellites.

Dr. Jerry Grey, who in January, 1982, was appointed a deputy secretary-general for the conference, observes that "these U.N. conferences are political in nature, not technical." Yet at previous meetings the United States has limited itself almost exclusively to technical presentations. As a result, both the USSR and the Third World have scored important political and propaganda victories at America's expense.

Because of this, it might be tempting to view America's early decision to boycott the Vienna conference as a wise refusal to join in an attack on its own national interests. In fact, the cause was simple politics. With, perhaps, some masterful orchestration from the Soviet Union.

In the U.N. hierarchy, responsibility for Unispace 82 falls to the director of the Outer Space Affairs Division of the Committee on the Peaceful Uses of Outer Space. When Unispace 82 was first put on the U.N. calendar, the division's head was Lubos Perek, of Czechoslovakia. His deputy was Marvin Robinson, an American.

Perek's five-year term was up in May 1981, and, according to normal U.N. procedures, he would have been succeeded by his deputy. But the Russians claimed that they had a verbal agreement with the United States to replace Perek with another Czech. They nominated Victor Kopal. The United States denied any agreement and opposed the Russian idea that U.N. positions should be "hereditary," that a position held by a Czech must always go to another Czech.

Kurt Waldheim was then running for reelection as U.N. secretary-general, and he wanted votes, not enemies. He refused to decide the matter. As the impasse deepened, the United States announced that it would not attend Unispace 82 unless a satisfactory decision was reached.

By December 31, 1981, Waldheim's bid for reelection was dead, and he finally appointed Robinson acting chief of the Outer Space Affairs Division. The American will become the full-fledged head of the division on the day that Unispace 82 convenes. Kopal will be his deputy.

Secretary of State Alexander Haig then decided that the United States will attend Unispace 82 after all. NASA Administrator James E. Boggs will lead the American delegation.

Attorney Dula is anything but optimistic that the United States will fare better in Vienna than in previous conferences. For one thing, the United States agreed to attend only at the last moment. Its representatives have been forced to squeeze two years of preparation into less than eight months. Dr. Grey has high praise for Ken Pederson, NASA's director of international affairs, and his assistant, James Morrison. They are, he says, "doing a fantastic job" in getting ready for the meeting on such short notice. Yet it remains an enormous task to be accomplished in haste.

But Dula's real concern is that the American emissaries simply are not prepared for an attack on the U.S. space program. As Grey sees it, the Russians have been far from hostile in the United Nations. "Their position in this conference is roughly the same as ours," he believes. "Both nations oppose more U.N. bureaucracy." East-bloc industrial nations as well as the West, he says, prefer agreements between individual nations to the U.N. machinery that the Third World wants to create.

Yet conflicts between East and West are far more frequent than attempts to seek common goals. The story of the NGOs—nongovernmental organizations—at the Vienna meeting is a case in point. At U.N. conferences, not only national delegations but private, nonprofit groups are invited to air their views. Their presence has long embarrassed delegations from countries in which organizations are either government-sponsored or prohibited. Unispace 82 nearly had to do without these private participants.

David Webb, an activist who founded the Campaign for Space Political Action Committee, worked hard to get American NGOs into the Vienna conference. When it appeared that the United States would not be represented at all, he formed a group called U.S. Space 82 as a rallying point for private American participants. In November 1981 the United Nations made him chairman of all NGO activities at the Unispace conference.

Neither the world body nor the participating nations have been willing to contribute money to support the NGO effort, however. Webb sees Soviet interference at work. "The Soviet bloc did not want NGOs at the conference in the first place," he says. "There are no NGOs in the Soviet system; everything is state-sponsored. They are very worried about NGOs, because it is the one area they cannot control."

As a result, all NGOs at the Vienna conference will be supported by voluntary donations. Webb has organized day-long seminars on space and the environment, remote sensing, communications, education, private enterprise in space, space transportation, and energy from space.

The NGOs will also devote a day to the demilitarization of space. Considered too hot to handle by the governmental delegates, space demilitarization was deliberately left off the agenda at the U.N. conference on disarmament, held in New York City in May 1981. Vienna is the only place where the subject will be discussed in an international forum.

As the Vienna conference approaches, Soviet planners can view their work with satisfaction. By branding the U.S. space shuttle a tool of military "piracy," they have undercut one of America's most spectacular achievements. They have delayed American preparations for Unispace 82 and have crippled participation by the NGOs. They have prepared world opinion for the idea that the entire U.S. space effort is a military program and that peace-loving Russians have the right to destroy the satellites of other nations—including the manned shuttle—in order to protect their own. Most ominous of all, they may well have missiles aboard *Cosmos 1267* capable of carrying out that threat.

The United States, with no weapons in orbit, is in the position of defending its intentions and trying to explain to the world that the shuttle is not a military weapon. It is not. But it may be a military target.

SHOWDOWN ON THE HIGH FRONTIER

By Tim Onosko

High over the Naval Weapons Center, at China Lake, California, a heat-seeking Sidewinder missile sizzled across the sky toward an Air Force Boeing 707. Suddenly the plane shot an intense ray, touching the Sidewinder's hull with a long, skinny finger of light. The missile's instruments were scrambled. Seconds later the Sidewinder veered off course, missing its target.

Lasers 1, Missiles 0.

On July 25, 1983, the Air Force announced the final score for this series of tests of its Airborne Laser Laboratory—Lasers 5, Missiles 0. It was a resounding success for the "star wars" theory of defense, a multibillion-dollar program that the Reagan Administration seeks to make national policy. And by revealing how advanced such directed-energy weapons already are, the laser tests raised a question that legislators and the voting public must answer: Who are the Darth Vaders?

Is the dark side of the Force with those who seek to

block this potentially powerful defense against nuclear attack? Or is it with those who would turn outer space into a high-tech battlefield, adding dangerous complexities to the already precarious balance of terror on earth?

Unfortunately, Han Solo, Luke Skywalker, and the dauntless Princess Leia are not here to simplify the problem into black and white. We're on our own, stuck with ambiguous gray. Meanwhile, ever since March 23, 1983, when President Reagan made his "star wars" speech calling for orbiting hardware to zap any Soviet missiles launched toward North America, the Force has been cracking through Washington. Pro- and anti-space-weapons partisans are doing battle in the Pentagon, and arguments will flash in Congress like light swords. Driving the debate is a sense of urgency because the first batch of new space weapons might be ready for launch during this decade.

Some Pentagon systems are straight-forward. The space mine, for instance, is a maneuverable satellite that parks next to an enemy satellite and blows up, destroying them both. Others use far-out techniques for knocking out enemy intercontinental ballistic missiles (ICBMs) with what amount to death rays.

In another area of technology, government researchers are testing the MAL (Miniature Air-Launched weapon), a small, heat-seeking rocket that's launched at high altitude from an F-15 fighter. It would ascend to an orbiting satellite and destroy it on impact. Testing for this antisatellite weapon has already begun.

More sophisticated space weaponry from the Pentagon harnesses the power of light to wipe out incoming ICBMs. Most advanced of the devices today are chemical lasers, which produce light by burning hydrogen and fluorine compounds, and amplify and focus the resulting deadly ray with mirrors. The infrared light such lasers produce, however, could be their weakness: The Soviets might simply make their ICBM hulls so shiny that they would reflect the rays like a mirror. Thus, researchers are now looking beyond chemical lasers to beams with shorter wavelengths, like highly energetic ultraviolet rays. These would be substantially harder to reflect.

Another idea calls for a powerful laser generator based on Earth but using orbiting mirrors to reflect its beam at incoming ICBMs. The laser generator might be a linear particle accelerator. Still another design, the excimer laser, generates the ray by passing an electric current through a mixture of a noble gas (like xenon or argon) and a halogen gas (like chlorine or fluorine) to produce a chemical reaction that in turn produces ultraviolet light.

Even further in the future are particle-beam weapons. These devices shoot a stream of particles that penetrate an ICBM and destroy its instruments. Particle beams, however, are apparently still far from being operational. As with other antimissile systems, the beam must be designed to withstand such potential countermeasures as using decoys and "spoofing" (electronically misdirecting) the weapons' intricate command and communications systems.

Now some researchers are looking into yet another far-out idea, which they call a fléchette. It would be a giant arrow, huge and full of mass, that would plummet from orbit and smash into a target on the ground with so much speed and kinetic energy that it would instantly hammer the sturdiest fortress into rubble.

While the Pentagon pushes ahead on star-wars projects, another influential group is touting the value of technologies from roughly the same era as the Fifties TV show *Tom Corbett, Space Cadet*. High Frontier, Inc., a Washington, DC, nonprofit group, advocates orbiting 17,000 to 20,000 conventional (nonnuclear) heat-seeking rockets. These would sweep down on incoming Soviet ICBMs. "It's more of an engineering problem than a science problem," says retired Army General Daniel Graham, who founded the organization in 1981. High Frontier's membership comprises conservatives who believe mounting an orbital antimissile system requires little more than money.

Graham, an affable warrior known in the defense establishment as Danny, says the rockets—attached to 432 launchers lifted into orbit by the space shuttle—would be one of three defense layers. Earth-launched antimissiles would blast any ICBMs that survived the first attack. And General Electric's new GAU-8 rapid-fire guns would defend U.S. missile silos with a cloud of 30mm shells against anything that squeaked through the first two layers. Also in the plan are a space station and a space transport tug with limited fighter capability.

Before he established High Frontier, Graham was candidate Ronald Reagan's military adviser in the 1976 and 1980 campaigns. Others on the organization's advisory board range from Air Force General Robert Richardson, Admiral Mark Hill, physicist

Arnold Kramish, and satellite expert Peter Glaser to science-fiction author Robert Heinlein and conservative activist Phyllis Schlafly. Also active in the organization are Republican congressmen Gordon Humphrey, of New Hampshire, and Kenneth Kramer, of Colorado, and Senator William Armstrong (Republican, Colorado). Thus, High Frontier has influence in the White House.

And the plan has another selling point: Since it includes the use of off-the-shelf technology, we can begin installing the system virtually anytime. As Graham puts it, High Frontier has a "kind of dumb, brute-force approach to things."

Arguably, it is a Fifties approach to things, a set of ideas pioneered in the age of tail fins and basketball-size satellites. John Bosma, an arms researcher working for Graham, takes pride in having unearthed details of Project Defender, a space-based defense study undertaken by the Eisenhower Administration in 1958. Parts of Defender bear remarkable similarity to High Frontier's plan. According to Bosma, it included a subproject that investigated laser weapons, particle beams, directed-nuclear plasmas, and other speculative technology. Another subproject, BAMBI (Ballistic Missile Boost Intercept), was part of the larger concept called SPAD—Space Patrol Active Defense. BAMBI presaged the orbiting missiles of High Frontier's proposal, and SPAD included plans for a "winged, recoverable, vertical-takeoff, horizontal-landing payload booster"—in other words, the space shuttle—to deliver BAMBI to outer space.

Some weapons researchers ridicule the High Frontier rocket system as too simplistic. "It won't drop a lot of money in Livermore's lap," responds Graham with aplomb, referring to the Lawrence Livermore National Laboratory, in California, where much of the country's weapons research is done.

The wide variety of exotic plans for new space-war technology contributes to the likelihood that at least some of the plans will be developed and deployed. Some observers suggest that means potential enemies will probably launch their own space-weapons systems.

"When they issued the six-shooters to the U.S. marshals, that was going to end it on the western frontier, but the crooks soon got them, too," says Senator Larry Pressler (Republican, South Dakota).

Pressler believes that if one side arms itself with orbiting six-shooters, the other side will soon match them. "Unless something is done, or some agreements are reached, or mankind somehow decides against it, I suppose space weapons *are* inevitable," he says in a sinking tone. "On the other hand, if the Russians are doing it, I suppose we have to. It's the old arms race extended to outer space. And that's a very painful direction if you look at the costs and the potential for destruction that could result."

Costs? Consider the plan that Republican Senator Malcolm Wallop, of Wyoming, is pushing: 24 laser stations orbiting the earth 800 miles up. According to one Wallop aide, each laser-tracking system would be so fine-tuned that it could be mounted on top of a New York City truck and keep perfect aim on a tennis ball bouncing on a London court. Each station, overseeing 10 percent of the earth's surface, would have enough fuel (hydrogen and fluorine) for about

1,000 shots. That capability would be enough to contend with "the theoretical contingency of one thousand missiles launched beneath it in almost simultaneous barrage."

The first laser battle station, by Wallop's estimates, would cost $3 billion to $5 billion, with each station thereafter costing $1 billon, for a total of $28 billion, plus shuttle-shipping costs. Some critics say the cost could be twice that figure or more.

Is it worth the price? "Oh, hell, yes!" says Wallop. "The dimension of the threat changes enormously if it can shoot down five thousand reentry vehicles [ICBMs] in five minutes." Wallop goes further: For the United States *not* to build an orbiting weapons system might be national suicide, he says. "Any nation that deployed two dozen of these first-generation chemical-laser stations would command the portals of space against any other nation," Wallop maintains, asserting that the Soviets might own the void if they were able to build such a system first.

"It depends on the capability of the weapons they launch and what they wish to do with that newfound capability," he says. "It's conceivable that they would *deny* us access to space."

The day after President Reagan's star-wars speech, Wallop and Senator Paul Laxalt (Republican, Nevada) introduced a joint resolution calling for a space-sited antiballistic-missile system "at the earliest possible date." Specifically, Wallop and his supporters want to speed up work on three Defense Advanced Research Projects Agency (DARPA) programs:

• Project Alpha: demonstration of a five-megawatt chemical laser by 1987, with TRW the prime contractor. Wallop says that a ten-megawatt laser would be possible with more money.

• LODE (Large Optical Demonstration Experiment): Lockheed is the prime contractor for this effort to produce mirrors large enough (13.1 feet in diameter) to direct antimissile laser beams and yet sturdy enough to survive the shuttle trip to orbit. Wallop says that, with more money, we could have 33-foot-diameter mirrors.

• Talon Gold: a superaccurate pointing and tracking system for laser weapons that would enable an orbiting laser to aim at a flying ICBM and lock on long enough to burn out its instruments. Again Lockheed is the contractor. Wallop is upset because funding reductions deleted a Talon Gold test with the shuttle.

Wallop feels that the greatest injustices being done to space-weapons programs are budget cuts and needless delays. "There's a bizarre level of conversation that comes out of the Department of Defense that says they're not ready" to go ahead with development, Wallop complains. "But their specific testimony is that they are."

As military strategy goes, it all sounds like Mom's apple pie. After all, if super-weapons in space mean we can neutralize a nuclear attack directed against us without having to destroy a large swatch of the earth with a counterstroke, who would oppose them?

Certainly when President Reagan issued his call for space weaponry, a strategy military experts have discussed at least since the Project Defender study, the idea seemed alluring. Not for nothing is the strategy for the present balance of nuclear terror called MAD, the apt acronym for mutual assured destruction.

MAD's premise is that no nation would take the risk of starting a nuclear war if its own annihilation were probably assured by its enemy's nuclear counterstroke.

MAD is virtually a legal entity in today's world, resting upon the Anti-Ballistic Missile (ABM) treaty. It bans defensive antimissile missiles because they would upset the evenly matched standoff that, so far, has saved all our skins. The treaty, however, was written before notions like orbiting laser weapons became serious, and does not mention space war. Thus, with the ABM treaty effectively finessed, the major powers are now poised for an out-of-this-world antimissile arms competition.

Weapons for attacking and defending satellites are part of the issue because, in today's warfare, satellites are vital for command, control, communications, and intelligence, known in military circles as C cubed I. Supposedly, the United Nations' Outer Space Treaty of 1967, which defines astronauts as humanity's international envoys in outer space, precludes space weapons. The treaty, however, specifically mentions only nuclear weapons and weapons that would destroy human life on a massive scale. Its writers did not foresee lasers, particle beams, space mines, and other star-wars concepts now on the military drawing boards. Wallop, for one, argues that existing treaties are no obstacle. And Leonid Brezhnev himself told the United Nations that the ABM treaty did not apply to space weapons, a stand that Brezhnev's successor, Yuri Andropov, reaffirmed in May 1983, Wallop claims.

In fact, reality already is sounding much like the

science fiction of a few decades ago. For instance, on September 1, 1982, the U.S. Air Force quietly activated its new space command, headquartered in Colorado Springs. The command was established to "push for understanding and awareness of the Soviet space threat," according to its charter, and to "develop space-defense doctrine and strategy." The Navy followed with its own space command in 1983.

But all of this activity has stimulated a backlash of protest. The opposition takes several forms. Senator Pressler, for one, has introduced a Senate resolution calling for a ban on the development of antisatellite weapons; this would be a first step toward prohibiting *all* space-based weaponry. Pressler is concerned that the focus on space war will slow the nonmilitary development of space. He points out that the Defense Department is already urging civilian space users to harden their satellites against attack. "This technology is being held up and could be destroyed by all of this," he says.

A pessimist, Pressler says that arms-control talk "really doesn't amount to much." He notes that the Soviets already have launched an antisatellite weapon. But he adds, "I'm a critic both of the Russians' and of our own operations." Pressler also is troubled by the cost of space weaponry; he cites estimates that range from $50 billion to $500 billion. "You're going to impoverish Earth by supporting these sophisticated systems," he says.

"I know that some people say, 'If we just get one step ahead and we build lasers and they're effective, it will give us superiority, and there will be peace.'" Pressler says. "That's also what they said about

MIRVs [today's state-of-the-art multiple-warhead ICBMs, which both the Soviet Union and the United States are now pointing at each other]."

Representative Joe Moakely (Democrat, Massachusetts) is even more opposed to space weapons. Moakely emphasizes, however, that he is no pacifist. In fact, during World War II he quit high school at fifteen to join the Navy. Cases like this underscore the fact that the arguments for and against the space-war strategy do not fit into neat ideological pigeonholes.

"I still get a thrill when the American flag goes by. I'm not a peacenik," Moakely says gruffly. "I'm fifty-six years old. I've been through a lot, and I figured, geez, somebody's got to do it, and somebody's got to have people taking a look at this." Scientists like Carl Sagan have joined Moakely in his space-war opposition, which was expressed in a House resolution calling for a sweeping ban on all weapons in space.

More than anything, Moakely is upset by the speed with which decisions are being made on these complex systems. The House Armed Services Committee, for instance, debated an antisatellite-weapons bill for what seemed to Moakley to be an unconscionably short time.

"Five minutes of hearings on the thing, and now they want us to embark on a brand-new kind of space war!" he fumes.

Moakely, along with many others in Congress and the science community, questions the new weapons' effectiveness and reliability. "I'm afraid of putting *anything* up there that's going to disturb any of those satellites doing the reconnaissance work, because if they start sending some funny signals back . . . you know . . . it could be *sayonara*." He also fears that as defense systems become even more complex, with far-out systems orbiting overhead, the chances for mistakes grow.

"As long as we've got humans living on this planet, we're going to have a lot of human error," he says. "So let's give them fewer things to have human error over."

Because Soviet ICBM's are in their boost phase for only a few minutes, decision-making time is limited and systems are highly automated. In military jargon, "they take the human out of the loop." Moakely's reaction: "I fear this may take the human out of the planet."

So complicated is the issue of space weaponry that the arguments cross over the old hawk and dove lines. Among the space-war lobbying groups, for instance, conservative High Frontier's natural enemy would seem to be the L-5 Society, a group that formed to support space-colony ideas such as those outlined by Princeton physicist Gerard O'Neill. O'Neill envisions giant artificial satellites parked at the L-5 point, where gravitational forces of the moon and Earth are equal. Critics have called L-5 members "space hippies," preoccupied as they have been with such notions as beekeeping in orbit.

But since High Frontier's Graham addressed the L-5 Society's national meetings in 1982 and 1983, the group has split, and some members now embrace High Frontier's arms-in-orbit theory for ensuring peace. Others want to maintain the original L-5 idealism. An article in a recent issue of L-5's magazine tried to heal the rift. Its author, Eric Drexler, of the Massachusetts Institute of Technology, proposed that the United States and the Soviet Union jointly establish an antimissile system that would be unable to differentiate between one country's ICBMs and the other's. Graham terms that idea "just plain silly," but it shows how difficult it is to maintain polarity in the wonderland of MAD.

Graham, meanwhile, has little trouble keeping his own perspective on the L-5 ideology of space as a workshop for the human-potential movement.

"That's what gets me about some of the people on the sweetness-and-light side," Graham huffs. "They want the poor old slob—Joe Sixpack, Joe Lunchpail—to pour his tax money in so that one day they could have this marvelous colony of *their* kind of people."

Some members of the opposition have impeccable scientific credentials. One is physicist Richard Garwin, who has worked on a variety of federal weapons-research projects, including satellites and nuclear warfare, and is currently an IBM fellow at the Thomas J. Watson Research Center, in Yorktown Heights, New York, an adjunct research fellow at Harvard, and a professor at Columbia. In February 1983 he led a blue-ribbon bloc of scientists, including Sagan, physicist Hans Bethe, former Johnson Space Center director Christopher Kraft, and formed Advanced Research Project Agency director George Rathgens, in petitioning world leaders for a ban on space weaponry.

"He is talking about rendering all nuclear weapons impotent and obsolete," says Garwin about President Reagan's star-wars plans. "That's nonsense; nobody in the community who is working on such things believes that is possible."

We need a strong defense, but the real purpose of space-defense systems is to preserve the U.S. nuclear deterrent—its ICBMs, Garwin argues. And for that purpose, he suggests a simple point defense of our missile silos: SWARMJET, a launcher that can shoot hundreds of miniature projectiles at incoming ICBMs. Ironically, that is the same weapon Graham at one point advocated as High Frontier's third defensive layer.

How complicated can the issue get? Very. Some six months after Reagan's speech there were rumors among informed scientists that the U.S. Arms Control and Disarmament Agency had drawn up an offer to the Russians to limit antisatellite weaponry. The rumors, which surfaced at about the same time the United States was about to test its fighter-launched antisatellite system, raised a few questions. If the offer were serious, wouldn't it have been better to delay tests and put a hold on development costs until after negotiations with the Russians? And what's the national policy on the need for such weapons? *New York Times* columnist Flora Lewis quotes one scientist on the prevailing confusion in Washington:

"Negotiations with the Soviets? Who worries about that? It's negotiations with the White House and the Pentagon that are the first concern."

Whether they are proponents or opponents of space-war preparation plans, national leaders today are contending with another set of difficult questions. These are among the thorniest:

If the United States decides to commit itself to a major space-war effort, could the government round up enough brainpower to design the systems? George Keyworth, the President's science adviser, believes the answer is yes.

He says that, after World War II, scientists appalled by the nuclear weapons they had produced believed in unilateral disarmament. But the Soviets were arming on a massive scale. "And here we sit in 1983, with the Soviets possessing an overwhelming land-based ballistic-missile capability." Keyworth says that many other scientists, still plagued by guilt, remain adamantly opposed to the arms race. But that attitude is "not so prevalent among the younger generation of scientists," he says.

Garwin agrees that the administration can find many willing hands among younger scientists to work on the new weapons. "I think there are lots of scientists who will work on anything that's not criminal," he says. He believes the effort could backfire, however, because the scientists working on the new weapons systems, eager for promotions, would be unwilling to tell their superiors when the designs do not work.

"There's really very little capability in the government," Garwin asserts. "Very few experienced, technically sound people of any independence at all. This government is worse in that regard than any other I can remember."

Even if the people could be found to build such systems, how vulnerable would the hardware be to countermeasures? Colin Gray, an arms strategist who is friendly to the idea of space missile defense, worries that there hasn't yet been enough thought or planning about how to defend the systems themselves.

"I have the impression that the weapons advocates have scarcely begun to think through the whole range of electronic, physical, and tactical countermeasures that could be taken to negate such systems," says Gray, a member of the White House Arms Control Advisory Committee and president of a Virginia think tank called the National Institute for Public Policy. Countermeasures range from throwing debris into the orbital path of a laser system to misdirecting control of a weapon's command systems: Garwin says that even the most sophisticated detection devices can be fooled with such simple decoys as balloons. "If you use plastic or aluminum-foil multilayer balloons," he says, "there is absolutely no sensitivity to whether there is a reentry vehicle inside or if they are empty. They look the same to radar."

Keyworth agrees it's a complicated problem. But he says there's a solution: "The thing to focus on is data processing. If you can handle enough data fast enough, you can do a pretty darn good job of discrimination." Garwin counters: "No kind of processing is going to help."

Even if a system survived countermeasures and worked well, would it make war more or less likely? Would it save lives? There are contrasting scenarios to answer these life-or-death questions. One somewhat hopeful picture comes from Gray.

"If a Soviet planner knows that he must duel for the first time with an American active defense that he has never faced before, that has got to increase the uncertainties of his offense to an unimaginable degree," he says. "It vastly reduces the calculability of an attack; so it's got to increase uncertainty, which has to be good for deterrence. Also, of course, at some unimaginable point deterrence may fail, and active defenses could make a life-and-death difference in the damage that North America might suffer. You're talking about saving tens of millions of lives."

By contrast, Garwin's scenario is terrifying. It opens with a kind of two-step dance: First we orbit an anti-ICBM system, and then the Russians put up space mines to neutralize it. Then the space-weapons proponents cry "Foul!" They will find it intolerable for us to allow the Soviets to put up space mines, Garwin predicts. "But," he says, "it would be intolerable to the Soviets to allow us to disarm them [neutralize their ICBM threat] by deploying something that is pictured as being one hundred percent effective.

"So they *will* put up those space mines," says Garwin. "We *will* shoot them in peacetime. They will shoot down our satellites in peacetime, and that's not going to do us any good. We will have *no* satellite-based defense system. We will just have a war that is totally unnecessary and will do no good because it will end up with us not being able to defend against nuclear weapons."

Not a pretty prospect. Even some proponents of space weapons agree that their plans open up new possibilities for conflagration. With automated systems in place on both sides, superpowers will be tempted to test the sophistication of their weaponry. After the first button is pushed, for several minutes the confrontation will be a kind of chess match between systems and countersystems and counter-countersystems. "As a prelude to a large nuclear campaign, it is very credible indeed," Gray acknowledges. "You're talking about very complicated military systems that have never been tested under operational conditions. You're talking in the context of the enemy having the maximum incentive to degrade, neutralize, or blow you out of the sky. And there are many, many vulnerabilities to [the proposed] space-based systems."

And there is the moral issue: Should we really ascend into what our forefathers innocently called the heavens and build killer satellites? Or should space be a peaceful sanctuary for all humankind?

Gray has a simple answer to the question of whether we can avoid sending military hardware into orbit. "The one-liner is 'No,' " he says. A virgin outer space, free of weapons, he terms "romantic nonsense. The notion of putting weapons in space to defend urban areas is morally salutary and not the contrary," he says.

Keyworth argues that MAD, the current chicken game whereby we and the Soviets try to scare each other out of making the first move in a nuclear war, is inherently unstable. "I think, looking back on history, the likelihood of mutual assured destruction's maintaining peace and stability for hundreds of years is not high," he says. "What the President did was to look at the roots, the very foundations of this reasoning, and ask, Aren't we capable of a more stable and more moral basis for defense?"

Garwin says that though such arguments have a certain ring, they lack substance. They are, in fact, simpleminded since space-based antimissile weapons, rather than precluding the need for a nuclear defense based on counterstroke, simply add a new level of complexity to the mind-numbing game we're playing.

"The fact that there *must* be another way, as the President says there is, does not guarantee there *is* another way," says Garwin. "There is no other way in a world that has vast numbers of nuclear weapons."

Daniel Deudney, a senior researcher at the Worldwatch Institute, in Washington, DC, believes we have arrived at one of history's turning points. He hopes that we turn away from space weapons. "I think that weapons in space bring us to a threshold as significant as the one we faced in the late Forties, when the atom bomb was invented," he says. "If we head off this military race in space, we will have closed off a major avenue of confrontation that's arguably as great as the problem we have had with the atom bomb and the subsequent diminishment of our security."

The arguments, pro and con, over the technical, strategic, and moral questions of space war are heating up. But Duedney has stripped the issue down to a single question: Should we have these weapons simply because we are able to build them?

"We have got to mature enough as a species so that every scientific principle we discover is not automatically fashioned into a weapon," he says.

Can we?

"*That* is the big question that hangs over the human species," he says. "I think that space will be the decisive arena for answering the question."

PART ELEVEN:
THE PAST IS PROLOGUE

"Penetrating so many secrets,
we cease to believe in the unknowable.
But there it sits, nevertheless,
calmly licking its chops."
—H.L. Mencken

THREE FUTURES

By Robert Malone

An awareness of the future is not a given in our universe. This concept, like the wheel, was invented. As with any invention, the future has undergone many revisions, just as the cultures it serves have themselves metamorphosed. One can, however, discern certain patterns throughout history in which our perceptions of *future* have been intimately linked with the way we regard our past.

Now, late in the twentieth century, humankind is still mired in a nonvisionary rut that traces its origins to the ancient kingdom of Sumer. Our tendency to define the future in terms of our past has become more sophisticated, but the method continues to obscure the best pathways to the *real* future. And yet what the Sumerians and other early peoples called future, what we call future, and what the people of tomorrow will call future are three concepts so dissimilar that to truly get where we're going, we had better first examine the key to any understanding of *future*. That key is *time*.

Future-past does not really exist! Like Arthur Conan Doyle's famous dog that did not bark in the night, future-past is interesting precisely because of its nonexistence. Precivilization man lived without a sense of either the future or the past. He was frozen in an all-pervading present. English author J. B. Priestly refers to this kind of existence as Great Time, a nonsequential, all-at-once existence rooted in nature.

The visions we do have of these people reflect the totality of their life within Great Time, and this totality cannot be broken down and analyzed separately as art, religion, or social custom. Cave paintings and fertility figures are what they are, no more, no less. If there was any substance to their future, we may guess that it was associated with the unknowable forces of nature or the mystifying actions of those peoples' gods. The future becomes recognizable only when a society begins to record its life cycle through some form of calendar, written symbols, and a structured mythology. The mythologies of Sumer and Egypt (5000 B.C. and after), with their concept of an afterlife, were built around a glorious, though mysterious, past. The events of this superpast constituted the major body of information passed on by priests, medicine men, seers, or leaders. Similar to an ingrown hair that returns to its host, the future was in the past. Who needs a future when the past is so available and filled with wonders? Eternal life was the one condition to look forward to, but as an eternal life in an eternal past. The Egyptian culture endured this static condition not for decades but for centuries piled on centuries. The primary focus of Egyptian life was to arrange for the proper "passport" to eternity. This passport consisted of reciting essential passages from the *Book of the Dead*, which were later inscribed inside the coffin's lid (no point in taking chances). Eternity became their one vision and a substitute for any real sense of the future. The Egyptians stuck to this grave vision for thousands of years. Societies that believe that time is cyclical may be extensions of this early view of time.

American Egyptologist James Henry Breasted pinpointed the "world's first individual" as being Akhenaton (Amenhotep IV, 1388-1358 B.C.). At some point in his life, old Akhenaton (not too old, since he died at thirty, like all his friends) tried to break out of the Egyptian mold by saying to himself, *I exist. I am. I am conscious. I can change things. Move men. Twist the course of events. Create a new religion if I wish.* Neither his vision nor support for his vision among his contemporaries came to pass. Akhenaton lacked a structured sense of time. Hours were not to be broken into minutes and minutes into seconds until the fourteenth century. He also had no way of knowing that he needed to invent not just himself but also the scientific method and thereby the key to evolutionary growth, both biological and technological. This was a tall order for any man, especially for one whose culture steadfastly clung to that continuous best-seller *Book of the Dead*. Yawn!

The future stayed put on the back burner. The past flourished for the next 3,000 years as Eden, Arcady, and the Golden Age. A place for heroic deeds. A place dominated by mythology. A limited, day-to-day vision was sustained by reading entrails and offering sacrifices in exchange for the latest news from an oracle. The future was limited to chance predictions of win, place, or show. Even Plato's *Republic* appeared less a vision of tomorrow than a simple restructuring of the priorities of the present. Plato created his own ideal vision of the present, which may have been the first step out of the past—to an intimation of the future— but the classical world of Plato was narrowed to the city-state in the everyday here and now, just as Plato's Christian counterpart, Augustine, limited the possibilities of the future to the achievements of an eternal city of God.

The Renaissance is popularly thought to be the breakout point for new ideas and new individualism. Leonardo da Vinci is often considered the darling of this period and, consequently, a modernist. But as Freud has said, "He was a man who woke too early in darkness, while others were still asleep." Three thousand years after Akhenaton, Leonardo tried his wings but essentially failed, for he was really grounded in the Middle Ages. His visions of flying and driving, unlike his public visions of equestrian figures, were private visions. Leonardo's ideas were not acted upon by his contemporaries. As a visionary, he never made it out of the closet. But he did, by sheer brilliance and an imagination no one has ever equaled, create on paper wondrous tools, machines, and architecture These were the end game of a deductive and medieval view of the world, however. He never made it to the scientific method and inductive reasoning; therefore,

401

he could see only the outside shell of reality and not the scientific principles underlying time and space. Sweet dreams, Leonardo.

FUTURE-PRESENT

Francis Bacon is a man of future-present. The late anthropologist Loren Eiseley said of him, "Bacon, more fully than any man of his time, entertained the idea of the universe as a problem to be solved, examined, meditated upon, rather than as an externally fixed stage upon which men walked." His *Novum Organum* (1620) and *The New Atlantis* (1627) were radically different from other works of his time and went a long way toward confirming the potential of the scientific method. Bacon saw the universe as a demonstration of knowable laws, not as an extension of mythology or fantasy. The only barrier to knowledge of these laws was spiritual hesitation and an adherence to dogmatic philosophies, which Bacon described as "idols of the theatre." Bacon lived in a world still dominated by dogmatic philosophies—philosophies of such power that in 1600 they could force Italian seer Giordano Bruno to be burned at the stake for expounding upon the existence of infinity. Better, of course, to die for infinity than for some smaller issue. Bacon's burning (no pun intended) occurred in later distortions of his thinking by otherwise noble historians. But Bacon moved us from myth to fact, from permanence to process, from alchemy toward chemistry, from squaring the circle toward calculus, from astrology to astronomy, from guess-and-by-gosh to observation and disciplined reason, from magic to science.

Bacon was not trapped by objects. He did not sit about, inventing specific objects, such as parachutes, machine guns, or submarines. His attention was fixed upon the relationship between events in time and space, but the world did not get into immediate step with Bacon or the scientific method. Nothing so complex could blossom all at once. There were other voices, retrogressive, tugging to maintain the status quo. One such voice grew out of the slightly earlier visions of Sir Thomas More, English writer and saint-to-be. His *Utopia* (which means "no place") reintroduced Arcady with shades of the *Republic*: a place of religious tolerance, an ideal state, a place where all folks shared, a commune (pre-Kool-Aid).

Only the good guys and gals needed apply. However, More's utopia and most utopias since had their roots in the values of the past (a simplicity real or imagined, our "old West," for instance), which magically circumvented lust, garbage, overcrowding, and, most important, any fully realized or individualized person. In the enlightened twentieth century we've learned to have second thoughts about visions that do not include telephone bills, divorce, and other sticky wickets, including an odd cavity or two. These views, however, can invariably be reduced to the Orwellian remark "If you want a picture of the future, imagine a boot stamping on the human face—forever . . . and remember that it is forever." Is there something else?

Contrary to George Orwell's tableau, the late nineteenth to early twentieth century held firmly to a vision of the future perfumed with optimism, sprinkled with the euphoria of progress, and distinguished by its mastery over nature. The future was conceived as the inevitable betterment of humankind. Ideally, everyone had an equal chance, yet we know, in retrospect, that relatively few prospered. Real power was gained from the scientific establishment. With the development and distribution of a massive new technology, the invisible power of principle was made visible in the form of goods and services.

This period not only shared with Leonardo a preoccupation with objects and inventions (which lingers to our day), as typified by Jules Verne and H. G. Wells, but also extended More's idea of a better social world in visions like Edward Bellamy's *Looking Backward*.

Future-present, therefore, is dominated by measured time and is limited to an overwhelming concentration on objects, mechanisms, and other practical inventions. Its measured time lifts out of Great Time to the first awareness of time as a three-part abstraction: past, present, and glimmers of a future.

A more complete vision of the future depends upon a view of time that offers progression both biologically and technologically. True science fiction poses fresh alternatives to the mundane constraints of future-present. It enlists the underpinnings, conceptual structures, and facts of the scientific and industrial revolutions (notably time, space, causality, energy, and evolutionary process) to create something recognizable. Fantasy, on the contrary, is oriented to deeds of past heroism and may be another disguise for mythology. Science fiction, at the very least, wears the mask of reason.

Science fiction is still with us and is now contending with the newer force of nearer-my-computer-to-thee futurists. Futurists are often unable to see the future for the statistics. Their statistics are a product of present readings, present values, and present visions. Statistics too often have a homing device that mirrors what already is, instead of giving a clue to what may be.

Futurists are, to a person, all honorable people, but they do bear watching, like those South American fish that have been observed climbing trees. A bit tricky. We will have more to say about the futurists in future-future.

Future-present has brought out, by one predictive vision or another, much that has come to pass. It has also goofed outrageously. Arthur C. Clarke, in his provocative *Profiles of the Future*, writes, "The facts of the future can hardly be imagined *ab initio* [from the beginning] by those who are unfamiliar with the fantasies of the past." He reviews the results and failures of both extrapolation from known facts and speculation in an imaginative vein. We might usefully review our own list of those things that have been predicted and pulled off: automatic factories, robots, death rays, doomsday weapons, spaceflight, impending solar energy, some replaceable human parts, home computers, wall-sized TV images, test-tube babies, hybrid crops, atomic energy, and so on.

Yet airships have not come back; we are not living underwater or in space; private airplanes for commuting are not commonplace, and could you imagine New York or Tokyo if it were (elbow to rotorblade)? Clothing is not disposable, home-delivered everything never got beyond the Avon lady, radiant heating and present electric heating are questionable, atomic energy is by no means infinite, cheap, or too readily available, cryogenic preservation is still real only in movies, domed cities do not exist, and high-speed mass transit seems more distant than near. Remember moving sidewalks and better taxicab service? Whatever happened to rotating houses, Wankel engines, monorails, picture phones, electronic newspapers, teaching machines, plug-in learning while you sleep, STOL aircraft, hovercraft on city streets, new steam-driven vehicles, electronically controlled cars on highways, and on and on?

There was a time in the nineteenth century when it was rumored that the Patent Office would close since everything that could be invented had been invented. We are no longer so naive. An object-oriented future may be as bereft of vision as one without any objects at all. The future is not a simple trick done at the end of a prediction. Still, we remain anchored in future-present, thanks largely to three venerable gurus, each in his own way dominated by images and methods of future-past. Buckminster Fuller, Marshall McLuhan, and Herman Kahn. If we were to accept Fuller's image of Spaceship Earth and position our three gurus on its bridge, they might advise us of our journey into the future in the following manners.

As the ship's rigger, carpenter, plumber, and engineer, Fuller would be in charge of mechanical existence. He would advise setting a "new" tension-compression mast to hold a triangular spinnaker that would, Christopher Columbus-style, sail us off to the future, using basic nineteenth- and twentieth-century technology. "When you want a new, greater-performance ship," he says, "you simply melt the old one, if it is made out of metals. You can use the same metals over and over again, ad infinitum." There would be Mason jars in the hold (we are reminded of the model boats in the tombs of the Egyptian dead). Mechanics are dandy, but the rum bottle had better be handy.

McLuhan, acting as the chief receptionist and assistant quartermaster, would call attention to what we received and how we perceived. When we looked ahead, he would remind us of the rear-view mirror; when we turned to the rear-view mirror, he would suggest we look ahead. "Societies have always been shaped more by the nature of the media by which men communicate than by the content of the communication," McLuhan instructs. He would tend to read all the "road" signs but help us miss the road. In a word, he would overreact to the changes in the delivery system of technology at the expense of its substance. Navigation requires knowing where you are going, not just a talent for playing with the quadrant.

Kahn, being in charge of lists, would immediately produce an Escalation Ladder (presumably our ship's condition and course is a little risky). His list: "16. Aftermath; 15. Some kind of "all-out" war; 14. Complete evacuation; 13. Limited nonlocal war; 12. Controlled local war; 11. Spectacular show of force; . . ." And so it goes. We might take issue with lists that start out backward anyway. Our ship's bridge now begins to parallel the bridge of *Star Trek*'s *Enterprise*. Kahn will shift us away from the doom ahead of us to the doom within. We have a "final" bomb in the bilge, and, statistically, our chances of survival are number 37. . . . ! What is supposed to be very new is often very old.

To recapitulate: Fuller offers us a technology for survival, but it is old and inadequate. McLuhan warns us that we are misreading technology and then jumps overboard. Kahn tells us that if we analyze technology properly, we can figure out a way for it to kill us. Great shipmates!

FUTURE-FUTURE

Whereas in future-past there was at best a crafted magical future for pharaohs only and in future-present a mixed technological bag for the right advanced cultures, future-future will surely be a time for the realization of all persons in a shared future. If as James Joyce says, "But Holy Saltmartin, why can't you beat Time?" we may have to give up trying and join it and blossom within it.

We should also acknowledge our need for a future. Without need, there is no fulfillment. As Simone de Beauvior has said, "There is no other justification for present existence other than its expansion into an indefinitely open future." An open future is one that sees time not as all-pervasive, nor simply as measured, but as something whose events are created in their own particular time-space; this is a time of many tracks, many awarenesses, and many positions.

An open future means recognizing that remnants of the past will get through to the future. Some things and conditions must perform as a necessary continuity. Others, like Pompeii, are accidents of capricious history. We may never know when we will be covered over by ashes and later pop up as a well-labeled exhibit in the Louvre. We will need new tools for

future prediction and a revised mind-set to face the future of the future.

Photographer Barbara Morgan noted way back in 1973, "As the life-style of the space age grows more interdisciplinary, it will be harder for the 'one-track' mind to survive. . . . I see simultaneous intake, multiple-awareness, and synthesized comprehension as inevitable. . . ." The searches of simple speculation will give way to new forms of thinking. There is no way to deal with the combinational possibilities of the future without, while actually searching, appearing to do something else, as when we are highly attracted to a sexual partner but pretend to be blasé before him or her, or when we spear for a fish and have to compensate for the light diffraction.

The closest thing we can suggest at the moment is to adopt the "science" that studies the laws of creative activity, namely, *heuristics*. Such an adoption means a more empirical approach to the future. Into the future with the rule of thumb. A leap of faith! We will have to seek answers that may confound our senses and mental conditioning, possibly even subvert the structure of our present minds. But isn't this what Johannes Kepler did as he substituted ellipses for "pure" circles when he calculated planetary orbits?

We must allow that part of us enriched by experience, rather than logic, to take control. To advance into the future, we should avoid projections of ourselves into "pure intelligence" or "bits of machinery." We must steer a careful course between these two extremes, as they have been articulated by Norman O. Brown and R. D. Laing. Brown has stated, "It is the essence of the scientific spirit to be mercilessly ascetic,

to eliminate human enjoyment from our relationship to nature, to eliminate the human senses, and finally to eliminate the human brain. Pure intelligence is thus a product of dying, or at least of becoming mentally insensitive, and therefore is in principle madness." Steady! And Laing states, "We shall be concerned specifically with people who experience themselves as automata, as robots, as bits of machinery, or even as animals. Such persons are rightly regarded as crazy." Steady, again; just a little bit longer now.

We may be now, and may continue to be, inclined in the direction of bits of machinery and/or pure intelligence. It will be to our advantage, however, to accept a symbiosis of mind and matter. As part of our self-realization, we will want to fill the sciences to a full rainbow rather than accept the discontinuities of today. Surely there will be closure between biology and physics. Biophysics will find itself under pressure to solve problems on the molecular level that require the combined wisdom of both former disciplines. One such problem will center upon the understanding of weightlessness in space.

As the closure occurs, we will have to adapt our understanding to conform to the change. We must direct, and not be directed by, the consequences of the new sciences. Technology will have to be approached not as something apart from us, like a perverted and out-of-control imp, but as an extension of us. It will need our stewardship. Technology will be the means by which we make peace with the "natural" world. Man and woman are the motile tissue of the universe as we know it. Their mission is to act as the mind and nervous system for that universe.

Yet it has always been the nature of human beings to connect mind and matter. Now only the scale will change. It is scale that will take into account our new consciousness of multiple time centers and multiple constructs of space. We envision a time that folds into itself our past and present attitudes and projects them toward time and the future. The scale of time is toward infinity; the scale of space is toward infinity. We may awake ever so slowly, but we will awake. Aware to the future! In order to act on the universe, we will have to leave Earth. However, two highly organized institutions will deal with those who stay: The Metropolitan Museum of Earth (under the good direction of Thomas Hoving, who will never die) and the United Sanitation Department (understaffed, of course). Everything on Earth will have become either an object of art or recyclable waste (is there anything else?), a true growth industry for curators and sanitation inspectors. Earth will be a nice place to visit or send radio messages to, but once we have reached another galaxy, return calls will necessitate our having become eternal in order for us to receive them.

Our departure from Earth will be by means of an advanced Universal Turing Machine. Based upon those self-replicating machines conceived by Alan Turing 40 years ago, the Turing Machine is an automaton that is theoretically capable of reproducing itself; its offspring have similar capabilities. They do this as life does, by containing within themselves coded instructions for their own duplication. Their duplicate contains reproductive instructions as well.

In the future of the future, the Universal Turing Machine will not only self-program and self-replicate but self-grow, self-regulate (given changes in the environment), self-regenerate, and self-repair. It will be mobile, environment-sensing, and structurally adaptive. Its human cargo will not be identifiable by the untrained eye as different from the automaton. But therein will lie a continuum of coded and charged matter!

How will we create a machine of sufficient scale to hold billions of assorted people? We won't! The machines will be measured in centimeters. There is no point in using up precious fossil fuels to loft a pack of now-aging bodies (they, too, are art objects or recyclable waste). Those who go will go as fertilized eggs or as potential zygotes in a molecular soup. These zygotes will be birthed in the Turing Machine. The zygote, like its host, has within its nucleus a blueprint of its own: the structure of its DNA. As it grows, it will be nurtured and educated by the Universal Turing Machine. Thus, the machine will grow along with the zygotes, picking up matter and energy as needed while moving out into space. In time, the Turing Machine will convert itself from a ship to a city. And as its citizens get too big for one particular Machine City, it will spawn another Turing Machine. The new ship will very probably look like a radiolarian to the casual eye and make use of some form of ion engine to move itself. Its human passengers will create not a utopia but, more probably, a world like our own (with some improvements, one hopes).

Picture yourself aboard a four-dimensional version of the *Queen Elizabeth*. As we sit in the bar lounge, we spot Bucky Fuller, Herman Kahn, and Marshall McLuhan in heated debate with Woody Allen. All the futurists would be aboard in cloned-zygote form at first. They would be granted first crack and reduced rates. Even Akhenaton might be there, having been cloned from a fingernail. Laugh! Will Isaac Asimov be there? Yes, and writing more robot stories. As writer Meridel Le Sueur has said, "For none shall die who have the future in them." Future is where we will share, as witnesses or participants, in the big bang 2, a future where we may hold infinity in our hands. We may create a new universe through cooperative human action that combines on an infinite scale all the aspects of a fine garden. Within this garden we may act as gods fully realized in our person in time, fully realized in our person in space. We will one way or another fully realize what it is to be human! Thus, time, like so many other concepts that we accept as given, will have to be invented all over again.

OMNI'S PROPHECY QUIZ

Arthur C. Clarke's answers:

1) a	26) a
2) d	27 d
3) b	28) f
4) b	29) c
5) a	30) a
6) a	31) a
7) a	32) d
8) c	33) a,b,c,d,e
9) b	34) a
10) b	35) a
11) b	36) b,c,d
12) b	37) d
13) d	38) a
14) f	39) e
15) e	40) b
16) a	41) b
17) a	42) a
18) a	43) b
19) a	44) b
20) e	45) b
21) a	46) a
22) b	47) a
23) a,b	48) a
24) b	49) d
25) a	50) b

ZEBRA'S SELF HELP BOOKS

SLEEP WELL, LIVE WELL   (1579, $3.50)
by Norman Ford
Here, finally, is a book that tells you how to improve the quality of your sleep, easily and naturally. This complete guide includes 41 medically proven sleep techniques.

FOOT TALK   (1613, $2.95)
by Dr. Barry H. Block
Reading *Foot Talk* could be the first step in relieving many of the uncomfortable problems people have with their feet. Dr. Block shares his knowledge of podiatry with facts on surgery, injuries, exercises, plus an invaluable Foot Health Test.

MAKING DECISIONS   (1634, $3.95)
by Dr. Andrea Williams
Now through the easy step-by-step procedure developed over seventeen years by psychologist Dr. Andrea Williams, you can sift through all those conflicting desires and fears and discover what is truly most important to you.

STOP SMOKING, LOSE WEIGHT   (1776, $2.95)
by Dr. Neil Solomon
There is new hope and help for smokers from noted endocrinologist Dr. Neil Solomon. Combined with a revolutionary new diet is an exercise plan that is easy to use and very rewarding. You'll not only look better but feel better too!

VOICE POWER   (1796, $3.50)
by Evelyn Burge Bowling
By discovering the hidden potential of your voice you'll not only be able to lead sales presentations and win over audiences, you'll also communicate better with friends and family.

Available wherever paperbacks are sold, or order direct from the Publisher. Send cover price plus 50¢ per copy for mailing and handling to Zebra Books, Dept. 1896, 475 Park Avenue South, New York, N.Y. 10016. Residents of New York, New Jersey and Pennsylvania must include sales tax. DO NOT SEND CASH.